Melanesian Odysseys

Melanesian Odysseys

Negotiating the Self, Narrative and Modernity

Lisette Josephides

Berghahn Books
New York • Oxford

First published in 2008 by

Berghahn Books
www.berghahnbooks.com

©2008, 2010 Lisette Josephides
First paperback edition published in 2010

All rights reserved. Except for the quotation of short passages for the purposes of criticism and review, no part of this book may be reproduced in any form or by any means, electronic or mechanical, including photocopying, recording, or any information storage and retrieval system now known or to be invented, without written permission of the publisher.

Library of Congress Cataloging-in-Publication Data

Josephides, Lisette.
  Melanesian odysseys : negotiating the self, narrative and modernity / Lisette Josephides.
    p. cm.
  Includes bibliographical references and index.
  ISBN 978-1-84545-525-5 (hardcover : alk. paper)
  1. Kewa (Papua New Guinean people)--Social life and customs. 2. Kewa (Papua New Guinean people)--Psychology. 3. Oral tradition--Papua New Guinea. 4. Identity (Psychology)--Papua New Guinea. 5. Papua New Guinea--Social life and customs. I. Title.

DU740.42.J65 2008
305.89'912--dc22
                                    2008028021

British Library Cataloguing in Publication Data

A catalogue record for this book is available from the British Library

Printed in the United States on acid-free paper.

ISBN 978-1-84545-525-5 (hardback)
ISBN 978-1-84545-706-8 (paperback)

Contents

List of Illustrations	ix
Dramatis Personae	xi
Preface	xv

Overtures, Ethnographic and Theoretical

1. The Aesthetics of Fieldwork among the Kewa   3
   The Style and Tone of Kewa Life   3
   Bickering, Bantering and Coming to Blows   4
   Place, Movement and Residential Mobility   8
   Daily Life   10
   *Scrambling into the Field: Mining the Field and
   Eliciting Minefields*   15

2. Self Strategies: Ascription, Interlocution, Elicitation   20
   The Person/Self/Individual   22
   An Archaeology of the Self   24
   *Ascription: Distinguishing, Co-creating and Merging
   Self and Other*   25
   A Modern History of the Self: Interlocution and Its Denial   30
   The Everyday Self: Language and Communication at Issue   33
   What Speech Does: Communication as Capability   34
   Strategies   36
   *Elicitation, Explicitness, Rehearsed and Rehearsing
   Talk and Action*   38
   Conclusion   43

Part I: Narratives

3. Narrating the Self I: Moral Constructions of the Self as
   Paradigmatic Accounts   53
   Theories of Narrative   55
   Narrative and Paradigmatic Thought   56
   Ethics, Morality and the Self in Paradigmatic Accounts   57
   *The Storytellers (Wapa, Ragunanu, Pupula, Yakiranu,
   Payanu)*   59
   *Kewa Pre-contact Practices and Persons: A Narrative
   of Many*   67
   Growing up   67
   Of Courtship and Marriage   68
   Of Magic and Gardens   71
   Spirit Houses   73

	Pig Kills	74
	Warfare and Pacification	75
	Conclusions: Moral Constructions of the Self as Paradigmatic Accounts	77
4.	Narrating the Self II: Metanarratives of Culture, Self, and Change	81
	The Storytellers (Rumbame, Alirapu, Mayanu, Mapi)	82
	Rumbame's Story	85
	Alirapu's Story	90
	Mayanu's Story (Excerpt)	92
	Mapi's Story	93
	Mapi: Visionary and Dreamer	98
	Four Features Revisited and Expanded	102
	Creating Moral Personhood	102
	Constructing Coherent Selves	103
	Constructing Critical Metanarratives	105
	Facing Modernity and Christianity	106
	Conclusion	107
5.	Narrating the Self III: The Heroic, the Epic and the Picaresque in a Changed World	112
	The Storytellers (Hapkas, Papola, Rimbu, Lari)	113
	The Stories: Third Set	118
	Hapkas's (Nasupeli's) Story	118
	Papola's Story	122
	Rimbu's Story	123
	Lari's Story	128
	Seizing the New World: Narrative, Consciousness and Communication	135
	The Heroic, the Epic, the Picaresque and the Symbolic	135
	Narrative as Form of Consciousness and Organization of Experience	141
	Experience and Consciousness	142
	Morality	144
	Narratives as Communication	146

Part II: Portraits
(Several Weddings, Some Divorces and Three Funerals)

6.	Portraits and Minimal Narratives: Elicitations of Social Reality	151
	Portraits, Stories and Minimal Narratives	153
	Elicitation and Explicitness	155
	Language, Talk and Action	156
	Norms and Claims: Rehearsed and Rehearsing Talk and Action	157
	Conclusion	158

7.	Love and All That: Negotiating Marriage and Marital Life	162
	Courtship	162
	Problems with Brideprice	167
	Irregular Unions	170
	Polygyny and Conflict	172
	Ainu and Yako	173
	Giame and Yadi	174
	Lari and Rimbu	176
	Liame, Rosa and Kiru	179
	Rarapalu, Karupiri, Foti and Waliya	181
	Negotiating Marriage and Marital Life	182
	Love and All That	184
8.	The Politics of Death	188
	Who's the Big Man of Us All? Rake's Death	188
	Duties to Persons, Rights in Persons: Wapa's Death	195
	Out with the Old, in with the New: Payanu's Death	202
	Death and Recurring Conflict: Conclusion	209
9.	Mimesis, Ethnography and Knowledge	216
	Stories, Ethnography, Theory	216
	Mimesis as a Way of Knowing	218
	Ethnography as Difference, Locality and Chronicle	221
	Cultural Region and the Tyranny of Theoretical Regionalism	221
	Ethnography as Chronicle of Cultural History/History of Consciousness	222
References		227
Index		233

For Marc

List of Illustrations

Maps

1.	Southern Highlands: Eastern Districts	xvi
2.	Approximate Locations of the Yala and Neighbouring Clans	xvii

Figures

1.1	Sugu Yala Settlements in December 1981	11
8.1	Rake's Grave and the Walk to Aliwi	190

Plates

3.1	Wapa drinking Coca-Cola. (8 January 1980)	59
3.2	Payanu with granddaugher Wapanu. (April 1980)	60
3.3	Ragunanu with cat. (17 May 1980)	61
3.4	Pupula (right). (25 November 1982)	62
3.5	Yakiranu. (April 1980)	62
4.1	Rumbame (left) with daughter Demanu. (15 January 1981)	83
4.2	Alirapu (centre) with husband Yembi. (25 November 1982)	83
4.3	Mayanu. (April 1980)	84
4.4	Mapi pretending to shoot cassowary. (27 September 1979)	86
5.1	Hapkas with son and paintings of his dreams. (December 1985)	113
5.2	Hapkas with son. (December 1981)	114
5.3	Papola with daughter. (1 January 1980)	115
5.4	Rimbu (right) with Councillor Mara. (26 September 1979)	116
5.5	Lari. (11 May 1980)	117
7.1	*Tanim het* courting session. (11 December 1979)	163
7.2	*Tanim het* courting session with Rimbu in the foreground. (11 December 1979)	165
7.3	*Tanim het* courting session with Rimbu in the foreground. (11 December 1979)	166

Dramatis Personae

Their Kinship and Clan Links and Place of Residence
Ainu Yako's wife living in Yakopaita.
Alirapu Yembi's wife living in Poiale.
Amasi Rimbu's and Lari's second daughter living in Yakopaita.
Ana Rumbame's husband, Yala clansman living in Tema.
Areali Wapa's deceased father's brother, Umba-Paripa Yala who lived in Agema.
Biru Department of Agriculture Extension Officer who lived in Yakopaita and eventually married Roga's daughter Ragunanu.
Foti Waliya's third wife living in Yakopaita.
Gapea Mapi's and Kumi's father, Tiarepa Yala living in Poiale, died 1980.
Giame Yadi's wife living in Yakopaita.
Hapkas (Nasupeli) Wapa's and Payanu's son, Rimbu's brother and Kambenu's husband, Umba-Paripa Yala living in Yakopaita.
Ili Lari's father's brother, acting as her father, living in Alomani.
Ipa A government translator ('tanim tok', office already defunct in 1980), Mapi's affine married into Tiarepa Yala and living in Paipanda.
Ipanu Yako and Ainu's daughter, Paripa Yala living in Yakopaita.
Kalinu Yasi's wife from Ialibu living in Yakopaita.
Kalu Yembi's brother, Rola Yala living in Poiale.
Kamare Pupula's daughter and Michael's sister, Yarepa Yala living in Puliminia.
Kambenu Hapkas's wife and Rorepame's older sister living in Yakopaita, died 1986.
Kaporopali Koai's senior brother who attempted to marry Kamare and Wareame. Ala clansman living in Roga.
Karupiri Rake's widow, repulsed his brother Wola and became Waliya's second wife living in Yakopaita.
Kengeai Took over Rake as Councillor, businessman and truck owner, of Perepe clan living in Aliwi.
Kiru Son of Noyopa (deceased) and husband of Liame, took Rosa as second wife. Umba-Paripa Yala living in Yakopaita and then moved higher up near Popa.
Koai Kaporopali's junior brother and Lapame's father, Ala clansman living in Roga.
Koipa Roga's younger brother, Umba-Paripa Yala returned from plantation in 1980 and living in Poiale.

Koke A widower with a bad leg, artefact maker, Rola Yala living in Aka.
Komalo Wapa's and Yalanu's son and Hapkas's and Rimbu's junior brother, Umba-Paripa Yala living in Yakopaita but spending much time on plantations in Mt Hagen.
Kongalepa Wapa's deceased father, Umba-Paripa Yala of Agema.
Kumi Mapi's junior brother, Tiarepa Yala living in Aka/Yadara.
Lapame Koai's daughter, whose epistolary marriage arrangements with a man from Kundiawa fell through.
Lari Rimbu's wife living in Yakopaita, mother of five children in 1993.
Liame Kiru's wife living in Yakopaita, died 1995.
Lisette Rimbu's and Lari's third daughter living in Yakopaita.
Loma Rama's and Mayanu's daughter living in Puliminia.
Lu Rola Yala from Erave, who shared Rimbu's Port Moresby adventure and later collected large compensation payment for his sister.
Mapi (Lopa) Gapea's son, Kumi's elder brother and husband of Ramuame and Noeme, village magistrate until 1983, Tiarepa Yala living in Aka/Yadara.
Mayanu Rama's wife and Loma's mother living in Puliminia.
Michael (Agema) Pupula's son, Yarepa Yala living in Puliminia.
Nadawa Rimbu's and Lari's son, Umba-Paripa Yala living in Yakopaita.
Nadisua Kiru's son, Umba-Paripa Yala living in Yakopaita.
Noeme Mapi's second wife living in Yadara.
Papola Wapa's sister's son, Umba-Paripa Yala living in Yakopaita.
Pasaroli Waliya's junior brother, Umba-Paripa Yala living in Yakopaita.
Payanu Hapkas's and Rimbu's mother living in Yakopaita, died 1993.
Pima Pisa's son, Paripa Yala living in Puliminia.
Pisa Father of Pima, Rero, Wareame; Paripa Yala living in Kerare.
Poreale Yadi's classificatory sister, whose marriage he terminated when other relatives received brideprice.
Pupula Ragunanu's husband and father of Michael, Kamare and Koipame; Yarepa Yala living in Puliminia.
Ragunanu Pupula's wife and Koipame's mother, living in Puliminia and then Yakopaita.
Ragunanu Roga's daughter, later married to Biru; living in Aka.
Rake Councillor, Perepe living in Sumbura then Aliwi, died 1979.
Rama Husband of Mayanu and father of Loma, Paripa Yala living in Puliminia.
Rarapalu Waliya's first wife from Erave, living in Yakopaita.
Rero Pisa's son, eventually married Komalo's betrothed Wata, Paripa Yala living in Puliminia.
Rika Roga's junior brother, Umba-Paripa Yala living in Aka.

Rika 'Companion of Wapa's youth', Wapia Yala who attended Wapa's funeral.

Rimbu Wapa's son, Lari's husband and father of Wapanu, Amasi, Lisette, Nadawa and Ruma; Umba-Paripa Yala living in Yakopaita.

Roga Son of Yamola (Wapa's brother, deceased) and Rika's senior brother; Umba-Paripa Yala living in Aka.

Rorea Pastor of Evangelical Church of Papua, Yarepa Yala living in Poiale.

Rorepame Papola's wife and Kambenu's younger sister living in Yakopaita.

Rosa Kiru's second wife living in Yakopaita and on a mountain near Popa.

Rumbame Ana's wife living in Tema. (Not Lari's mother, also called Rumbame.)

Rusa Village Magistrate, Koiari living in Puri.

Sipi Pisa's son, Paripa Yala living in Puliminia.

Waliya Son of Adawi (deceased), Pasaroli's elder brother and husband of Rarapalu, Karupiri and Foti; Umba-Paripa living in Yakopaita.

Wamili Lari's cousin living in Puli, who contrived to receive her brideprice.

Wapa Old warrior, husband of Payanu, father of Hapkas, Rimbu and Komalo, Papola's sister's brother. Umba-Paripa Yala, lived in Wapia, Popa and Yakopaita, died in 1980.

Wapanu Rimbu's and Lari's eldest daughter, living in Yakopaita until marriage.

Wareame Pisa's daughter and sister of Pima and Rero, Paripa Yala living in Kerare.

Wata Komalo's betrothed then Rero's wife, Amburupa living in Puliminia after marriage.

Wola Rake's older brother who propositioned his widow; Perepe living in Aliwi.

Yadi Son of Renali (deceased, brother of Pisa) and Giame's husband; driver, Paripa Yala living in Yakopaita.

Yakiranu Widow of Kale living in Poiale.

Yako Ainu's husband, self-proclaimed 'half-man' (because small), Umba-Paripa Yala living in Yakopaita.

Yalanu Wapa's deceased first wife, Komalo's mother who lived in Popa.

Yamola Wapa's deceased senior brother, Umba-Paripa Yala who lived in Agema.

Yasi (Etali) Kiru's junior brother and the anthropologist's assistant; Umba-Paripa Yala living in Yakopaita.

Yembi Alirapu's husband, Rola Yala living in Poiale.

Note on Settlements and Clan Names

In Kewa country and beyond, settlements take their names from the plots of uncultivated land where men erect their houses, singly or jointly with other clan-related men. Moving to another site or settlement following a quarrel or disagreement is not uncommon. Among the Yala, the Umba, Paripa and Yarepa are closely associated clans whose members sometimes double up their names (e.g. 'Umba-Paripa') or (more rarely) use them interchangeably (Paripa for Yarepa). Whether they do so or not depends on their desire to stress or deny a close bond and common origin.

Preface

In a series of epic self-narratives, ranging from traditional *Bildungsgeschichte* (where narrators epitomized the 'cultural persons' passing through life cycles) to Christian epiphanies, and from the picaresque adventures to the psychological traumas and transformations of more fragmented lives, Kewa persons of the New Guinea Highlands attempt to shape and control their selves and their relentlessly changing world. The autobiographical narratives then give way to accounts of interactive encounters, whose analysis arrives at a startling conclusion: that the reflection by which we know our own self involves self-externalization rather than self-introspection, with the correlation that the process of knowing others is not essentially different from that of knowing one's self.

Since the book deals with what it means to be human – conceptually, morally and emotionally – its relevance transcends any one discipline or culture. *Theoretically* it develops an understanding of culture and self as constantly created in people's interactions, not already there and waiting to be discovered by the anthropologist. *Methodologically* it brings to bear interdisciplinary philosophical perspectives on anthropological and local knowledge, through attention to elicitation (how people locally create their worlds) and mimesis (how anthropologists can produce ethnographies). *Ethnographically* it presents lively narratives by named individuals whose stories and escapades can be followed through, enabling the reader to observe how people finish up in a different place from where they started, transported by their own interactive exchanges. A dialogue, generating its own values, is allowed to develop between people's own words and actions.

Using approaches from the philosophy of mind, phenomenology, existential philosophy and narrative theory, the book outlines the connections between narrative, self, and morality. The investigation is tackled through an examination of different types of stories and experiences: self-narratives (the odysseys of the title) and accounts of events as they unfold ('minimal narratives'). While in classical ethnographies anthropologists may homogenize the subjects of their enquiry, here I personalize them, but never relativize their stories or lives.

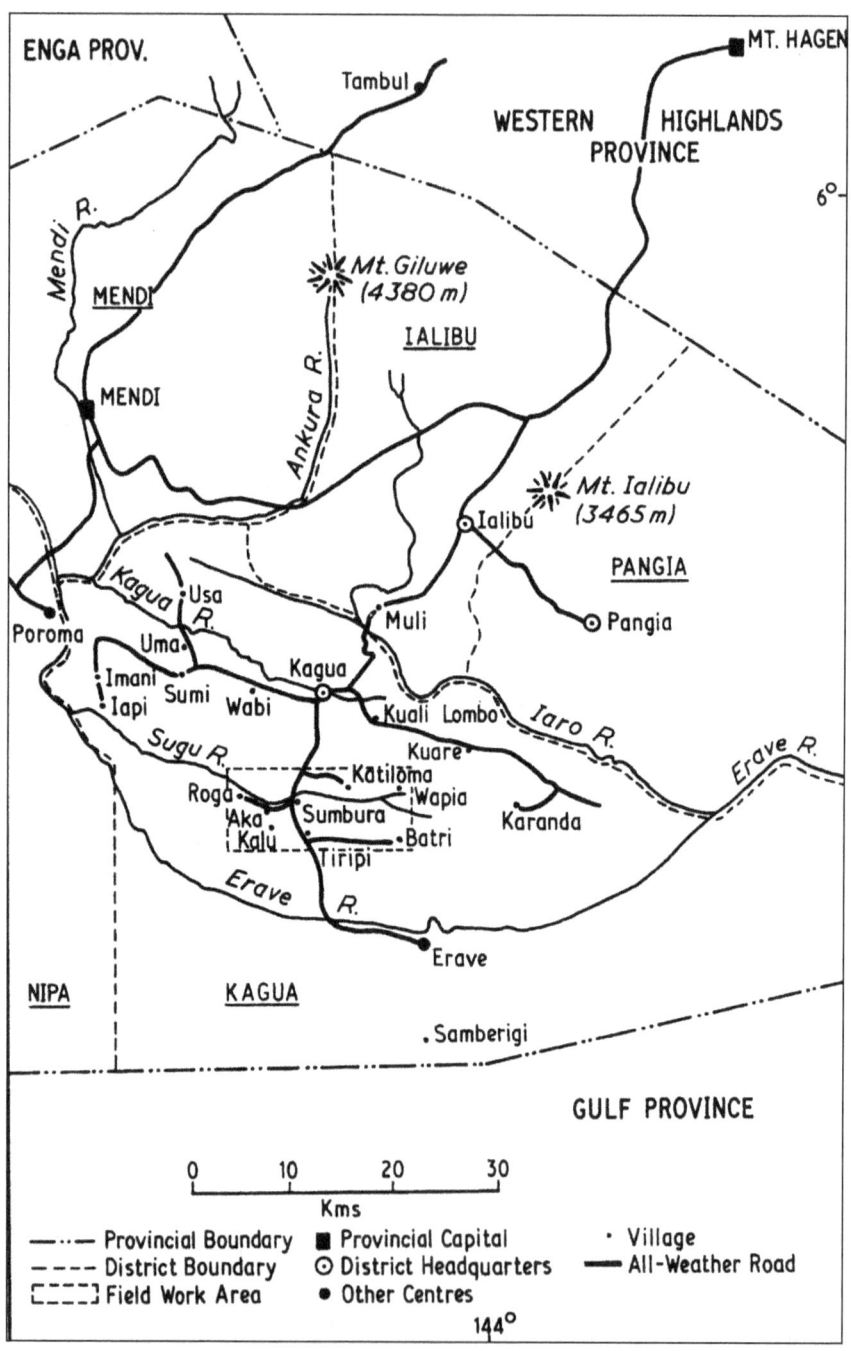

Map 1. Southern Highlands: Eastern Districts

Map 2. Approximate Locations of the Yala and Neighbouring Clans

(To help the reader identify the characters in the stories, a list of Dramatis Personae appears just before this Preface.) As the stories unfolded on the pages of the book, I became aware that what anthropologists compare is not local cultures, but forms or aspects of universalism – as indeed people everywhere universalize their lives and their experiences

My own intellectual trajectory is part of the background to this book. Straight after completing a degree in philosophy, whose final phases led me, unaccountably, to Lévi-Strauss's *Tristes Tropiques*, I fled to Berlin for a year. My first introductory classes in ethnology at the Free University quite decided me, and I returned to London to enrol in the two-year postgraduate Diploma in anthropology. Andrew Strathern had just been appointed to the Anthropology chair at University College, and in his office I had my first iconic encounter with Papua New Guinea: beside the plumed head of a man, an enormous bird of paradise fixed its steady gaze upon me, while the distant figure of a woman with a netbag on her head was sketched in the background, surrounded by gambolling pigs. The bold inscription revealed this to be a poster advertising the national airline of Papua New Guinea: 'Papua Niugini: the Last Place You've Never Been.'

I knew right away I had found my field-site. Two powerful memories of my first arrival at the Highlands airport of Mt Hagen in 1979 are etched on my consciousness: the warm, acrid smell of wood fires on people's skins and their clothes, and the feeling that nothing here was strange to me. I had come to the last place on earth, yet felt quite at home. This attitude may be reflected in one aspect of my theoretical approach: in my ethnographic analyses I tend not to stress differences between practices in different cultures, being instead struck by underlying similarities – even though, within cultural exchanges, I stress conflict rather than consensus.

My doctoral fieldwork was foreshadowed by my Diploma dissertation, which focused on how inequalities developed in so-called egalitarian societies. It resulted in an analysis of gender relations as modelling and disguising relations of inequality. While I wrote an ethnography that recorded the observed surface of things, my aim, in faithfulness to the theoretical interests of my discipline, was to uncover a hidden structure. This required that I analyse action in order to discover what it covers up or mystifies. Bourdieu was all the rage at the time, and coupled with my own Marxist leanings, which looked for alienation, exploitation, and smokescreens disguising relations of production, it was almost inevitable that I should produce a book titled *The Production of Inequality*.

The present work inverts this analytic logic. It is concerned instead with bringing to view the process by which explicit knowledge is constituted through the efficacy of speech and action. The point of departure for this enquiry is that social knowledge is established through negotiation, which takes place in the process of making that knowledge public or explicit. Explicitness is a locus of disclosure. The key term I use for this process is 'elicitation'. Elicitation denotes the contestability and negotiability of meanings and intentions. It is part of a theory of pragmatics.

My concept of elicitation has its antecedents in the work of Roy Wagner and Marilyn Strathern. Strathern's *The Gender of the Gift* described Melanesian action as realized only in its effect. According to her analysis, gender is created from the actions men and women elicit from each other, and each sex depends on the other to bring out the effects by which both may know that their action (as a cause) has taken place. My own work has developed along parallel lines, but in a different register. My field notes bulged with unwieldy stories: self-narratives, observations of events unfolding, exchanges and accounts heard through flimsy bamboo walls; and all augmented by daily briefings on the latest local chicaneries. How was I ever to present this excessive, irrepressible material? To shape it into the form of a monograph proved to be the labour of Sisyphus, as excised materials kept rolling back. While Strathern's work drew my attention to key theoretical concepts, the ethnography stretched those concepts and took them in a different direction. My use of elicitation stresses the open-endedness of agency, as I discuss below. It links back to an earlier influence, that of Roy Wagner, whose *The Invention of Culture* set out the creative relationship between 'invention' and 'convention', defined as the individuating versus collectivizing aspects of action.

Everyday Kewa exchanges are often elicitations in the form of claims. A particular exchange begins as a confident or even aggressive claim, until it is checked by those addressed. At this stage, misunderstandings may be revealed in the responses. The claim may then be retracted or turned into a conciliatory negotiation, intended to ascertain how far the elicitor's project can be made into a shared project. On the one hand, one attempts to work out the meaning of other persons' words and actions by offering different responses; on the other, one tries out on other persons possible variations of one's own meaning, for acceptability, coherence, and intelligibility. In the first case, the talk of others is considered more or less as veiled speech, hiding their meaning and desire; in the second, one elicits, bit by bit, the acceptability of one's own claim before committing oneself outright.

In this context of constant and delicate negotiations, the activity of making social knowledge explicit is simultaneously the activity that modifies that knowledge. Other claims, or different reasons for the claims, are substituted for unsuccessful ones. New intentions develop in the interaction itself, adapted to responses to the original statements. Communicative intentions are additionally obscured by the tendency to use a form of veiled speech (*siapi*), out of caution or uncertainty. Eliciting talk is thus always a line with a hook, fishing for responses. Social knowledge is not created as an external reality by an already constituted person; that person is inextricably bound up with its world, so that world creation coincides with self-construction. The concrete demonstration of such creative activity, with an elaboration of self theory as its foundation, is at the core of this ethnography.

Notwithstanding the centrality of personal strategies in this presentation of Kewa lives, it would be a mistake to infer that Kewa persons act without reference to cultural norms or rules, or to the larger social structures that are the subject of most ethnographies. Rather, my arguments rest on these shared understandings of social practices, developed in my earlier work, in at least three ways. First, as contexts already described and therefore requiring only brief reference. (Thus I allude to gender inequality as flowing from the relationship between production and exchange and resting on women's dependent relationship to land as the means of production.) Second, I signal these understandings as points of contrast against which the present work takes shape. The ethnographic aim here is to understand Kewa culture 'in action', through accounts of people's talk and interactions as they go about their everyday lives. Third, early and present work converge in the kinds of appeals made in the arguments that people use to support a particular claim to social knowledge. The ethnography will show that the arguments people use in their personal strategies are usually stated as redefinitions or true definitions of rules, not as exceptions. Even if a particular case giving rise to conflict enjoys extenuating circumstances, the plaintiff or disputant will generalize his or her argument in terms which regularize the exception within a body of common practices.

Thus what is made explicit, by being openly named in public or acted upon, is a common understanding on which to operate. So-called structures are appealed to as 'rehearsed talk', equivalent to 'precedence' in legal terms, examples of occasions when certain claims were accepted. But the act of appeal is always in the form of 'rehearsing talk', containing claims that may not be successful. Despite these claims to shared understanding, it should be clear that the activity of making social knowledge explicit is achieved through negotiation, trial and error, claims and rebuttals. It is never a matter of ascertaining what the relevant norms are, but of negotiating what they might be. (This point is made theoretically in chapter 2, section on 'Ascription: distinguishing, co-creating, and merging self and other', and ethnographically throughout chapter 7.)

Since an account of how people come to consciousness of their selves requires a demonstration of how the ethnographer attained that knowledge, I conclude with some comments about the construction of anthropological knowledge. I adopt the term 'mimesis' for the ethnographic project, taken from Michael Taussig's book *Mimesis and Alterity*. For Taussig, the ethnographer who has the urge to get hold of something by means of its likeness needs a good mimetic faculty, 'the faculty to copy, imitate, make models, explore difference, yield into and become Other' (1993: xiii). I add the facility to accrue roles and predicates, without becoming lost in them or losing previous ones. This activity also has a knock-on effect: Rimbu's action in making a copy of me (as a sister) enabled me to make a copy of him as a brother, but also allowed me to write an ethnography, a sort of 'copy' in the terms discussed in chapter 9.

The book's organization in three parts reflects these theoretical concerns and builds on other intellectual antecedents. In the first part, Overtures, I begin in chapter 1 with a description of the place and the people as I knew them. Chapter 2 follows with a theoretical introduction to topics and concepts. I start from the self and distinguish three aspects or stages of its construction: the archaeology of the self, the modern self, and the everyday self. The archaeology of the self describes the process of self-construction that takes place in all societies and at all times. My account is taken from social psychology and philosophy, specifically the work of G.H. Mead, Strawson, Sartre, Ricoeur and Taylor. These theorists describe self-construction as a process of co-creation which implicates the self with the other through such processes as intersubjectivity, interlocution, self-externalization and self-objectification. Language stands for a 'public space' for the articulation of a common act of focus; being a person is a capacity acquired in conversation (premised on embedded social relations) with other persons and maintained through conversation with them. From these philosophical debates I draw several conclusions relevant to the method of anthropological fieldwork: if our relationship to others is built on the process of externalization, in which the self is experienced indirectly as another, it follows that the reflection by which we know our own self involves self-externalization rather than self-introspection. In order to become self-conscious, individuals must become objects to themselves.

A further corollary is that the process of knowing others is not essentially different from that of knowing one's self.

The second stage, the modern history of the self, adds cultural and historical dimensions to this construction. The modern person, as described by Taylor, ascribes all its powers to the individual, losing sight of the formative dependence on conversations with others. Personhood becomes interiorized, and this generates the notion of the individual as monad who imposes values and makes choices. While this perception does not alter the basic process of self construction described earlier, it does cause persons to misrecognize it. Finally, my discussion of 'the everyday self' turns a direct beam on theories of speech and utterance and introduces the concepts derived from my own ethnography: elicitation, making explicit, rehearsed and rehearsing talk and action.

To a large degree, chapter 2 deproblematizes the process of knowing the other, by pursuing a philosophical enquiry that instead problematizes the self. Several chapters then follow that tell stories of and by Kewa themselves. In Narratives (part I), chapters 3 to 5 present people's life stories. Spanning three generations, these accounts provide rich biographies of social, psychological and material lives and the trajectory of change. The narratives are organized in groups that show a shift in people's understanding of themselves and their environment. Chapter 3 opens with a discussion of theories of narrative (drawn chiefly from the work of Bruner, Carrithers, Benjamin and Ricoeur), then moves to the stories of old people 'close to death', who offer their lives as paradigmatic accounts or cultural glosses for how the Kewa in general live. Chapters 4 and 5 continue the exposition and analysis of autobiographical narratives through to the second and third descending generations, developing arguments about 'self narration' at times of rapid social change. These self constructions reveal, almost in equal measure, the heroic, traumatic and creative effects of moral and political strivings, in narratives of sometimes epic proportions. Chapter 4 gives voice to the narratives of middle-aged people, who straddle two worlds and can no longer take for granted a representative moral personhood. In their strivings for coherence and identity, their stories become metanarratives, consciously critical attempts to negotiate change and shape the future. The younger storytellers of chapter 5 directly seize the new world. Their narratives of the heroic, the epic and the picaresque form their consciousness and organize their experiences as denizens of this world.

In Portraits (part II), three chapters focus on the analysis of 'minimal narratives' (Carrithers' term), accounts and observations of interactions as they are played out. Here I develop aspects of the negotiability of social reality and social knowledge in concrete slices of ethnography.

Chapter 6 provides a background to theories of communicative practices, introducing the theoretical concepts of 'narrative thought' and 'paradigmatic thought' and elaborating on the concepts arising directly from my ethnography: elicitation, making explicit, rehearsed and rehearsing speech. Chapter 7 shows how individuals negotiate marriage and marital life, displaying eliciting strategies in their pursuit of self-acknowledgment. By contrast, chapter 8 focuses on group concerns around three deaths. These events easily map onto the three groups of narratives in part I: worries with big-man politics, puzzles over changing socialities, and anxieties about the disappearance of the old order and its replacement by the new. In conclusion, chapter 9 recapitulates the themes of this book and sums up its theoretical contribution.

Inevitably, many debts have accrued in the writing of this book. I will not save the biggest till last: I cannot think of a way in which Marc Schiltz has *not* contributed at all stages, from fieldwork to the creative conception of the monograph through to the manuscript's many incarnations. His genius is to see the bigger picture and make connections. He praised the project unfailingly when my own confidence flagged, insisting it was worth the pursuit. His support in myriad other ways must remain unacknowledged, lest it divert attention from the intellectual and creative input. Our daughter, Leda, kept me grounded, providing a mysteriously calming effect.

My gratitude to and affection for my Kewa friends, especially Rimbu and Lari, should be evident in the book, which could not have been written without them. They are best at describing their own contribution. I agonized over the decision whether to use pseudonyms. After struggling with Merleau-Ponty's admonishment that ethnographers should take off their own mask, I could not, in all fairness, put masks on my friends, especially against their wishes. Their names are in any case already out in print.

I am grateful to various authorities and persons in Papua New Guinea for facilitating my fieldwork at various points: The University of Papuan New Guinea (and in particular Kewa students Stephen Rambe, Justin Yatu and Martin Yakopa), the Office of the Premier of the Southern Highlands, local officials in Kagua (especially Paul Fearman) and Mendi (where Marc and I did archival work). I thank the ESRC for my initial doctoral studentship, as well as one year's Postdoctoral Fellowship at the London School of Economics in 1989 (award number R000231053), when this project first took seed. Grants from the American Philosophical Society and the University of Minnesota funded sub-sequent fieldwork in 1993; I thank those institutions for their support.

For the University of Minnesota, where I taught for seven years, I have both debts and grievances. The present book cancels out the latter, but the former live on: to Allen Isaacman and other members of the MacArthur Program, for their unfailing support; to Richard Leppert and Bruce Lincoln, for their collegiality and friendship; and to Hal Schwartz, my true knight whose canticles I have sung elsewhere. For their direct feedback on an earlier version of this manuscript, I thank Alfred Gell (now sorely missed), Roy Wagner, and Marilyn Strathern. In her generous comments, which gave succour at a critical time, Marilyn Strathern alluded to the agonistic relationship of our different approaches, from which I continue to derive creative energy. At Queen's University Belfast I benefited from Kay Milton's thoughtful comments on a section of the manuscript, in addition to her collegial help throughout my time here. Michael Carrithers read and commented helpfully and encouragingly on the penultimate version. Thanks also go to Nigel Rapport and Bruce Kapferer, for general encouragement and helpful feedback, and to the two anonymous readers, who provided thoughtful, critical comments that forced me to reconsider several formulations in this book.

Overtures, Ethnographic and Theoretical

Chapter 1

The Aesthetics of Fieldwork among the Kewa

The Style and Tone of Kewa Life

In my imagination I often return to my thin-walled house in the Highlands of Papua New Guinea, surrounded by houses of similar light bamboo construction. Dusk is falling and the breeze carries the gossip of the village, almost in circular motion, in and out of houses, through flimsy walls and onto open porches.

Gossip, talk of all humans 'sibbed in god' (godsibb), thus beyond blood and semen links, is the breath of daily life. Its incessant low murmurings like monologues break off here and there, dying away only to rise up again, sharply to admonish a child or as accompaniment to some exacting indoor task, unseen but imagined by the listening anthropologist. It fans out, directed at unseen others and covering countless topics. It ebbs and flows, part of the rhythm of life. Onomatopoeic talk, it draws out the last syllable as if to show the passage of time: 'Tupela wik igooooooo' ('two weeks agoooo'). Warm and reassuring, it lulls children to sleep; suddenly violent and jarring, it wakes them up to the volatility of social life. Children do not talk. They cry, complain, demand. A little girl farts uncontrollably, her parents scream at her, prod her. This talk is the constant input from community members: of knowledge of outside events, of attitudes and perceptions, interests and changing trends, feelings, new technologies, tentative revisions and redefinitions, strategies, negotiations, making 'public', giving advance warning, dropping hints, sowing doubts, foreshadowing claims or troubles, redressing the balance of discourse, complaining, consoling and praising, expressing aesthetic pleasure, frustrated desire, sorrow and support. The talk goes back and forth, not put in a basket in the middle of the open ground for all to partake but passed around, elaborated upon, internalized, transformed, allowed to die in its dying fall. It comes o'er one's ear like the sweet sound that breathes upon a bank of *kunai* grass, stealing and giving meaning. Meanings are negotiated, appropriated, transformed. Whines remain: persistent, grating, 'eating ears', provoking, irritating like children's paroxysmal, intermittent coughing, malingering in the air. The evening breeze is caressing while the falling darkness is still a soothing glow, not greatly impairing vision but removing harshness. But as the night wears on the talk that lingers has no happier or more soothing message than the child's dry cough, thickening the air with portents of doom.

This is how the talk appears to the ethnographer, who participates in tentative fits and starts in the rhythm of this life. Certain talk only is to be recorded, analysed to provide support structures for my arguments, bridges for my understanding: important talk, 'culturally salient', affecting those structures which it helps me to construct. Other talk I feel only through the various conditionings of my senses and emotions; it is to facilitate fieldwork, not be the object of it. Thus facilitations and enablements are already divorced from objectives, theoretical conclusions, cultural representations and understandings, the 'meat' and final academic message of fieldwork. Yet how does the talk appear to those who participate in it, how does it construct that social life which I thought adequately understood without it in this role? What do people talk about all the time, seemingly casually and disinterestedly, sometimes dully and tonelessly, at other times excitedly and angrily, vacillating between laughter and tears?

Bickering, Bantering and Coming to Blows

Throughout the day and well into the night the squabbling continues. At first it alternates with laughter, but less and less as the night wears on. People bicker, banter, bait each other, stake out their claims and negotiate meanings. A man reproaches some women for allegedly not working; a mother argues with her son's bride's brother, following the bride's flight, for the return of money given in brideprice. Some men meet to discuss pig stalls ('they should be built on the other side of the road so that the pigs don't overrun the village') and childcare ('women should not leave their children behind when they go to their gardens, because children left alone can hurt each other'). A woman and her brother-in-law argue over rights to a banana tree; a son and his father have a serious disagreement over the grandchildren's unruly behaviour, the son retorting that his father always picks on *his* children and never on his other sons'. The same old man, armed with bow and arrow, struts up and down the settlement vilifying his daughter-in-law after a massive row over childcare, which he claimed she delegated too often to him. A woman delivers a monotonous homily to her sister-in-law, whose chickens have been taking the thatch off her roof. The sister-in-law listens with silent resignation, 'she has no talk'. A husband and wife argue about everything: housecleaning, childcare, pig care, pig distributions, coffee-garden care, equitable distribution of proceeds from coffee sales. A father berates his sons for not building him a new solid house, threatening to move to the deserted ancestral settlement, where he will surely die. A group of women relay information that in a neighbouring settlement a man had been seen, he was given the chase but got away, he meant to poison everyone, so 'let's do something'. Some men retort in sarcastic tones that the women should give chase with their bows and arrows. One brother complains to another that he was never adequately compensated for his work on a coffee garden, whose proceeds are now being enjoyed by this brother as the nominal owner.

Much of this kind of talk is said to the wind, shouted by one brother inside his house so that the other brother inside his may hear. An elderly matron accuses a youth of taking her money, which he falsely denies. When it is found on him he owns up, choking back tears of vexation. The same woman is teased on account of her defective knowledge of Tok Pisin, which she is baited to pronounce with her droll accent. An old woman and her daughter-in-law fight over the distribution of the old woman's recently deceased husband's things. A fight between husband and wife leads to the involvement of their grown children, his severe injury, and her imprisonment. Another daughter-in-law has it out with her husband's stepmother, and her husband's father's brother's wife comes to berate her: she always quarrelled with her husband's father's brother while he was alive, and no sooner does he die than she starts on another in-law. The men do not interfere, the older woman storms off flanked by her daughters; the younger woman follows, weeping and protesting. The implied charges are grave: that the husband's mother will die as the husband's father's brother did, with her son's daughter partly responsible and wholly unreconciled.

There is also much 'hiding talk' that reveals anger by pretending to hide it. Anger is not good. If another person feels your anger, she or he will become sick. Roga was made ill by the resentment of Mapi's lineage; Yadi took sick when he smoked a cigarette given to him by a brother who bore him a grudge. Ragunanu quarrelled with her stepson over his card-playing and left her settlement to come and live in ours, where she now sits husking coffee. When I see the stepson he denies both the quarrel and the card-playing, insisting that he was just visiting in another settlement. Rimbu resentfully avoids me but sends messages that he is not angry, protestations that always signal the opposite. Impossible for him to say he is angry because his attempts to control me were thwarted, equally impossible that his anger should make me ill. His *siapi*, 'veiled speech', is, of course, 'hiding while revealing' talk par excellence.

Moods are mercurial. The whole place seethes with tensions that a peal of laughter momentarily dissolves. The day before Wapa's death, following his threatened move to the stony ancestral home, the settlement sways to the rhythm of the saddest threnodies; but a moment after, the chief mourners sit a little apart and engage in mirthful conversations. At her unofficial court session Rarapalu laughs through her tears, while her male opponents threaten and joke by turns. Older, more 'traditional' men's bodies easily assume a fighting posture, head cocked and face set in a ferocious frown. But just as suddenly the frown crumbles into a wide smile, or breaks out into helpless laughter.

Some grudges fester and fights erupt afresh. Yadi comes home drunk and begins to taunt Kiru, a 'brother' from a closely associated sub-clan, calling him a 'bush man' who doesn't know how to enjoy money. Kiru retorts that Yadi is drinking other people's money; he should first return the K10 he owes him. (Lari, listening from inside my house, assents: 'It's true, this man doesn't repay his debts, he owes us money too.') The K10 debt has a twisted history. Kiru was playing cards when Yadi borrowed the money from him to buy pork from another card-player. In a run of good luck Kiru won the K10 back from this man and told Yadi that the debt was cancelled. Yadi cooked the pork and everyone on the settlement had a share. So now he shouts, 'I ate your K10 in one day, it wasn't big money.' Retorting, Kiru piles on the complaints. He had helped Yadi plant his coffee trees and given him K10 for a pig kill, but Yadi never reciprocated properly. As they come to blows Rimbu tries to intervene, but gets it from both sides. Yadi is hit on the head with a stone, but by the time his brothers come from Puliminia to defend him the fight is over. Rimbu and Ipa say it will be forgotten now. It may be brought up from time to time when the two men are drunk or in need of cash, but they are brothers after all and can't go to court over such matters.

On another occasion the ill-feeling between Rero and Yadi, classificatory brothers' sons, breaks out when Rero's father invites Yadi to his house to discuss the impending pig kill. Rero complains that Yadi has no business to call himself the 'mother' or 'father' of the longhouse built in preparation for the pig kill. The argument escalates and Rero snatches a log from the fire, knocking Yadi out with a blow on the head. The reasons for this attack come in layers. Rero has had a grudge against Yadi since Yadi crashed the clan's truck in an accident resulting in heavy compensation payments, to which Rero contributed a large pig. But he should not hold it against Yadi, said Rimbu, since Yadi did not 'eat' the money but had himself been injured in the accident, and served a prison sentence into the bargain. Then Rimbu goes behind this reason: Yadi is always pouring scorn on Rero, calling him a rubbish man and challenging him to show his wealth and his mettle. 'How can I do this,' Rero retorts, 'when Yadi himself brought about the ruin of the whole clan with his irresponsible bad driving?' And so the talk drones on into the night.

Other talk sounds lighter, but has serious undertones. Sexual bantering abounds. One young married woman sits morosely for hours, complaining about her husband's habit of sleeping at other people's houses. She got so upset that she fell ill and almost died, quipped one old man. So people teased her: 'What are you imagining, what's making you ill?' They treated her answer – that her husband did not want to sleep with her – as a huge joke, but in between peals of laughter they also advise her to pull herself together and stop talking like this. Now she is sitting in the settlement looking glum. 'Why won't he sleep with me,' she asks of no one in particular, 'what's wrong with me, am I dirty or something?' The men bait her: 'So your husband hasn't been sleeping with you, eh? Ha, ha, ha.' (Sixteen months later the woman ran away and the husband had to propitiate her to return.)

One day while I was in a discussion with a group of women it became obvious that two of them were having an indirect argument through me. Liame asked who had given me the rubber band I wore on my wrist, and on hearing that it was Lari she remarked that it was cheap to wear just one band. I said one was enough for me, and Lari suggested that Liame should give me some of her own bands, if she was so concerned. (I had declined Lari's offer of more rubber bands in the past, but she was too proud to mention this now.) Though she wore no bands herself, Liame kept repeating that she would not wear just one. A group of men who had been chatting a little way off filed into the longhouse at that moment. One of them, Yasi, a returned migrant who considers himself quite a lad ('Women just can't leave me alone') called out laughingly, 'Don't listen to women's ingratiating talk!' I responded in a similarly playful tone that men were more likely to talk 'grease' than women, and that I hadn't come to Papua New Guinea just to talk to the men. The women nodded vigorously and appreciatively. It was female solidarity now, though they also laughed in recognition that this was banter.

Perhaps they were also laughing at Yasi and his preening. This kind of teasing is not limited to cross-sex exchanges; anyone can put anyone else in his or her place and cut down to size inflated egos. On the occasion of a brideprice exchange, many pigs were tied to stakes while transactions took place. In the midst of this Kumi, a local big man's younger brother, appears on the scene and begins to scold everyone in general: 'Look at the pigs, fainting away in the scorching sun while you chatter on! The poor pigs will die!' 'Oh, Kinyoko has come,' the cry goes up. Why Kinyoko? Not so long ago members of the Yala clan were invited to sing in a fairly distant area, where they had to wait a long time for the local big man to show up. They became very uncomfortable in the hot sun and constantly asked, 'When will Kinyoko come?' Finally the cry went up: 'Kinyoko has come!' They all turned to see the big man, but all they saw was a 'half man', a rubbish man. Yako, a puny Yala man, quipped: 'He was just like me, my double.' Thus the Yala were now telling Kumi that he did not have the power or equipment to order anyone around. It was humorous teasing, but it made the point firmly. By alluding to an occasion when they themselves were roasting in the hot sun like pigs, they sent out a warning to Kumi: don't presume to treat us like pigs who need a 'rubbish man' to point out the obvious.

Place, Movement and Residential Mobility

As I walk along a deserted path, a rare event in this populous region, I become vividly conscious of being surrounded by a green stillness broken only by the murmuring of the water in the stream and the faint fluttering of birds and butterflies in the luxuriant growth. All movement and time are suspended in an intense straining to become part of what the senses open out to. Green mountains rise up to the sky, a circle of azure light over their high steepness. The verdure around is not yellowish or lank or lustreless, but alive and glistening, with shades of reddish brown. When dusk is falling the darkening landscape becomes enveloped in a light mantle of coolness and a still clarity. There is no other place on earth whose recollection could supplant this reality, now.

But for long periods the rain falls and hazy mists descend. Then the paths turn to thick mud and everybody keeps indoors. Not only are the roads unmotorable, they become unwalkable. I park at the end of the good road and wade ankle-deep in mud, each step claiming a flip-flop. The wind howls, and all night the rain cascades deafeningly down on the tin roof. Torrential downpours all day and all night; then waking up to constant, miserable drizzles. It never dawns on some days. Children and adults wearing pandanus capes and carrying any watertight vessel they can lay their hands on come to fill it at my water tank's overflow. There are two different kinds of rain. *Ropa pia*, torrential rain, is always followed by *kala para*, an irritating non-stop drizzle, which confuses people by turning bananas the colour of ripeness. But when they cut them down and take them home, they find them unripe and inedible.

In contrast to the usual still clarity of the landscape, people's movements are often incessant. Always going from one settlement to another, walking for hours, deciding on the spur of the moment, because they see a truck is bound for there, to go into Mt Hagen, and then going only as far as Kagua or even Sumbura, but sometimes all the way to Mt Hagen and staying there for some days or even weeks. It seems excessive to someone who sees these movements as motivated actions to be judged by their rate of success in attaining a stated objective. A whole family goes to the village of Roga to receive medication, but returns unministered because following some whim of the orderly the aid post was shut. They meet with similar lack of success at Kagua hospital, after almost a whole day's round trip on foot or the outlay of a few kina on fares. I rant and rave, curse the administration, threaten law suits and complaints in high places. They nod sympathetically, as if I had been the injured party. Trips to administrative offices, almost invariably closed; wrong or misunderstood information concerning shotgun licenses, car and driving licences, road-work contracts; missed rendezvous, the two parties waiting at different places or one party giving precedence to another matter; longish journeys to pig kills or other distributions that have already taken place or been postponed or moved elsewhere; trips to collect pigs, ornaments, money, or other gifts from partners or affines, and empty-handed returns because of the purported donor's absence, the gift's inadequacy, or the inaccuracy of the word of mouth information that set the quest in motion; treks to the market loaded with coffee in response to a rumour that 'a car will come', but returns without sales either because the rumour proves false or the buyers are paying too little.

Yet no exasperation accompanies such 'unfulfilled' returns. Life is not fully described by or measured out in constant goals, and every activity is not only such a goal that will be crowned with success or suffer failure. If it were necessary to account for life in terms of 'economic use of time' it would be possible to do so. One could say that these trips built up and maintained relations that in the end reaped those benefits that the ethnographer may describe as social successes. But they were not necessarily subjectively motivated by these end-products. People lived, acted, did what they did for any ostensible reason. At the same time it would misrepresent local notions to assume that time is of no consequence to them. Time combines in important ways with activity to construct personhood. To be let down, kept waiting, employed in tedious and thankless tasks, is to be treated as a person of no consequence who inspires little regard.

Aka, Poiale, Yakopaita and Puliminia are 'pulsating' Yala settlements of the hamlet type (see Fig. 1). Among them and other settlements there is constant residential mobility, following political, economic and social imperatives. Yadi moved out of Yakopaita as soon as the pig kill was over. Koke lived near his lineage brother Yembi when the two ran a trade store together, until Yembi accused him of 'eating' the store money, and physically attacked him. Seizing the opportunity to gain a valuable ally, Roga, who lived in the same settlement, offered to build Koke a house near his own rather than let him move back to his mother's place. Rama and Mayanu came to live with their nephew Yadi because of a disagreement with Pisa, Rama's older clan brother, while Ragunanu left her husband and children in Puliminia and came to live in Yakopaita for 'ideological' reasons (her husband's refusal to embrace the Catholic faith, her son's persistent gambling at cards). Kiru threatens to leave Yakopaita whenever he argues with his brothers. Fear of living too close together is an important factor in residential changes, yet it is also desirable to have a central social meeting point. The porch at Rimbu's and Lari's house fulfilled this function; when it collapsed, social and communal life suffered greatly. While Hapkas's porch provided social space during this period, it could not replace his brother's porch, just as Hapkas's influence was no match for Rimbu's.

Daily Life

Seeing me chop firewood, Lari hurries to my assistance. She breaks the thin wood on her head and bites off small bits with her teeth. (Coke bottles are also opened with teeth.) Now Lari sits in the dirt hugging her naked baby, renamed Lisette after me, while her other daughter, Amasi, mischievously beaming and charming despite her shaved head, entertains little Lisette by feeding her tasty morsels. When Lari's own hair was shaved she became very shy with me, running her hands uncertainly over her shorn head. As evening creeps in the family sits cosily around the fire, preparing food. Ever since their porch collapsed Lari and Rimbu have been living in the longhouse. (A year later they had built a new house nearer to mine.) They have a spacious sitting room (literally a 'sitting room', being too low to stand up in) with a mud floor and a hearth in the centre. One pig sleeps there too. The children (Wapanu, Amasi, Lisette – two boys will be born in following years) sleep around the fire, though there is an area in the back with a large raised bed. But most of the

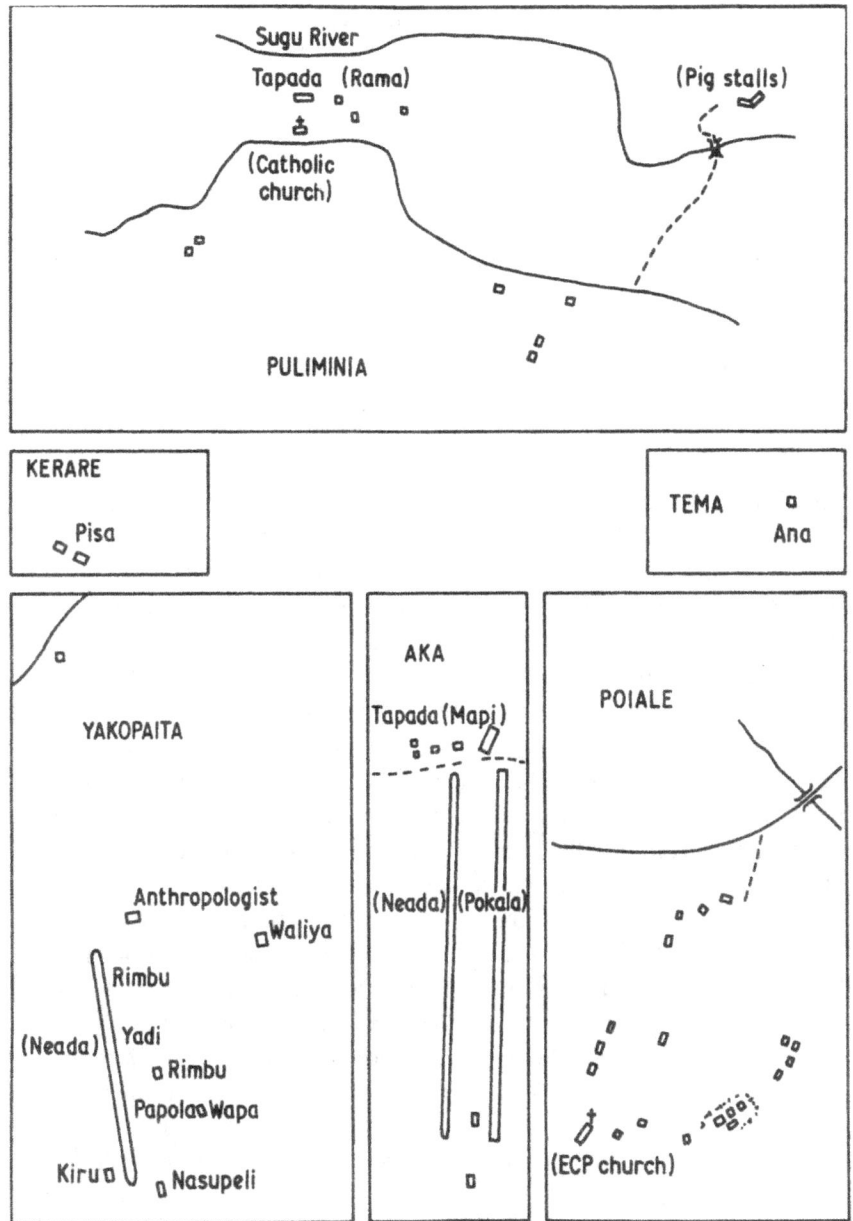

Figure 1.1. Sugu Yala Settlements in December 1981

day is spent out of doors. There is a cosiness in people sitting together and performing one task, such as peeling vegetables or husking coffee. At housebuilding time, how companionably we sit on the ground, stripping and flattening the cane that will be woven into house walls.

Food prestations go back and forth, both in the village and between villages. Some offerings are taken to the church, where men squat on the floor in a long row on the left side and women on the right. The pastor repeats one rhetorical question: 'One thing we may not eat. What is it?' 'It's blood,' Kumi whispers in my ear. Men drank pig's blood in traditional Rimbu Rombake ceremonies, but now they may not drink it, 'because it is the source of all life'. The service drags on as non-attendance grows and parents take out their boisterous or tearful children. Later the congregation discusses a new project for a coffee nursery.

Life in the village is not so uniform as to allow the construction of a typical day. I once attempted to obtain daily accounts of people's activities. For a month I had an assistant follow and record the activities of a different person each day. The only recurrent 'facts' obtained by means of this exercise were that people woke up, washed, ate, emptied their bowels, went to the garden or to the market, and always ended their days in sleep. The details of actual activities, the specifics of a particular event or exchange which reveal its contribution to the understanding of a practice or an intention, resisted typification. Most of my accounts are thus anecdotes or vignettes, into which general statements (such as 'Hunting is not an important subsistence activity') provide a sort of entry.

Hunting is not an important subsistence activity, especially as catch is often consumed in the bush, but men enjoy prolonged hunting trips, alone or in groups of two or three. Sometimes they build tree houses in which they sit for days on end, making leisurely attempt to catch birds. Late one evening Kiru returned from the bush carrying a possum he had killed. He hung it outside and went inside to sleep. In the middle of the night his wife Liame, woken by the dog, saw the possum and took it into her room. When later in the night Kiru found out what she had done, he was furious. He told Liame that the possum was not for her to eat, but for his clan brother's wife. Liame went into a screaming fit that roused the whole settlement. At first light she packed the dog in her net bag and took off for the bush, swearing she would kill her own game. When she had not returned by seven in the evening, Kiru, who was in the habit of saying he had married a hard woman, ventured the wistful opinion that she might have fallen off a tree and died in her pursuit of game. She returned in a complacent mood late in the night, having killed and eaten some bush rats.

The night before, Sopo, newly returned from plantation labour on the coast, went off to the bush with a tin of fish that his clan brother Rimbu had given him. He used the fish as bait to catch a large pig foraging in the bush. Having tethered the pig securely, he proceeded to make preparations for cooking it in an earth oven ('mumu') – fetching firewood, stones and leaves. In the late afternoon he returned to the settlement, where pork from a neighbouring pig kill was being cooked. As they were eating he whispered in Rimbu's ear: 'Brother, with the fish you gave me I lured a wildcat and tied it up. Shall we go and look at it?' Rimbu responded: 'If you've caught a wildcat give it to some old woman, they like looking after them.' 'Brother, I am talking about a pig. Shall we go and mumu it? We'll eat it and no one will know.' Rimbu was cautious. They should wait until the following evening, he said, and if no enquiry was made, then they could eat the pig.

Early the following morning a man approached the settlement and asked if anyone had seen his pig. Rimbu listened to the description, and turned to Sopo. 'Yes, that's the pig.' The man was told that he should compensate the finder, who lost a tin of fish and tore his trousers in the pursuit, and he agreed to the payment of K3. When Sopo started to give the man details of the pig's whereabouts, Rimbu stopped him with the whisper: 'The man will see all your preparations, brother; you must fetch the pig yourself.' Sopo went off in a huff and was seen no more that day. Later he grumbled that the man never paid the compensation.

The saga of Komalo's bride flavoured daily activities for some months. One night Komalo, Rimbu's younger brother, returned to Yakopaita from a plantation in Mt Hagen, bringing a woman and her child from an earlier but not yet dissolved marriage. Rimbu publicly shamed Komalo for his inability to produce the K700 her brothers wanted in brideprice. Mapi, the village magistrate, was fetched, who 'reversed' Rimbu's decision, allowing the woman to stay and make gardens until Komalo could retrieve his savings from his many years of wage labour on plantations. Rimbu gave way reluctantly, muttering that Mapi would be responsible if trouble came of this. Who was to know if the husband would not turn up and sue him for sheltering his wife? The woman (Wata), with her baby daughter, her mother and her sister's son, took up residence in Rimbu's house, as did Sopo, who had returned from the plantation at the same time.

There were objections to the woman herself. Rimbu's wife Lari complained that she and her mother never cleaned the house or helped in the gardens. They went to the coffee garden, supposedly to work, but fell asleep. It was not their job, said Lari and Rimbu, to police them. And Komalo had left no money for their maintenance. The women had spent K14 of their own money and were now broke. While Rimbu did not like to keep them on short rations, nor did he want to use up Lari's money or the petty cash from their trade store. 'Everyone suffers because they are here,' he complained. Then there was the daily nuisance of having to look after so many people, Lari added. Old Ragunanu was living there as well, and the strain showed. The place was always dirty, and the noise level, especially at night, had become intolerable, what with the talking and the playing of recorded tapes. Arguments were becoming frequent. As Lari put it, 'The more people you have living together, the more they will talk. The more people talk, the more likely they will disagree and fight.' People commonly warn against too much talking, and recommend silence as a form of avoidance, but taciturnity was not most people's preferred lifestyle.

Wapa, the father of Rimbu and Komalo, died while the issue of Komalo's marriage was still unresolved. Wata's brothers sent word that they would not press for brideprice payment until funeral expenses were absorbed. While welcoming this gesture, Rimbu felt increasingly irritated by Wata's mother, who could talk of nothing but the brideprice. Eventually he asked her to leave. As she would not go without her daughter, the two women slowly and mournfully collected their belongings, and the baby, and began to make their doleful way out of the settlement. Wata was too upset even to shake hands. By Wapa's grave at the entrance of the settlement she broke down completely, and wailed aloud. Rimbu remembered the threnody (*temali*) Wata had sung for Wapa, and was softened. 'Come back,' he shouted, 'you've been with us for so long and you have wept for us so much, come back.' Rama, an older clansman, led Wata back by the hand. Rimbu told me later that he was also mindful of his accountability should anything happen to the baby while Wata was on the road. If her brothers had taken her away his responsibility would cease, but now she was under his care. (While this reason does not cancel out his emotional response, at the time I thought, 'ah-hah!' – as if I had penetrated deep into the underlying reasons, simply because they concerned a material economy whose determinant imperatives I was more prepared to recognize.)

Komalo returned empty-handed, with the story that the plantation manager in whose safekeeping he had left his K200 was away on holiday in Australia. Wata's kinspeople agreed to wait on condition that Wata return home with them, but she gave them the slip and made her way back to Yakopaita. As a matter of form, her kinspeople conceded that women who run away weaken their claims to brideprice, but this did not prevent them from reaching a settlement. This marriage was not destined to come off, however. Some months later Wata accepted from Rero, Komalo's clan brother, the brideprice of four pigs, six shells and K100 in cash. Komalo himself eventually married another woman. When Rimbu and I met the new couple in Mt Hagen, Rimbu would not give them the time of day. Undaunted, they made their way to Yakopaita, where Rimbu reproached Komalo bitterly for his behaviour, but still gave houseroom to the wife.

The tensions of cohabitation were serious during this time. One day Rimbu returned to a home packed with people and filthy with food leavings. Angrily he asked Lari to clean up, but she retorted that she was in the middle of preparing a meal. With vague threats of notifying health inspectors, Rimbu stormed off to the market. Ragunanu's stepdaughter Kamare heard Rimbu's ranting, and lost no time in reporting to her mother. No sooner had Rimbu returned than Ragunanu confronted him. She reminded him that she had been invited here when her troubles started at home, yet now things were being said behind her back about destroying houses. 'No, no,' Rimbu reassured her, 'you are not the only one responsible, stay.' He made his peace with her by explaining that he was not singling her out for blame.

While Ragunanu was being mollified, Kamare took her story to her brother Michael, who hurried down to Yakopaita. When he found the affair settled amicably he returned to Puliminia, and attacked Kamare for lying. Then Pupula, the father of Kamare and Michael, entered the fray. Desperate to save her skin as well as some of her fabrication, Kamare now cried that Rimbu was thrashing Lari and had drawn blood. Brother, sister and father beat a path to Yakopaita yet again. Kamare had a lot to answer for when everything was found to be peaceful there.

Scrambling into the Field: Mining the Field and Eliciting Minefields

In May 1979 I found myself scrambling up a mountainous village in the Kagua area of the highlands of Papua New Guinea, accompanied by two local men and a whole retinue of children. Half an hour later I was climbing down again, carrying an indignant cockerel. The villagers had insisted on giving him to me when I told them, in my best Tok Pisin, that I had been referred to their village by one of their young men who was a student at the University of Papua New Guinea in Port Moresby. Luckily I was able to dispose of the cock further down, in return for a gift of boiled eggs, which in turn I offered to my companions. I was a doctoral student at University College London looking for a site for my ethnographic fieldwork. With Andrew Strathern as my supervisor and an intense desire to experience life in far-flung places, the choice of the New Guinea Highlands seemed almost inevitable. By a stroke of luck that would have seemed contrived in a novel, the University of Papua New Guinea had some months earlier advertised a vacancy for an anthropologist. My partner Marc Schiltz, also at UCL and in the throes of completing his PhD thesis on the Yoruba, was offered the job, and his domicile in Port Moresby provided me with a base for this exploratory trip.

As I walked through the village of Yakopaita, Rimbu, clearly the most prominent man there despite his comparative youth, enquired pleasantly after my business. I wanted to live in a village, I said, to learn their language and customs and collect their stories. The lush vegetation dazzled with shades of green and purple, and the less elevated situation – offering a stunning view of the mountain I had just descended from but requiring less expenditure of daily climbing – was enticing. No sooner had I taken my leave than I heard the patter of feet pursuing me: Rimbu had held a speedy consultation with his companions and now invited me to settle in his village, even pointing to a spot where my house could be built. I accepted his offer, and returned some weeks later to take up residence. This time the student had armed me with a little Kewa, the local vernacular, so I could explain to villagers in their own language why I had suddenly dropped in their midst.

Rimbu immediately set about selecting ten men to work on my house. We agreed they would be paid K10 each on completion. In the meantime I lived in an abandoned shack on the main road, the ill-famed Highlands Highway, which appeared safe from highwaymen at this extreme southern end. But the building progressed slowly and sometimes I found nobody working on the site at all. One day, when attendance was slightly better than usual, I made some pointed remarks about work patterns in England, citing the five-day week, eight-hour day. Rimbu said that this pattern obtained in Papua New Guinea towns, but different rules operated in bush *kanaka* villages, where 'contract' work was abandoned on feast days, court days, mission days, community work days, and for any other reason. Koai, a non-Yala workman, responded with the suggestion that I pay an extra K20 for work done on Fridays. 'No', I said; '*dia le*', was promptly translated to him. He then tried another tack: I should pay the workmen K12 each instead of K10, or else employ five men instead of ten and pay them K20 each. I launched into a speech in Tok Pisin, with two salient points: that I had spent a lot of money on the materials for the house which I would eventually bequeath to them, and that we had made an agreement which they should honour. The Yakopaita people nodded in assent, and Rimbu explained that 'this big man' had just wanted to speak his mind. But Koai had not finished. He wanted to make me aware, he said, that he and another two men from Roga had come 'inside' Yakopaita to help with my housebuilding, cutting down trees in other men's forests; the implication being that they would not enjoy the benefits of the bequeathed house and water tank. I said, all right; I spoke my mind and you spoke yours. We parted smiling, but little did I know then that Koai would triumph in the end. Despite my best precautions in writing down the names of the workmen, I found when work was completed that I had unaccountably picked up an extra two, and was obliged, after all, to pay K120.

These were my first few days in the village, and Rimbu appeared reluctant to translate what he later called Koai's 'bad talk'. He now told me that Koai and other non-Yala men had been talking in this vein for some time. Koai himself claimed he was offering the idea in case I found merit in it. This is part of a well-known Kewa strategy: statements are made in the form of claims, but no sooner are they challenged than they become relativized. At this stage, different justifications are sought for the same end-result. Thus Koai began to look for other ways in which I could be prevailed upon to pay more for the construction. His search indicated the various ways in which something may be justified, but it also showed how the value and the power of the end-result is constantly seeking its own justification, and, in a sense, is revealed to be overdetermined.

Koai was not the only one 'testing the waters' here. Rimbu had allowed him to speak on this occasion by translating his talk to me (Koai spoke no Tok Pisin, and I had virtually no Kewa at the time). I suspect that Rimbu often used this ploy. Hiding behind a professed reluctance to interpret, he could find out my feelings, and ascertain how far I would go in certain matters, without running the risk of displeasing or upsetting me; or, to put it differently, without creating for himself in my eyes a personhood of which I might not approve. He was constructing a selfhood in relation to me, while at this early stage, although I was anxious to understand, I was less concerned with his approval of my rather less flexible self.

I refer to this kind of probing as 'eliciting talk'. Though it is a general Kewa principle to claim never to know what is inside somebody else's head, it is everyone's constant endeavour to discover the intentions of others. While talk externalizes and insinuates, it also elicits, probes, and provokes responses. It is used to find out from others and to test the ground, perhaps to muddy the waters or to sow seeds (cf. Josephides 1998a). A Kewa form of veiled speech, *siapi*, is crucial in this endeavour. In my early days in the field I thought that *siapi* was understood in the same way by all adults who had been initiated into this alternative language. I soon learned that no clear-cut rules existed, and the meaning of *siapi* had to be worked out in each concrete case of its use. Nor could it be assumed that it had only one meaning, or that the person using it had decided on its meaning, or that a few minutes later she or he would not change or add to it. I have witnessed many instances of grown people puzzling over someone's *siapi*, considering and rejecting several possible interpretations.

Elicitation can be gentle probing, or it can be used like a goad, pushing people to act. Not long after the pig kill was held in Yakopaita, Rimbu began to goad the Paripa and Yarepa men of the neighbouring agnatic settlement of Puliminia into making public their long-term pig-killing plans. (The Yala tribe is made up of several clans, the three most closely connected being the Umba – Rimbu's clan – and the Paripa and Yarepa.) His questions were pointed and persistent. Did they intend to build a church, a longhouse for a pig kill, or what? Perhaps, Rimbu suggested to Rama, an older but not prominent member of the group, they had no plans. They were too dispersed and divided and their opinions too diverse to pull off a major joint venture.

Michael reported this goading to his father Pupula, the Yarepa clan elder. Pupula hurried down, and Rimbu rashly repeated his remarks. 'I told Michael you should all go to your village and make a longhouse or build a church. It's not so long since I bought the truck and gave it to you. Rama said he would get some wild game [*siapi* for pigs] and come and stay with me. I killed my pigs. What will you do? Rama, Rero, Pisa, Yadi, you haven't yet decided on what you will do. You wouldn't like it if I didn't help, that's why I'm asking.'

Though Rimbu justified this piece of importunity as concern with helping his clan brothers, the implied challenge was unmistakable. He was uninterested in the ostensible reason for the pig kill – it could equally well mark a traditional occasion or the building of a church. He suggested that Rama would 'defect' to him, implying that he was recognized as the most prominent Yala man in the area. As an additional prod, he referred to his contribution to the purchase of the truck, which Yadi (a Paripa) had crashed – thus reminding the Paripa of another area of their incompetence. Pupula's response to these taunts was direct and unambiguous.

> You've just killed pigs in your name, and your thing is finished. Everyone helped Rake [a recently deceased prominent man whose death is described in chapter 8] in his pig kill, but I was the only one of your father's generation to help you in yours. Rake's brother Wola said he would help you, but he didn't. Don't follow his example and make promises you won't keep. I saw the money and pigs at your pig kill, it wasn't an impressive line-up. But when I brought mine, then you saw something. So don't shoot your mouth off. These are your brothers, they are not women and you can't push them. You will see later what they will do, and if you have something to contribute, you can join them. You've already beaten some men, you bought the car from the white woman, you made your prestations to her and she will leave you all her things. Now rest and keep your mouth shut. You asked what Michael and Pupula would do, well, we will do something bigger than yours. You can't just send for people and make speeches. You've eaten your pigs, what sort of talk are you making now, who is hungry? It's my turn to talk. I thought the child would live, I carried it and was happy. But it was smashed, it didn't live very long.

This dressing down did not immediately strip Rimbu of all hubris: 'It's true that I am just one big man, but when I prepared for the pig kill all my father's agnatic lineage brought pearl shells; they made their own pig-killing shelters and brought ten or fifteen pigs to kill. When you do your thing, I will come.' Pupula's response was unanswerable: 'If you talk like this, when your father dies [that is, Pupula himself] this bad feeling will go to your wife's belly and your child will be stillborn.'

The sparring ended with Rimbu acknowledging the fairness and wisdom of Pupula's remonstrance and thanking him for it. 'Pupula explained the matter to me and I am satisfied,' he reported to me. Rimbu had been eliciting two kinds of responses: a disclosure of Paripa pig-killing plans, and an acknowledgement of his pig kill as his own unmatched prestigious initiative. Pupula objected to Rimbu's pressure on the Paripa to 'match' his achievement, branding this behaviour as characteristic of a *rawa*, a traditional practice of destructive largesse, frowned upon by Christian missions and modern secular authorities alike. Rimbu was pushing to have his achievement recognized and his worth affirmed as a major pig killer and big man, but Pupula withheld such unconditional recognition. He rejected Rimbu's claim that big men of his father's generation had supported him, stressed his own contribution to Rimbu's pig kill, and compared Rimbu unfavourably with Rake, thus diminishing Rimbu's claims to big-man status. Both before and during the pig kill itself there had been strong and resentful resistance to Rimbu's forceful attempts to extract this regard from his brothers and fellow pig killers. As a result, the major speeches at the pig kill had been made by other men, who though having prestige could not claim the occasion as theirs.

Pupula and the younger men active in the pig kill had thus decided on the boundaries of the recognition they would grant. If some lines were crossed, male egalitarianism, and more specifically the status of Yaripa and Paripa men, would be threatened. Pupula also threw back in Rimbu's face the implied charge of responsibility for the truck's ill-fate. But the last card was of a different colour, reminding Rimbu of the deadly dangers of creating bad feelings in others, especially those who will become ancestral spirits. This caution, together with the other rebukes, had force, and brought about some short-term closure. It would claim too much, however, both for the neatness of Kewa social life and the operation of its norms, to assume that Rimbu ever entirely left off pushing.

Chapter 2

Self Strategies
Ascription, Interlocution, Elicitation

In the previous chapter I attempted, using all the arts at my disposal, to convey to the reader how my field-site had impressed itself on my consciousness, and how I perceived daily life to be lived there. I presented the vignettes with little commentary, almost like pictures at an exhibition, but I also intended that they should serve to introduce the ethnography's theoretical aim: to provide, by means of narratives, 'portraits' and elicitations, a concrete demonstration of people's strategies as they negotiate their social world and their own place within it. Reversing the usual sequence, the second chapter will provide what is normally expected of an introduction: a summary of the argument, an indication of the methodology and materials used, and a brief discussion of the key theoretical concepts and topics through which the argument is made.

This book is an account of social strategies and techniques for living: how people negotiate social knowledge and make it explicit in their talk and actions; how their own selves, their self understanding and self worth, become implicated in this negotiation, and how they respond to the necessity for constant testing and renewal of selves, relations, and shared understandings of practices and values. In keeping with these interests, my writing strategy develops a narrative that combines people's life stories with the 'minimal narratives' made up of their talk and my observation of their actions (referred to as 'portraits' in Josephides 1998a) – thus allowing a partial ethnography of the Kewa to emerge over the course of the book. Self theory and concepts of the person are the tools of analysis for these materials, as well as language-based philosophies such as speech-act theories and theories of narrative and communication. The theoretical focus on the self and communicative practices signals my interest in this book: to examine how people in their talk, actions and interactions make use of the 'rehearsed talk' of their institutions, their traditional beliefs and practices – in short, their 'culture' – rather than how such institutions, beliefs and practices rule over *them* and determine their actions.

With a view to developing a conceptual vocabulary tailored to my needs, I introduce several terms suggested by my ethnography: elicitation, rehearsed talk and rehearsing talk, and making explicit. 'Elicitation' is the key term which denotes the contestability and negotiability of meanings and intentions. As Wagner was first to introduce the term (in his book *Asiwinarong*, 1986), I avail myself of his perspicacious discussion, beginning with his definition of elicitation as an appeal: '"Elicitation" implies a seemingly indirect and reactive, or competitive, inducement to action, analogous perhaps to Bateson's notion of schismogenesis; instead of literally commanding or explaining what the actor is to do, the actor is confronted with the contingency in which he is to act' (1986: 215). Thus 'the actor is put on his mettle, thrown back on his own resources, in providing a response' (1986: 215–16). This inducement to action in effect challenges a relationship by forcing it to renegotiate its parameters: 'To the degree that others respond to the challenge, and in the manner that they respond, the elicited relationship can be seen as affirmed, or at least ... tacitly acknowledged' (1986: 54). The object of elicitation is a comportment that Wagner (after Geertz) calls 'ethos', a concept also generalized as 'respect' (1986: 45). Ethos can be seen 'as the object of creative elicitation along the lines of Bateson's "This is play" to emphasize that the most elemental relations of culture may be cogently understood as being continually invented or synthesized out of one another' (Wagner 1986: 176).

So far, my use of elicitation largely overlaps with Wagner's – Kewa constantly attempt to elicit acknowledgment and respect – with the whiff of a caveat: Kewa elicitations create room for innovation that breaks out of the cycle of invention and convention (Wagner 1975). Both caveat and overlap grow with Wagner's further elaboration: 'Every trying or hazarding of a relationship in this way leads to its renegotiation, and the normative means of elicitation, the taboos and restraints customarily imposed in kin protocols, are the techniques by which the renegotiation is effected' (ibid.: 53). Though the powers of renegotiation are stressed, the techniques are normative, involving protocols. While Kewa present their eliciting claims as 'true' understandings of social relations, and appeal to cultural norms as final arbiter ('rehearsed talk'), I argue that these claims are personal elicitations open to dispute, not, as Wagner suggests in his ethnography, limited to 'eliciting the significant relationships of [Barok, New Ireland] culture' (ibid.: 45. In the section on speech as capability I return to Wagner's further work on 'hazarding intent'.) In the Kewa context elicitation is well served by *siapi*, a form of veiled speech already mentioned in the preface, which acts both to elicit talk and as a safety-catch.[1] As I discuss there, Kewa verbal exchanges often appear in the form of claims, understood as hiding meaning and requiring further negotiation.

Following a brief explanatory discussion on the relevance of self theory to this study, the rest of this chapter is organized in three main sections. 'An archaeology of the self' gives a short history of the problematizing of the concept of the self, followed by an account of how the self is constructed, drawn from social psychology and philosophy (using the work of Mead, Strawson, Ricoeur and Sartre). Noting the key role of language in self construction I nevertheless postpone debates on theories of utterance and concentrate instead on the symbiotic relationship between the self and the other, traced through theories of ascription variously understood as distinguishing, co-creating and merging self and other. Looking ahead at speech-act theories, I introduce Kewa 'eliciting strategies'. The ethnographer's experience of kinship-ascription in the field concludes this section, by demonstrating the power of ascription for self-consciousness and self perception. The next section, 'A modern history of the self', discusses philosopher Charles Taylor's account of the changes that led to the modern person's loss of the sense of being an interlocutor and constructed in (language) exchanges with others, and its replacement with the illusion of being a monad who imposes values and makes choices. The discussion underscores the general applicability of the process described in the first section, by identifying the cultural overlay as a slant in perception; far from altering the basic process of self construction, it only causes us to misrecognize it. Finally, the section on 'The everyday self' turns a direct beam on theories of speech and utterance, and introduces the concepts derived from my own ethnography: elicitation, making explicit, rehearsed and rehearsing talk and action.

The Person/Self/Individual

A debate on the person and the self is key to all aspects of enquiry in this study, for several reasons. First, persons are the basic units whose actions and communications provide the materials through which I make my arguments about the negotiable nature of social knowledge. Second, social knowledge is interpretively made explicit by persons. Third, I argue that in their personal strivings people are engaged in developing a worthy selfhood or personhood, one that is active in constructing a moral or political world. In this endeavour one is always concerned with understanding others, convincing others, having the input of others in one's constructive conceptions, through eliciting talk and action. Since I am engaged in the concrete demonstration of this creative activity – people creating their moral world by placing themselves at its centre – an examination of what is a self and a person is essential.[2] Finally, from the perspective of fieldwork, it is as a person and through personal relations that the anthropologist constructs anthropological knowledge. Here, questions about knowing others and how others can be known become crucial.[3]

Much has been written about the distinction between the concepts and entities of person, self and individual (Rorty 1976; Kondo 1990).[4] I follow Cohen through some of the swathe by insisting with him that 'a concern with selfhood should be clearly distinguished from an infatuation with individualism' (1994: 168. Cf. Mauss 1985: 3: 'there has never existed a human being who has not been aware, not only of his body, but also at the same time of his individuality, both spiritual and physical'). Cohen is right, it seems to me, to question anthropologists' assumptions that 'selfhood' is a culturally alien concept for many societies in which they work, and to argue instead that these assumptions are misconstructions, deduced from 'publicly expressed and affirmed *principles*' rather than observed '*practices* of selfhood' (1994: 109). A focus on these practices would reveal (as many Kewa narratives demonstrate) the store of pride people derive from their selfhood, which they burn to have recognized as something they have authored; and, conversely, the degradation they suffer when selfhood is subordinated to another category (1994: 102–3).[5] Moreover, to assume an 'axiomatic difference between the anthropological self and the anthropologised other' would be 'to deny to cultural "others" the self consciousness which we so value in our selves' (ibid.: 4–5).

Since I attach so much importance to the individual person for the development of Kewa culture and the daily construction of social knowledge, I must give an account of what I take an individual person to be. 'Person' is an entity denominated from the outside; from the inside, each of us thinks of her or his self. The term 'self', then, has an intimate character that more easily spans the insider and outsider perspectives. I will use both terms, but not contrastively. Strawson uses 'person' because he sees 'self' as too closely connected to 'oneself', but as Ricoeur argues 'To say *self* is not to say "I"' (1992: 18). I will use 'person' when I am considering how characteristics are ascribed, and 'self' when discussing consciousness and the construction of the self and its relationship to the other, but it is not a lexical distinction to which I attach much importance for my present purposes. What is more important to remember is that whichever term we adopt, we are still obliged to offer an account of how that person is constructed on a concrete, individual and everyday basis. Social psychology cannot be satisfied with anthropological offerings that deduce the nature/form/category of the person from the structural requirements of specific forms of social organization. The section below takes up this construction from a level that is both basic and concrete. It describes a process as it takes place in the person, not the culture or society, though it can only take place within a social milieu. It is a social process that happens in all societies.

An Archaeology of the Self

The problematizing of the self has a long philosophical history. Lévi-Strauss notes how, in a twist of the Cartesian cogito ('I think, therefore I am'), Rousseau questioned the self rather than existence, arriving at the startling statement that 'I am not "me," but the weakest, the most humble of "others"' (Lévi-Strauss 1977: 39). This paradoxical proposition captures the ambiguous nature of the concept (and entity) of 'self', but also provides a clue to its construction. Nowhere is the process of this construction more lucidly described than in the work of the social psychologist G.H. Mead.[6]

For Mead (1964), the self is a social structure, constituted by an organization of particular attitudes and social attitudes. A consideration of the two aspects of the self, the 'I' and the 'me', will clarify this organization. The 'I' is the self's response to the particular attitudes of other individuals. This response is expressed as, and takes the form of, an attitude towards others. The others in turn respond to my attitude towards them with an attitude towards me. The 'me' is this attitude of others towards me in response to my attitude towards them. Internalized as part of my self, it has become what Mead calls the 'generalized other', a vigilant organization of social attitudes within me.[7] As the active self, the 'I' always strains beyond the constraints of the 'me', and this is what gives our actions a sense of freedom.[8] Despite this freedom, my own action is always different from what I anticipated, for at least two reasons. First, the vigilance of the 'me', which as 'generalized other' acts as a censor, constantly modifies the intention of the 'I'. Second, actions undertaken by the 'I' are intrinsically inconclusive, having always to await their completion in the response of others. Unpredictability arises in this relationship, for no matter how meticulously we plan the future, it will always turn out differently from our envisioning.[9] This underlines the formative importance of the other in all our actions.

The self's self-construction in the process described above is based on what I would call self-consciousness, an objectification, externalization or distancing of the self. The objectification of the self and the censoring of the excessive 'I', which seeks self-expression and initiative, but also takes responsibility, are elaborated in Mead's discussion of the essential role of language as a process and a system of communication. He observes that while we speak to others, our listening self acts as a censor that may check us in mid-sentence, affected by our talk as an addressee. Thus we act both as subject and object of (and therefore external to) our speaking. From Mead's account I draw some conclusions that are relevant to the method of anthropological fieldwork: if our relationship to others is built on the process of externalization, in which the self is experienced indirectly as another, it follows that the reflection by which we know our own self involves self-externalization rather than self-introspection. In order to become self-conscious, individuals must become objects to themselves. A further corollary is that the process of knowing others is not essentially different from the process of knowing one's self.

Ascription: Distinguishing, Co-creating and Merging Self and Other

The last point is stressed by Paul Ricoeur. Elaborating on the work of fellow philosopher P.F. Strawson, Ricoeur writes that 'we have to acquire simultaneously the idea of reflexivity and the idea of otherness' (1992: 39). In a seminal essay titled *Individuals*, Strawson develops an argument for the 'primitiveness of the concept of the person' (1959: 101). The aspects of his argument that are relevant to my enquiry are contained in his discussion of states of consciousness and how they come to be ascribed. Using some deft reasoning, Strawson argues that if states of consciousness were to be ascribed to anything at all, it should be to the very same thing as corporeal characteristics. Since it is not possible to refer to particular states of consciousness except as the states of consciousness experienced by some identified person, it follows that they must be possessed by or ascribable to a person.

Once it is accepted that states of consciousness are ascribable, the next question is how we actually ascribe them. Do we do it 'from our own case'? The difficulty with this answer is that the method of ascription in the two cases is different: I experience my own states of consciousness whereas I observe those of others. It cannot properly be said that I 'ascribe' states of consciousness to myself when I experience something, such as pain. Self-ascription of a state of consciousness takes place only when I have to let others know that I am in pain. In almost Meadian fashion, Strawson refers to the *language* of ascription: 'we *speak* primarily to others, for the information of others' (1959: 100). I could not have learnt this method of ascription from my own case, but only as part of the experience of the whole language-structure of communication, in which I ascribe to others the pain which I observe in them and simultaneously hear their self-ascription of that pain. This line of reasoning ramifies into many arguments: that I cannot ascribe states of consciousness to myself without ascribing them to others, that others are self-ascribers just as I am, that the act of ascription places me in a world of self-conscious persons. Most immediately, it leads Strawson to his main contention, that we must acknowledge the 'primitiveness of the concept of the person' (1959: 101), which entails that the concept of the person is 'logically prior to that of an individual consciousness' (1959: 103). There is no 'pure subject' of individual consciousness, but a person to whom both types of predicates, those ascribing states of consciousness and those ascribing corporeal characteristics, are equally applicable (1959: 102).

In order to state the case more accurately, Strawson redraws the two sets of predicates. He distinguishes between a set of M-predicates ('is in the drawing room', 'weighs 10 stone') which may also be applied to material bodies to which we do not ascribe consciousness, and a set of P-predicates ('is smiling', 'is thinking hard', 'believes in God') which we apply to persons. Earlier discussion has already clarified why it is essential to the character of P-predicates 'that they are both self-ascribable otherwise than on the basis of observation of the subject of them, and other-ascribable on the basis of behaviour criteria'. As Strawson goes on to say, '[t]o learn their use is to learn both aspects of their use' (1959: 108). The concept of X's depression, to give Strawson's example, must cover both what may be observed but not felt by others, and what is felt but not observed by X. Therefore P-predicates are both self-ascriptive and non-self-ascriptive, and neither aspect of their use can be taken as primary (1959: 109). With almost anthropological insight, Strawson explains that such predicates get their meaning from the whole language-structure to which they belong (1959: 110).

The implications and ramifications of Strawson's concept of the person are wide-ranging, and are designed to counter both solipsism and ego-centrism. Since I cannot ascribe states of consciousness to myself without also ascribing them to others (1959: 99, 104), my awareness of others as conscious persons precedes (or is at least contemporaneous with) my awareness of myself, making it impossible to base my awareness of them on my self-awareness. The direction of inference shifts from self to other, from a necessity to extend to the other a state of consciousness I ascribe to myself, to a realization that '[o]ne can ascribe states of consciousness to oneself only if one can ascribe them to others' (1959: 100). Moreover, one can ascribe them to others 'only if one can identify other subjects of experience. And one cannot identify others if one can identify them *only* as subjects of experience, possessors of states of consciousness' (ibid.). Ergo, the world is peopled with particulars who are persons identifiable by corporeal characteristics and states of consciousness. The act of ascription itself places one in a world of self-conscious persons, others that are self-ascribers just like me, and whom I *see* as self-ascribers. To take another of Strawson's examples, I do not have to observe myself playing ball to know I am playing ball. When I observe other persons playing ball, I see this action as belonging to a class of actions that I ascribe to myself without observation. Consequently I see those others also as self-ascribers not on the basis of observation, as I am a self-ascriber of what I ascribe to them on the basis of observation (1959: 112).

A crucial aspect to remember about Strawson's concept of the person is its inextricable link to particularity (hence the title 'Individuals'). Though it happens, as Strawson observes, that on occasion groups of human beings may think, feel and act 'as one', 'it is a condition for the existence of the concept of an individual person, that this should happen only sometimes' (1959: 114). It is a condition of reckoning others as subjects of P-predicates 'that one should be able to distinguish from one another, to pick out or identify, different subjects of such predicates, i.e. different individuals of the type concerned (1959: 104). The individuality of this difference, but also pride in the self, will be seen to motivate the narratives of many Kewa persons in subsequent chapters of this book.

In a book that wears its heart on its dust jacket, Ricoeur builds on Strawson's propositions concerning the relationship between oneself and others. *Oneself as Another* 'suggests from the outset that the selfhood of oneself implies otherness to such an intimate degree that one cannot be thought of without the other, that instead one passes into the other' (1992: 3). Ricoeur underscores Strawson's insistence that the concept of the person is 'logically prior to that of an individual consciousness' (Strawson 1959: 103), and hence that consciousness is prior to self-consciousness, by stressing that 'To say *self* is not to say *I*' (Ricoeur 1992: 18). In this statement Ricoeur also separates the 'hermeneutics of the self' from the philosophies of the cogito. As an epistemology, hermeneutics can claim only the sort of certainty afforded by a combination of analysis and reflection. Its method, appropriately, is 'attestation', the 'alethic' or 'veritative' style of truth-confirmation which lacks security both as self-founding and ultimate knowledge, being instead a sort of belief: not a doxic belief ('I believe that'), but a kind of trust or credence ('I believe in') in the testimony of others (1992: 21). While attestation can offer no guarantee or make a foundational claim, it relies on the sort of verification (or falsification) familiar to ethnographers: 'there is no recourse against false testimony than another that is more credible; and there is no recourse against suspicion but a more reliable attestation' (1992: 22). I shall link Ricoeur's 'attestation' to my notion of 'elicitation'.

Ricoeur puts a phenomenological spin on another of Strawson's propositions. When he argues that 'we have to acquire simultaneously the idea of reflexivity and the idea of otherness' (1992: 39), he posits a stronger correlation than Strawson did between someone and someone else, by abandoning the third person ('someone' and 'someone else') and employing instead the first and second persons, 'I' and 'you'.[10] His stress on reflexivity, as a self-awareness that is expressed in acts of focusing and externalizing, facilitates the passing from the self into the other, which transforms the self.[11] Ricoeur takes Strawson further by following a 'theory of utterance' path in which the subject appears as a couple (rather than as a basic particular) made up of the speaker and the addressee, to the exclusion of the third person. In acts of ascription, the agent designates herself by designating her other (Strawson 1959: 111).

Though using a different conceptual vocabulary, the existentialist distinction between the in-itself and the for-itself also deals with the acknowledgment of other subjectivities, experienced simultaneously as one's own malleable objectivity.[12] The distinction is useful, as it ushers in a transformational process that may be applied to fieldwork. 'Being-in-itself' merely names the absoluteness and contingency of something's existence (for Marx, the working class in its objective existence, passive and inert, without subjective consciousness of itself as a revolutionary class). 'Being-for-itself', on the other hand, transcends into a consciousness of oneself as absolutely intentional and responsible for one's own existence (for Marx, the working class becoming revolutionary and, in the process, changing the basis of its existence). Sartre describes the externalizing process of the act of becoming for-itself (and thus capable of perceiving oneself critically as both consciousness and the object of consciousness) as one in which one also becomes *le pour-autrui*, 'being for others' (Sartre 1973: 318–19). As Sartre argues, it is always in the presence of another that one's existence is affirmed, and qualities become attached to one as a distinct individual.[13] My very actions reveal me as 'being for others', in the following ways. First, they are constituted by all the conventions and symbolizations of social being (Mead's 'universals', or the institutions congealed in the 'me'). Second, they have an *outside*, a meaning which escapes me (Sartre quoted in Mudimbe 1991: xii. See also Sartre 1973: 492, and compare with Mead's statement that my action has to await completion in the response of others). This 'being for others' must of course reduce me to 'the status of a sign-object, to be reflected or commented upon' by others (Mudimbe 1991: xii–xiii).

Right from the beginning of my fieldwork, in the village where I had settled following Rimbu's invitation, Rimbu conferred on me the kinship title of 'sister'. Being familiar with this practice from ethnographies and the personal communications of other anthropologists, I accepted the classification as a conventional strategy and attached little meaning to it. But as time passed I became used to this kinship fiction and it coloured my relationship with Rimbu. Much later, I heard stories that threw a darker mantle over this sibling bond: Rimbu had had a baby sister whom his mother, in a conventional response to her husband's attempts to remarry, threw into a 'hole in the ground'. The longer I stayed in the village, the more the sibling classification, which at first I considered an abstract formality, acquired a particularity and a specificity of its own, eventually disengaging itself from the class of conventional cases by its unique emotional associations. I *became* Rimbu's sister in my own eyes, even though I knew this to be his construction. My mode as Rimbu's sister can be said to 'depend upon and express the other's power of representation and his or her capacity for objectifying me' (Mudimbe 1991: xiii). It added a dimension to my identity, actualized new structures and uncovered new types of consciousness. Though the initial act of sibling-classification treated me as a sign-object, the externalizing process in which my existence as Rimbu's sister was affirmed was my own act. In this act I perceived myself critically as both consciousness and the object of consciousness, becoming what Sartre calls 'being for others'. This mode of being revealed to me an ontological structure that is mine without 'being-for-me', being more than myself and incorporating the other *as other* in me.[14]

It is clear that the work of the major thinkers examined above – Mead, Strawson, Ricoeur, Sartre – elaborates how the self is constructed in its relationship with the other, not how an essential self is defined by attributes. It outlines an 'archaeology of the self', applicable to all times and escaping the charge of a narrow cultural ethnocentrism. In the two paragraphs that follow, I explain how these theoretical concepts and processes are demonstrated in Kewa strategies of self construction. The exercise allows me to test the applicability of the method, but also to expose areas where the model needs to be expanded in another direction.

In chapter one I presented instances of 'eliciting strategies', ways in which Kewa people construct their selves by testing their understanding of the 'generalized other' while pushing their own agency (the 'I') to its limits. They 'externalize' themselves by taking a stand which they want to be understood as expressing the view of the generalized other, while as agents they are prepared to fight for the claim that their stand does indeed represent that view. Thus 'eliciting strategies' are both a response to the generalized other and the action of an agent within specific historical, cultural and political contexts. To Mead's insight that we listen to ourselves speak and judge our speaking as an 'other', I add that 'eliciting talk' elicits judgment *of* an other, forcing the other to respond and acknowledge the appropriateness or otherwise of one's behaviour. Political context and power relations will determine whether a particular eliciting strategy succeeds as a representation of the 'generalized other'. But even when its lack of success modifies the claims of that agent, it also modifies the generalized other: it has made a difference, by pushing agents (or actors) into positions that are somewhat different from their previous ones.

This forcefulness of eliciting behaviour calls for a modification of Mead's understanding of meaning as a pre-existing system of universally significant symbols. Kewa practice, by contrast, constantly strives to achieve agreement about meanings and the significance of symbols. The symbols to which one appeals must of course be found in the other's experience, but the contextual meaning of a symbol is left to forceful elicitation. As prefigured in the preface, and illustrated in chapter 7, an understanding of the symbolic meaning of a spouse's desertion of the marital home is not a matter of *ascertaining* what are the relevant pre-existing cultural norms or symbols; it is a matter of *negotiating* what they might be.

A Modern History of the Self: Interlocution and Its Denial

While the archaeology of the self describes a social process that takes place in all societies and at all times, the modern history of the self provides its cultural and historical dimensions. These added dimensions cannot change the basic process of self-construction, whose general applicability they underscore, but they affect our perception of the process. In so far as these additions may cause a misrecognition or a denial of the process of self-construction, they may appear as deformations, a sort of false consciousness. Charles Taylor describes such a case in his contrast of two views of the person, the representativist view and the view from self-interpretation. The representativist view is that of the modern person who, seen as an 'agent-plus', is self-aware, imposes values and makes choices. But this person, Taylor warns, enjoys 'freedom, responsibility, and individual originality' at a cost – that of 'interiorizing personhood' and losing sight of the formative dependence on conversations with others. The view from self-interpretation, which Taylor advocates, involves a rediscovery of the archaeology of the person in a context of freedom, as an almost existentialist act of free will and awareness, rather than out of narrow necessity and dire ignorance. Taylor gives this account of what I have called the archaeology of the self: self-awareness, first and foremost, is bound up with language (Taylor 1985: 272). There can be no self-awareness, and therefore no self, without a bringing into focus in a public space. 'Public space' here stands for an act of communication, when what is articulated involves 'a certain coming together in a common act of focus' (1985: 273). Placing in a public space in this way 'is not just a matter of using other people as checks on ourselves, tests of our understanding'; it also underscores our need of them even to understand what we ourselves feel (1985: 275. Cf. Carrithers' [1992: 174] discussion of anthropological knowledge as 'verified or corrected in public'). Being a person is a capacity acquired in conversation with other persons and maintained through conversation with them.[15] The representativist view of the person, by contrast, ascribes its powers to the individual and suppresses altogether 'the sense that we are persons only as interlocutors' (Taylor 1985: 278).[16] This interiorization of personhood, which generates the notion of the individual as monad (1985: 281), characterizes the modern person seen as possessing freedom, responsibility, and individual originality.

Taylor traces three sets of changes that have led to the modern person. The first set was the reduction of the public 'spaces of disclosure' (the locus where what has been disclosed most fully reveals its meaning) to just human language, discounting those mythologies and regions of the cosmos empowered by non-human sources, and the subsequent interiorization of that space within the 'mind'. The second set of changes, following on the placing of the space of disclosure inside us, was the elevation of human articulacy or language to the role of creator of meanings and classifications of things in the world. The third set of changes, made possible by the abolition of external spaces of disclosure, 'gave us a view of the subject as capable of purely inner, monological thought ... preceding any conversation' (Taylor 1985: 278). A fuller quotation from Taylor clarifies the role of language: not only does it carry and disclose, it also shapes 'evaluations', those influences on the person having a stronger force than mere fancy ('preference').

> Being a person is being self-aware, but this is inseparable from being open to different significances, the specifically human ones, which can't be reduced to the vital and the sentient. These involve our being open to strong evaluations, which have to be treated as assessments, rather than as conferrals of preference. And they are bound up with language, disclosed in language. They are shaped by the language in which they are disclosed ... But language as the locus of disclosure is not an activity of the individual primarily, but of the language community. Being a person cannot be understood simply as exercising a set of capacities I have as an individual ... On the contrary, I acquire this capacity in conversation, to use this as a term of art for human linguistic interchange in general; I acquire it in a certain form within this conversation, that of my culture; and I only maintain it through continued interchange. We could put it this way: I become a person and remain one only as an interlocutor. (Taylor 1985: 276)

It is clear from this excerpt that Taylor's modern person continues, just as before, to be constructed through interchange with the other. The difference is that now some of the public spaces of disclosure, such as those posited by cosmological and mythological beliefs, have been eclipsed or denied; but (in my analysis) these belong to culture and not to archaeology. Misrecognition comes about when external spaces of disclosure are altogether denied, and the modern person imagines herself or himself to be entirely self-constructed by an internal creativity and will.

Nigel Rapport's work provides a good illustration of the modern self in such a state of hubris, having lost an understanding of the significance of being an interlocutor. He describes the people of Wanet (a rural English village) as living in a world in which people simply do not communicate, but talk past each other. They have completed the elevation of their personal articulacy to the role of creator of meanings: 'Through language, individuals become origins of action upon the universe and centres of experience within it' (Rapport 1993: 152). To put it in Taylor's words, Wanet individuals have become 'capable of purely inner, monological thought ... preceding any conversation' (Taylor 1985: 278). Rapport's intention is to demonstrate the fallacy of assuming a culturally-induced uniformity. Though individuals in Wanet believe they share meanings, their different personal experience results in different worldviews, leading each to attach a different significance to the words they use. Rapport makes individual selfhood dependent on the appropriation of such different, even antagonistic meanings in cultural forms. As Cohen puts it (in a favourable review with different interests from mine), '[w]e find them seeing what they expect to see ... their worldviews acting as self-fulfilling prophecies whose meanings are self-sustaining' (Cohen 1994: 117).

In the next section I present quite a different picture of communication and speaking. Verbal exchanges among the Kewa are constant negotiations, attempts to fathom the meaning of others and test the acceptability of one's own meaning. Misunderstandings, cross-purposes and disagreements are revealed in, or betrayed by, the action and speech of others in response. Though individual Kewa people may try to make their speaking as persuasive as possible, they are aware that they cannot control its effects on the ability of others to act, and would have agreed with Foucault that 'People know what they do; they frequently know why they do what they do; but what they don't know is what what they do does' (Dreyfus and Rabinow 1982: 187; see also note 9). As people see the effect of their talk in others' responses, they may choose to renegotiate their own meaning.

The self is expressed not only in different understandings but also in *negotiations* – in attempts to compromise with others. The self is not solid and unchanging. Perhaps, even, the self is not 'expressed'. What is expressed is rehearsing talk, messages from the self, not the self itself. In circumstances where responses, both in the form of action and speech, are likely to occur, even Wanet people might find it difficult to persevere in mutual misunderstanding. Levinson (1995: 234), paraphrasing Sacks and Schegloff, put it very simply: 'if B responds to A in such a way that it is clear that B misconstrued what A said, there's a good opportunity provided in the third turn for A to correct, clarify or elaborate'. Fragmentation, multiplicity, contradiction and ambiguity, suffered by other groups of people as well as the people of Wanet, do not have to mean non-communication.

The Everyday Self: Language and Communication at Issue

It became evident early in this chapter that any investigation of the self and how it is constructed resorts to a debate on the use of language. Speaking becomes an act that constructs the self and the other, intertwines the self with the other, and elicits the self from the other. The language of ascription is the cornerstone of Strawson's category of the person, while for Mead the self acts as both speaker and addressee in the social construction of persons. This section turns a direct beam on theories of speech and utterance. In so doing it also reveals the difficulty of separating speech from action, whether as 'kinetic clues' that allow inference of meaning as a supplement to what is said, or as response that acts on a statement in agreement, disagreement, misunderstanding, or to elicit clarification.

Kewa social interactionist practices do indeed appear to construct selves by means of externalization and objectification in a relationship with a generalized other. Mead, and the other thinkers whose work I have discussed, analyse this process as foundational for the self. My study is more modest. I offer no developmental material on the Ur-construction of a self, but accept the premises of its formation as describing a permanent process that accounts for daily acquisitions and rejections of possible additions to the self, as well as the successes and failures of the 'I' to attain its object. I follow the actions of an already formed (but necessarily flexible) self in its daily strivings to attain or maintain integrity, agency and perspective by means of forceful elicitation. Though I draw on philosophical insights, I take them in a direction unavailable to philosophers, whose theories I test and expand through examinations of the minutiae of daily life. Rather than unconscious or subconscious formative events, I describe concrete daily happenings and actions, where disagreements, conflicts and negotiations are clearly visible.[17] In this analysis, the success of any claim is revealed by its power to become explicit.

I begin this section with a consideration of the 'doing' of speech – the capabilities of communication and the effectiveness of actual utterance. I include a discussion of the linguistic distinction between pragmatics and semantics, placed within the larger umbrella of Levinson's 'interactive intelligence'. In the second sub-section (Strategies) I present two nuts-and-bolts accounts of social action (through language) and link them to the conceptual vocabulary and ethnographic observations from my own study. In the final section I elaborate on the concepts derived from my own fieldwork: elicitation, making explicit, rehearsed and rehearsing talk and action.

What Speech Does: Communication as Capability

Ricoeur's reflexive theory of utterance postulates that utterance 'comes to influence the referential intention itself' (Ricoeur 1992: 41). It recalls Mead's formulation – that our listening self acts as censor that may check us in mid-sentence, affected by our talk as an addressee – but Ricoeur is pursuing a different interest, that of the simultaneity of differentiation and interlocution. Concerning differentiation: any utterance, being addressed to someone, implies simultaneously an 'I' and a 'you'; I always need the help of the other, even to maintain my identity when I am alone (1992: 332). But though the utterance begins by delineating an 'I' and a 'you', it does not end by separating them. A single utterance does not complete an action, which is the product of the entwined speech-acts and actions of many agents. For this reason, any attribution to an agent of a particular series of events is a *distribution*, an adjudication about the range of the action rather than a factual determination about the place where one's action ends and another's begins.

Concerning interlocution: though it is true that in retrospect 'attributing is distributing', as I utter my own utterance I am engaging in an act of 'representation' in that I assimilate to myself whatever I am representing and hence deny its otherness (1992: 336). The recipient of the sense assigned to my action-sentence (the addressee) moves towards me in equal measure, '[incorporating] himself or herself into the meaning of the sentence' (1992: 155) in an 'internalized interaction', which Ricoeur dubs 'interlocution'. '[U]tterance equals interlocution', he concludes (1992: 44). As characterized in the work of Paul Grice, interlocution 'is revealed to be an exchange of intentionalities, reciprocally aiming at one another' (Ricoeur 1992: 44). This, as I elaborate in the last section, is largely how I would define 'eliciting talk'.

The interactive character of most practices relies on the sort of understanding that goes beyond the speech content of an utterance. As Grice has observed, what is said is typically only part of what is meant. This fact, Brown and Levinson (1987: 49) remind us, has led to the split of the theory of meaning into two camps, semantics and pragmatics; the former being concerned with the meaning expressed by the linguistic properties of the proposition (the 'said'), the latter with the principles the listener must use in order to calculate the contextual implications needed to understand the meaning of the proposition. In Levinson's further elaboration (Levinson 1995: 234), linguistic pragmatics includes forms of 'inferential enrichment' such as intention, attribution, ascription, and mind-reading. These are part of a practical reasoning or interactional intelligence, notions drawn from Esther Goody's model of Anticipatory Interactive Planning (Goody 1995). Such notions recall Grice's category of implicature, which, as Strecker (1988: 50) observes, requires 'an anticipatory notion that includes alter as well as ego and mobilizes a jointly shared knowledge about the world in motivated and practical speech acts'. Pragmatic or practical reasoning, according to Levinson (1995: 233), enables inferences by the use of pragmatic heuristics, where utterance-type triggers off expectations: a normal expression indicates a stereotypical relation, a marked description indicates an abnormal relation. The 'shared knowledge' here relies on a kind of reasoning about others' intentions; and this leads Levinson to conclude that language is parasitic on interactive reasoning, that is, on the conceptual abilities that make social interaction possible (1995: 238).

My own work is less concerned with the relative ranking of interactional intelligence and language as means of communication (Levinson 1995: 232), but stresses instead their necessary combination, not only for communication but also for the construction of selves, relations, beliefs and practices. Though social relations are realized in interaction, I cannot agree with Brown and Levinson's claim that individuals merely replicate structured patterns (Brown and Levinson 1987: 240). The reasons for my disagreement can be found in Levinson's own work on intention-attribution. Levinson (1995: 241) shows that while we accept as determinate the inferences we make from intention-attribution, we are also ready to revise them when our understanding is corrected by our interlocutor. In my own work, I do not see such revision as representing a more accurate understanding of a cultural practice or state of affairs (Brown and Levinson's 'structured patterns').[18] It is, rather, a response to a claim too forcefully made for the claimant's current ability to carry it through. My accounts thus suggest a degree of 'agonistic exchange' or 'Machiavellian intelligence' as necessary for advancing social action (see Josephides 1999).[19]

This agonistic exchange, or overblown claim, also arises from a basis of uncertainty. No one says what they mean because the linguistic channel is not capable of such precise expression, writes Levinson (1995: 238). But is the human intellect capable of such knowledge? Though I accept Brown and Levinson's assertion (1987: 7) that communication is a special kind of intention designed to be understood, I also argue, in support of the interactive picture presented so far, that people rarely, if ever, speak from a position of complete certainty. First, they must work out what is left unsaid in their interlocutor's speech, using variants of what Levinson has called mind-reading; second, they must establish how far their own claim will be acceptable. In both cases Kewa linguistic strategies employ 'eliciting talk', which attempts to bring out a positive response from the listener. Depending on the response, people may accept different but equally satisfactory interpretations of their statements; or they may withdraw their statements altogether.[20]

Strategies

What I have called capabilities from one perspective are of course strategies from the viewpoint of the agent, who must act. I present two accounts of the dynamics of social action, at two different levels of agent intervention. They provide the theoretical background required for the introduction of the conceptual vocabulary I shall be using throughout this study.

A summary should suffice for the first account, which was presented more fully earlier. Taylor (1985: 273–76) uses the term 'interlocutor' to describe the self-aware, self-reflexive person, whose awareness and reflexivity are expressed in acts of focusing and externalizing through language. Nothing can be focused on and made part of the shared world if it is not externalized and placed in public space; conversely, this 'placing in public space' is precisely the coming together in a common act of focus – 'common' not only because public space is by definition a shared space, but also because the language through which it is carried out is a community language. Language is thus not only a tool for expression, but also the locus of disclosure, since it is within language that disclosure is possible; and this disclosing activity is a capacity of the language community, not the individual, who acquires the capacity in conversation with others and maintains it through interchange. 'Placing in public space' is an act that brings together all the operations of self construction which I have discussed so far. Our understandings of others, of our very selves and even our own feelings, are dependent on our conversation and interchanges with other people. This is what Taylor means by an 'interlocutor'. My concept of 'elicitation' is intended to convey the everyday aspects of such acts of focus, as negotiations in which people attempt to reach a common understanding of the world, and their place within it. My other key expression, 'making explicit', by treating 'explicitness' as a locus of disclosure, denotes precisely the operation of 'placing in public space'.

The second account, similarly summarized and adapted to my purposes, is a segment of Ricoeur's theory of action (Ricoeur 1992: 110). With an action that sets a closed system in motion, an agent isolates a segment of the system from its environment, explores its inherent possibilities of development, and learns about its resources. Ricoeur calls this an 'initiative' or 'interference' by the agent. Translating into my own conceptual vocabulary, I may say that the agent 'elicits' the possibilities of the system at (cutting back again to Ricoeur) 'the intersection between one of the agent's abilities and the resources of the system' (Ricoeur 1984: 135). This, says Ricoeur, is to determine the system's conditions of closure.[21]

To clarify this operation, I use an ethnographic example from my own analysis of interactive practices among the Kewa (Josephides 1999). Kuri, a young unmarried woman, comes across Mada, a young unmarried man, and addresses him in a manner he considers improper for interactions between unmarried people of the opposite sex. She asks him where he is going. This may seem like innocent 'phatic communication' (Favret-Saada 1980), conveying sociability rather than meaning. But with this simple greeting, she mobilizes the gender system, by isolating one of its segments, that of interaction. Fulfilling Von Wright's criterion (quoted in Ricoeur 1992: 110), Kuri is confident, on the basis of past experience, that her action will set in motion the dynamic gender system. The exponential effect of her action results from this, that in addition to being a segment of that system, interaction also belongs to the larger system of communicative practices. Among the Kewa these practices are fluid and flexible, based on negotiation and elicitation through innuendo or overstatement or veiled speech, requiring interpretation and enabling retreat.

These features allowed Kuri to use language in a particular way. Her initiative lay in her use of segments from one system to 'elicit' the possibilities of another, thus fully utilizing the resources of both systems, and exploring the possibilities of development inhering in each. Her action '[determined] the system's conditions of closure' (Ricoeur 1992: 110) through expansion. By interfering in a closed system (gender) through the use of a segment of a more open system (communication), she brought the two systems into open confrontation, thus extending the possibilities of one system through an application of the possibilities of another.

Reinforced by other developments in the community, this initiative contributed to the inevitability, in the long run, of a renegotiation of the gender system's conditions of closure. The action taken by Kuri had led to the development of new possibilities in the gender system, what Ricoeur calls new facts or systematic segments. These new facts are then assumed by agents as circumstances from which to launch new acts of practical reasoning. (I use 'system' in deference to Ricoeur's vocabulary, whose formulations expand my theoretical insights; my own preferred words would be 'practice' or 'sets of practices'.)

Elicitation, Explicitness, Rehearsed and Rehearsing Talk and Action

Writing about Kewa communicative practices in an earlier work (Josephides 1999: 139), I observed how they were marked by an 'openness and ambiguity', seeming 'almost to be searching for their own meaning in interaction'. This strong premise continues to inspire my work on this subject, primarily because it brings the boldness of Kewa interactions vividly to mind. I credited elicitation for this flexibility, identifying it as the larger category of discourse strategies. From my observation, common everyday exchanges were often elicitations in the form of claims. This is how it worked: a particular exchange begins as a confident or even aggressive claim, until it is checked by an addressee. Depending on the strength of the resistance, the claim may either be retracted or turn into a conciliatory negotiation, intended to ascertain how far the elicitor's project can be made into a shared project. In this process other claims, or different reasons for the claims, are substituted for unsuccessful ones. New intentions may develop in the interaction itself, adapted to responses to the original statements. In addition, communicative intentions are obscured by communicators' tendency to cover them up, out of caution or uncertainty. Eliciting talk is always a line with a hook, fishing for responses, so the original statement may not necessarily represent a strong commitment to a claim. Rather than seeking an absolute social 'truth', these strategies are akin to Ricoeur's 'attestation', susceptible to a more credible or persuasive claim (see section on 'Ascription').

'Eliciting talk' is often a strategy for understanding what is left unsaid in *siapi*. As well as being the formalized language of ritualized activities – such as courting songs and dirges, political oratory and ceremonial exchanges at pig kills – *siapi* is also a form of veiled speech with daily currency. More than an alternative language for the initiated, its metaphorical meaning has to be worked out on each occasion of its use. Thus it provides a forum for negotiating meaning and signalling an undercurrent of unexpressed intentions and desires. Attempts to understand *siapi* often come in the form of action, or by means of eliciting talk. Misunderstandings are revealed and may be corrected at this stage, or else lead to changes in strategic intentions. Veiled speech may be eliciting talk, and eliciting talk may be a response to veiled speech. Both play on intention and pragmatics, inviting/requiring 'inferential enrichments' (Levinson 1995: 234); and both are a set of strategies for intention-concealment, intention-negotiation and intention-modification.

Some of the tactics and linguistic forms discussed so far recall Brown and Levinson's studies of the principles of polite speech. Can Politeness Theory adequately account for the presence of these forms among the Kewa? Like any other language, the Kewa language has a rich reservoir of stock phrases which refer indirectly to various activities. A statement having recourse to this reservoir of metaphors does not bind people right away to specific action, because it constructs meanings that must be interpreted and are liable to revision. It thus allows for the 'righting' of the possible affront contained in any of its interpretations, by means of face-saving devices that also acknowledge that humans are 'rational' and that they have 'face' (Brown and Levinson 1987: 283; Josephides

1999).[22] Eliciting talk, just like politeness, is a major source of deviation from Grice's four maxims of rational efficiency (Brown and Levinson 1987: 95).[23]

Notwithstanding these points, *siapi* is more than a secret code and eliciting talk is more than a polite, face-saving formula. Elicitation, as Levinson (1995) argues for interactional intelligence in general, is based on the pragmatics of mind-reading and intention-attribution, but its aim is not always to achieve better co-operation. At times the elicitor uses pragmatic knowledge to avoid offence; at other times insult is the aim, with the shield of indirection adding frustration to injury. How *siapi* and elicitation are used depends on particular circumstances, on kinship relations and on relative power. But at all times and whatever the circumstances, the main aim is to carry through the elicitor's own project. To the extent that success depends on how far the project is recognized as a joint project, it may be counterproductive to offend those whose interests must be assimilated. A successful endeavour may thus require a long process of negotiation and modification.

In view of my description of the forceful character of elicitation, what are its affinities with perlocution? In *Speech Acts* Searle (1969) warns his readers not to confuse illocutionary acts with perlocutionary effects. An illocutionary act takes place when a listener has recognized what the speaker is trying to do when uttering a proposition; perlocution is achieved when the utterance has the desired effect on the listener. Consider the following speech event from my fieldwork: Lari tells her husband that it is undignified in a man of his years and standing to engage in public courting sessions; he should marry his courting partner if he is serious about her. Despite the meaning of the words (the locutionary force), the illocutionary intent of Lari's utterance was to shame her husband into giving up both the woman and participation in courting parties. Her husband understood the illocutionary intent well, but did not succumb to the perlocutionary force; he still married the woman (see chapter 7).

Whereas elicitation and *siapi* invite interpretation and negotiation, illocution is a less permeable category that does not take into account the viewpoint of the listener. Elicitation can thus be seen as mediating between illocution and perlocution, through compromise, negotiation and the incorporation of the perspective of the other. This is not to say that the final perlocutionary effect will represent a 'democratic' act; but it will depend on the mutual permeability of the speaker's intention and the listener's response.

The example just examined, as well as the one I am about to give, will benefit from the introduction to my conceptual vocabulary of a pair of new terms, metaphoric speech and metonymic pragmatics (for a fuller account, see Josephides 2001). Metaphor openly calls for interpretation. When a young man says 'I want to eat sweet potatoes', listeners who know that sweet potato is the staple food and that wives cook for their husbands will understand immediately what the young man means – he wants to get married. But Lari's case was different. Rather than speak metaphorically, she was eliciting, by her use of metonymic substitution, a specific response from her husband. I use 'metonymic substitution', acknowledging the possible pleonasm, to denote a speech event in which a whole statement is intended to achieve an effect which is quite different from – in this case the opposite of – its ostensive meaning in terms of word content. Metonymic substitution is a sort of pragmatics, when the whole of the 'said' is really a vehicle for saying something else. My next example carries this point further.

At the death of clan elder Wapa, Roga told Wapa's son Rimbu that the festivities he had planned for the impending pig kill would have to be scrapped. With these words, Roga, as Rimbu's senior, was laying claim to the authority of clan elder. His proscription, the whole of the 'said', was thus a statement about authority (Josephides 2001). Bloch (1989), adopting Searle's categories, refers to this form of communication as perlocutionary force, with the sole purpose of making a statement about authority and intent. In the Kewa case, the rhetorical use of metonymy, rather than formalized language (as in Bloch), conveys the perlocutionary force. The distinction is significant. In Bloch's theorization, the use of formalized language results in the restriction of political options and a decrease in the potential for communication. The elders who use formalized language present themselves as the unmediated mouthpieces of the ancestors, whose words do not need to be understood, because negotiation with their authority is impossible.[24] The coercive power necessary for these measures cannot, however, be mustered, nor is coercion the optimal political strategy in the general Kewa context, which includes such components as fierce male egalitarianism, competitively achieved status, fragile political relations and precariously established influence. Here no allusion or invocation, whether concerning a deity or an ancestral authority, is capable of determining conclusively between particular competing claims. Instead, the most powerful invocation is found in the innovatory potential of language itself, lodged there by the openness and ambiguity of communicative practices. Such cases call for an addendum to the contrast between semantics and pragmatics: the correlation between semantics and illocutionary force on the one hand, and between pragmatics and perlocutionary force or effect on the other. Metaphor belongs in the first set, metonymy in the second.

My characterization of elicitation inhabits an ambiguous sphere between concealment and explicitness. Eliciting strategies suggest concealment, negotiation, modification. What is the part of explicitness in his process? Part of the process of 'making explicit', in Taylor's description, is that of 'placing in public space', the place of disclosure. Eliciting talk likewise puts something in public space in order to bring it into focus. The process of bringing into focus is a negotiation which comes to a determination – even if reversible – about what is agreed, or at least conceded. Something is made explicit as agreement about it is reached. I have dubbed 'rehearsing talk' the language that is used in this process of negotiation, especially when it is concerned with the applicability, definition and effect of a cultural practice. In one example, a wife fights in court her husband's attempt to divorce her for desertion by citing what she claims are traditionally acceptable reasons for her absence. Although she operates in a pre-existing situation with whatever cultural materials are available, her actions entail a redefinition of those materials and her relationship to them. Acting as both cosmologist and bricoleur, and always placing herself as a person within particular social relations (Josephides 1998a), she uses 'rehearsing talk' to construct her own understanding of the entailments of marital relations. On their part, the husband and the village magistrates offered their own versions of what they claimed was acceptable social practice. The judgement of the court, though presented as 'rehearsed talk', is thus not a final decision or an impartial consensus at which one arrives by following the correct cultural rules. It remains a claim of social reality that seeks wider support, leaving a space for subsequent challenges from 'rehearsing talk'.

These strategies suggest that there is no cause, in the Kewa case at least, for concern about the impoverishing effects of explicitness. Writing about a different case, Marilyn Strathern observes that 'Morality made public became respectability ... once something was brought outside and made an object of knowledge, it stayed there ... there now seem only surfaces. There are no more depths' (1992: 130). The difference between 'morality' and 'respectability' may provide the contrast I need for 'rehearsed' and 'rehearsing' talk. Once something is made explicit and becomes accepted, or enforced as 'rehearsed talk', it acquires the easy power of a weapon. It has been acknowledged as 'right'. But attempts to challenge the authority of the established object of knowledge, as 'rehearsing talk', will not cease following such acknowledgement (see, for instance, earlier discussion on the necessity for selves to be made the objects of knowledge, in order to be selves, without loss of depth).

A good part of Kewa semiotic cultural interplay consists in attempts to make explicit both meanings and intent. Strecker (1988: 22) says of the ritual life of a people that it can function very well without any exegesis. This may be so, but the everyday life of Kewa people, as I experienced it, requires the daily acts of eliciting meaning and making social knowledge explicit as an agreed project, for a basis on which to act. Eliciting, externalizing, rehearsing, putting into public space and making explicit are moments in the operation of focusing, as described by Taylor. (Part II will provide ethnographic instances of how this is done.) The flexibility and negotiability of these interactive practices make social encounters unpredictable. A common Kewa saying, in the face of this unpredictability, is that 'we don't know what's in other people's heads'. By this they do not mean that other people are inscrutable or mysterious; only that they are capable of thinking and have the right to their own thoughts, which cannot be nullified by the disagreement of others.

This attitude implies taking seriously other people's thoughts about how things are or should be.[25] It also acknowledges the existence of other subjects, other selves who have thoughts different from the speaker. The acknowledgment entails a recognition that these thoughts are more accessible to the other subjects who have the thoughts, than to the speaker, who thus becomes aware of different understandings and different perspectives. The need to elicit the meaning of others and negotiate understandings becomes even more pressing with this awareness. Marilyn Strathern declares she is 'wary of "the self" as an object of enquiry' – other people's selves are accessible only to them (1992: 153). The Kewa would agree, but still continue with their attempts at guessing, or 'mind-reading'. This negotiation is, after all, the basis of their self- and world-construction.[26]

Conclusion

Anthropologists (and other social scientists) often describe the decisions of socio-political institutions as authenticating a culture's practice. They are the 'final word', whereas daily strivings appear as prevarications or corrections. My focus on communicative practices, by contrast, proposes a particular understanding of the effectiveness of social action which challenges taken-for-granted causal hierarchies in descriptions of social determination. It suggests that 'institutions' (such as mediated conflict settlement and local court hearings) do not operate as cultural forms which are essentially different from everyday strivings towards specific social ends. Outcomes of events, even when couched in language that claims cultural inevitability, are far from predictable or irreversible. The taken-for-grantedness described by Michelle Rosaldo ('[Culture's] truth resides not in explicit formulations of the rituals of daily life but in the daily practices of persons who in acting take for granted an account of who they are and how to understand their fellows' moves' [1984: 140]) is often just a contested claim. Though Gricean implicature as an 'anticipatory notion' presupposes the existence of social norms contained in co-operative principles and conversational maxims, it also negotiates by making claims.

In the Kewa case these claims are possibly more aggressive than elsewhere, because of the openness of Kewa communicative strategies and the negotiability of the meaning of social practices. Elsewhere I have characterized eliciting talk and action as being a measure of the absence of frame, yet simultaneously as serving as a sort of frame (Josephides 1999: 152, 5). On the one hand, elicitation is a strategy necessitated by the instability or unpredictability of audience response, due to the absence, within the frame in which a message is contained, of a reliable metacommunicative device for deciphering the message. On the other hand, elicitation also serves as a sort of frame, in so much as it delimits expectation, preparing listeners to treat a message in a particular way.

Throughout the discussion I have drawn parallels between my conceptual categories and those developed by other thinkers. The effect of this should not be to overburden a concept or reduce another to it. My strategy here is itself a sort of elicitation, 'placing into public space' and 'making explicit' – through conversation, analogy and comparative analysis – the several categories that have been used to explain the operations of constructing the self and its world: externalization, the 'I' and the 'me', ascription, being-for-others, self-consciousness, interlocution, attestation, elicitation, negotiation, metonymic pragmatics, making explicit, rehearsed and rehearsing talk.

In contrast to my earlier ethnographic work on the Kewa (especially Josephides 1985), my strategy here is not to analyse action in order to discover what it hides or mystifies; instead, my intention is to bring something to view, namely, the social processes by which explicit knowledge is constituted, through social action and speech, as Kewa persons create the discourses of their world and their self at its centre. In addressing this issue, an earlier essay identified the acknowledgment of one's self as a major motivation for these strategies. This led to the insight that people did not merely respond to situations; they responded to their implications for the perception of the self. Their actions, then, subverted many popular generalizations about social action and cultural institutions (Josephides 1998a: 163–64). Subsequent chapters will present ethnographic materials that put flesh on these arguments, which were suggested by ethnographic observations in the first place.

Notes

1. There are commonalities and differences between Zande *sanza* and Kewa *siapi*. Evans-Pritchard describes *sanza* as 'a characteristic mode of speech, an indication of [Zande] mentality' (Evans-Pritchard 1962: 227). As with *siapi*, what is important in the use of *sanza* is to 'keep under cover and to keep open a line of retreat' (ibid.: 222). When Kewa avail themselves of this line of retreat, it is not because, like the Azande, they want to conceal their affairs (ibid.), but because they want to give their interlocutors a chance to negotiate meaning, and thus avoid undue offence.
2. Here and elsewhere in this chapter and in chapter 6 my perspective is similar to Ingold's (2000: 1), when he argues that 'persons come into being as centres of intentionality and awareness within fields of social relationships, which are in turn carried forward and transformed through their own actions'.
3. Cohen writes that as an anthropologist he must admit that 'the starting point for my interpretation of another's selfhood is my own self' (Cohen 1994: 3). He cites Wendy James: 'Self-knowledge is intimately linked with the possibility of understanding others' (1994: 53). Following Strawson, I seek to make this claim more complex.
4. In a literary postscript to a volume on the identity of persons, Amélie Rorty (1976: 303) explains the relevance of our word choice: 'Our powers of action are different, our relations to one another, our properties and proprieties, our characteristic successes or defeats, our conception of society's proper strictures and freedoms will vary with our conceptions of ourselves as characters, persons, selves, individuals.' Rorty elaborates further that *selves* are 'possessors of their properties' while *individuals* are 'centers of integrity' whose rights are inalienable' (1976: 302). *Persons* evolved from *dramatis personae* on the stage, in combination with the legal or structural positions which they represented (see Mauss 1985). Rorty traces a transition from *person* to *self* and thence to *individual*: 'When a society has changed so that individuals acquire their rights by virtue of their powers, rather than having their powers defined by their rights, the concept of person has been transformed to a concept of self' (Rorty 1976: 313). Individuality is seen as the expression of an inchoate friction between the person and society: 'It begins with conscience and ends with consciousness ... The rights of persons are formulated *in* society, while the rights of individuals are demanded *of* society' (1976: 315). The categories that Rorty describes have heuristic value, but they are too cut-and-dried and need some scrambling. As we shall see, 'persons' and 'selves' cannot be unscrambled among the Kewa. The powers of Kewa persons may well be defined by their rights, but precisely what rights belong to specific socio-structural positioning is often contested. Moreover, those positionings or statuses are usually of the achieved kind and leave room for manoeuvring. Thus, persons may have to use their powers of persuasion or influence to convince others to acknowledge their claims to their rights. Dorinne Kondo has offered two arguments against philosophical and anthropological concepts of the self: they are essentialist, because they assume a core self

constructed without regard to power relations and cultural or historical context, and they effect a split between the person 'as bearer of social roles' and the self as 'the inner, reflective essence of psychological consciousness' (Kondo 1990: 12). These definitions are based on a reading of Mauss (1985) and do not take into account the philosophical traditions which I consider here.

5. Two examples: Cohen (1994: 37) cites Briggs' account of how the Utku Inuit train their children to acquire an *isuma*, defined as the ability to act autonomously and self-sufficiently. The ability is gained by achieving a mastery over emotions, but emotions are not cultural givens and hence the acquisition of *isuma* is not once and for all but must be constantly tested. He also cites Myerhoff's (1978) account of very elderly East European Jewish immigrants in California, who cling to their 'insistent selfhood' by demanding that others should be aware of it, and of themselves as its authors (Cohen 1994: 102–3).

6. All page references are to *George Herbert Mead on Social Psychology*, edited and with an introduction by Anselm Strauss, Chicago, 1964. Mead's work from an earlier volume (Mead 1934) is to be found here. The American tradition of social psychology can be traced back to Cooley (1902), who takes the self to be a social product, developed in interaction with others. For Mead, mind, body and behaviour were inseparably linked, and human intelligence was a product of evolution. Thus human behaviour includes past experience and future hopes, as through language we represent others and their imagined responses to us. This view of the interaction of self and society became known as symbolic interactionist social psychology (see Hewitt 1991). Mead's name is also associated with the philosophical doctrine of pragmatism, according to which the values, meaning and truths of propositions are taken as equivalent to the practical consequences derivable from them. In Peirce's formulation, the meaning of a proposition is its logical (or physical) consequences. Thus a pragmatic concern stresses outcome rather than process, preferring the practical and the concrete over the theoretical and abstract.

7. In Freudian terminology, the ego corresponds to the 'I' and the superego to the 'me'; Mead leaves no conceptual or psychological space for an id. Bourdieu's (1977) 'habitus' may also be seen as a variant of the 'me'.

8. For William James, 'me' referred to the empirical or known self, while 'I' referred to the knowing self.

9. Compare Merleau-Ponty (1974: 146): 'Is the meaning of our actions to be found in our intentions or in the effect they have on others?' And Bourdieu (1977: 79): 'It is because subjects do not, strictly speaking, know what they are doing that what they do has more meaning than they know'. Marilyn Strathern's *Gender of the Gift* (1988) also speaks to these questions.

10. It could be argued that in their ethnographies anthropologists achieve a stronger difference, rather than correlation, by using the first person for themselves and the third for the studied 'other'. The second person is the reader.

11. Elsewhere Ricoeur (1981) expounds on the hermeneutical circle, the comprehension of the self by the detour of the other ('appropriation'), by means of which the self also changes.

12. Drawing on the work of Merleau-Ponty, Jackson (1996: 26) expresses this point neatly: 'A person becomes a subject for herself by first becoming an object for others – by incorporating the view that others have of her.'

13. For Sartre, there is no reality outside human action, and the unconscious does not exist. Therefore unconscious mental structures become unthinkable. Instead, we

have the pre-reflective choice of being. Against historical dialectic, Sartre emphasizes the primacy of consciousness as absolutely intentional and dialectical, and individual praxis as the only ontological reality.

14. Favret-Saada provides an instance of the ethnographer being invented as an 'unwitcher' by her informants in the Bocage, in an example that demonstrates the perils of such a local placing of the ethnographer (Favret-Saada 1980: 173).

15. Like Ingold (1990: 220), I have so far assumed all persons to be human; unlike him, I have not taken up the case of non-human persons in another publication focusing on self-awareness in non-human animals (Ingold 1988). In a personal conversation, Kay Milton pointed out this possible lacuna in my argument, which, by making acts of communication within a public space the linchpin of personhood, excludes the possibility of non-human persons. The best service I can render the reader is to refer her or him to Milton's *Loving Nature* (2002), which discusses personhood from a perspective that is inclusive of all animals.

16. Carrithers (1985: 255) argues that Taylor's notion of the interlocutor is too simplistic, as it forgets that since 'culture' is not singular each individual is inducted into several great conversations. What constitutes an interlocutor, Carrithers rightly points out, is different in each case, sometimes being a soul and sometimes a citizen. I think Taylor's notion should be able to take this amendment on board.

17. This statement must be qualified. In their autobiographical stories people did in fact recount traumatic or formative events, of whose full workings they may not have been entirely conscious (see Lari's story in chapter 5). I simply mean here that this study cannot and does not attempt to trace an 'original' formation of the self from infancy.

18. In their edited volume *Dangerous Words: Language and Politics in the Pacific* Brenneis and Myers (1984) focus, as I do, on cultural meanings as they are constituted through interactional practices, but their thesis is closer to Brown and Levinson's in assuming that such practices reproduce norms rather than challenge them, as in my analysis.

19. Building on Goody's notion of Anticipatory Interactive Planning (Goody 1995), Levinson opts for the superiority of 'cooperative, mutual intersubjectivity' (Levinson 1995: 253) over agonistic exchanges. He uses the models of 'Machiavellian' and 'Humeian' intelligence to identify, respectively, agonistic interaction and co-operative, intersubjective interaction co-ordinated 'through implicit contract' based on mind-reading and intention attribution (Levinson 1995: 227). See my elaboration of these types of interaction in Josephides (1999).

20. In his intricate discussion on 'hazarding intent' drawing on the *habu* ritual of the Daribi people of highland New Guinea, Wagner reflects on the double sense of 'hazard': 'daring and being at risk because of what one has dared or chanced' (1995: 164). Starting in a Meadian vein, he describes how my reactions to others qualify their reactions, 'and feed back into my own self-expression' (1995: 163). In our quest to understand our intentions, our actions and our world, we must objectify; but objectification severs action and intention from me as an agent, and in an act of 'spontaneous and intentional' self-recognition I must then 'claim' some intentions as my own and impute some to others (1995: 164). Despite this, the subject remains estranged as subject, as the mode of knowledge is objectification. In an intriguing conclusion, Wagner depicts 'culture' as intentionality's 'photograph'; we should not expect to find intentionality itself in

the picture, 'for the simple reason that intentionality took the picture. And intentionality is out there taking pictures at this very moment' (1995: 174).

This humorous depiction recalls Italo Calvino's medieval tale of the *Nonexistent Knight*, the quintessential superego, empty inside his well-polished armour but able to perform exemplary knightly deeds. (I am grateful to Marc Schiltz for pointing out this connection.) When Charlemagne asks how he does his job, if he doesn't exist, the knight answers: 'By will power, and faith in our holy cause!' (Calvino 1977: 7). In Wagner's ethnography (1995: 168), *habu* men are the 'catchers' of intentionality, in 'a ritual of subject-object displacements' which requires them to penetrate the designs of malevolent intentionality. In a world of constant objectification, they must act confidently without knowing why they are acting, except to avert some feared calamity. They are seekers who in the end may don the nonexistent knight's armour – but perhaps only so that they may hide inside it.

Where Derrida's *différance* is the endless slippage of meaning from sign to sign, in Wagner's hazarding of intent agency slips from subject to subject. Because subjectification of intentionality is forever deferred and the subject objectified, the product and meaning of intentionality must also remain indeterminate: one intention, as a 'snapshot' of an act or a real thing, has its meaning deferred, being seen as the intentionality's depiction of its act rather than the act itself. The world is locked in a perpetual petitio principii. We do not know which is the act, which its depiction – but it seems to us that the nonexistent knight is very knightly.

21. The problem Ricoeur (1992) addresses concerns what makes possible the link between means and ends. The 'means' (C) in this case is a system, or a system segment which can be seen as a 'fact', amenable to causal explanation (D) (for instance, the gender system is a dynamic system whose origin, operation, function, and role in society may be explained in terms of cause and effect). The 'ends' (A) is a teleological segment, or a circumstance mobilizing the agent's action, which is amenable to practical reasoning (B); that is to say, the agent is motivated to offer cogent arguments for its desirability. It may be a belief system, or a value encoding the agent's desire. A by-product of these arguments (practical reasoning – B – to which Ricoeur refers as 'real action') is the introduction of new facts, or system segments (C), which in turn set off a new series of causal explanations (D). The process now goes into reverse, and the new causal explanations (D) lead to new facts (C). The final move links means with ends, when the new facts or means (C) are assumed by an agent as circumstances worthy of being seized or appropriated as ends. A teleological segment (A) is amenable to practical reasoning or syllogism because its explanation is tautological, by definition in terms of ends: 'an event occurs because the conditions that produced it are those required to produce this end' (Ricoeur 1992: 78). I cut with a knife because a knife is made for cutting. I learn to read and write at school because schools are designed to teach reading and writing. The syllogism goes like this: schools are designed to teach reading and writing. I attend school. Ergo, I learn to read and write. A teleological explanation does not have to be causal; it is contained in the antecedent conditions of a system. But when we come to the semantics of action, the motive that classifies an action as intentional requires that it is also a cause. I cut with a knife, not because knives are made for cutting, but because I intend to make sandwiches, and my action causes bread slicing.

22. Public self-image equals 'face'. In terms of wants, 'negative face' refers to the desire that one's own actions should be unimpeded by others, and 'positive face' to the desire that one's own wants be desirable at least to some others (Strecker 1988: 62 citing Brown and Levinson 1987: 67).
23. Grice's four maxims, as reproduced in Brown and Levinson (1987: 95), are as follows: 'Maxim of Quality: Be non-spurious (speak the truth, be sincere). Maxim of Quantity: (a) Don't say less than is required, (b) Don't say more than is required. Maxim of Relevance: Be relevant. Maxim of Manner: Be perspicuous; avoid ambiguity and obscurity'.
24. In the practice of witchcraft, words are also naked power, as Favret-Saada observes: 'witchcraft is spoken words: but these words are power, and not knowledge or information' (1980: 9). The difference here is between power and authority. A link with ancestral authority may render negotiation impossible, but Favret-Saada's ethnography on witchcraft in the Bocage (1980) describes the negotiations and 'mind-readings' necessary for such relations of power to be established.
25. I use 'taking seriously' in the sense of Heidegger's 'care' (*Sorge* or *Besorgen*), an existential or ontological condition of the Dasein which indicates a comportment or 'turning towards' things in the world (Heidegger 1988: 312, throughout).
26. Favret-Saada's ethnography on witchcraft in the Bocage again provides a comparative example from an entirely different society (rural France). She describes in strong words local people's watchfulness of the ethnographer: 'Let him open his mouth, and his interlocutor immediately tries to identify his strategy, estimate his force, guess if he is friend or foe, or if he is to be bought or destroyed' (1980: 11).

Part I
Narratives

Chapter 3

Narrating the Self I
Moral Constructions of the Self as Paradigmatic Accounts

The previous chapter provided a conceptual framework for understanding human interactions as operations that construct the self and the other in a reciprocal activity through forcefully eliciting practices. The same operations simultaneously negotiate understandings of cultural practices and social knowledge. Subsequent chapters will show how much of this activity is telescoped in the accounts that people give about themselves, their lives and their achievements. The importance of narrative, then, is from the outset analytically bound up with the human interactions that are central to this study. The present chapter does something different: it uses older people's narratives to provide for these later accounts a backdrop of Kewa culture, a context of practices, events and expectations constructed in almost 'doxic' terms of taken-for-grantedness (Bourdieu 1977). Introducing the Kewa through life stories avoids the reification of culture usually encountered in first chapters of classical ethnographies, when we are given a 'base' on which the ethnographic edifice rests. Here, instead, old people simply talk about what they do or did. The chapter also begins the theoretical discussion of narrative which is at the heart of this study.[1]

The narratives I present throughout this book undergo two different kinds of divisions. First, they are divided into three generational sets that coincide with formal as well as substantive differences: in addition to having a different theoretical focus, each set will also be telling a different story, covering a different aspect of Kewa life and experience. Old people's stories (set 1) are presented in this chapter, the stories of those in their middle age (set 2) are the subject of chapter 4, and the stories of married adults in their thirties (set 3) follow in chapter 5. Second, the narratives are divided into two categories: maximal narratives and minimal narratives. 'Maximal narratives' are the life stories of people who were consciously and deliberately giving me accounts of their lives; 'minimal narratives' are accounts I have put together from a variety of sources and to which I have referred elsewhere as 'portraits' (Josephides 1998a). I borrow the term 'minimal narratives' from Carrithers (1995: 268), who defines them as 'compact utterances' which work through implicit inference. But while his work illustrates how such utterances evoke stories that 'orient' people in their understanding of events and actions, I have a different focus. My use of 'portraits' reveals my interest in how people's personhood is made up of a combination of the following elements: their own speech, actions and interactions; other people's perceptions of them; and their perception of other people and events. By sinking my concept of 'portrait' into the meaning of minimal narratives I include my own act of gathering such narratives together from a living mêlée of interactions. The concept of 'portrait' should also clarify why, despite the division I began with, 'minimal narrative' traces always cling to maximal narratives, linking personal stories with the actions and responses of others before the latter have been appropriated and assimilated. My minimal narratives are thus interactive, displaying the achievements of social action.

This chapter begins the debate on narrative with a consideration of the maximal narratives of the older generation of Kewa villagers. (Minimal narratives will be the subject of part II) As I string these together into an almost seamless account, a picture of precontact Kewa life emerges as a shared or interpersonal experience. In Carrithers' (1992: 164) words, this is an example of the 'consensibility' of narratives. (Following Ziman 1978, Carrithers [1992: 155–56] investigates 'reliable knowledge' as resting on conceptual consensibility, that is, 'the ability of people to perceive things in common, to agree upon and to share perceptions'). Thus one aim of this chapter is to depict, as far as possible, a shared culture as the baseline or background to the more contested picture of narratives in subsequent chapters. From another perspective, I link this consensibility to a crucial distinction in the theory of narrative – that between paradigmatic and narrative modes of thought (Bruner 1986). Though I do not argue that old people's maximal narratives contain paradigmatic knowledge (which is generic, impersonal and based on abstract reasoning), their stories undoubtedly claimed a certain generality for their personal experiences, thus serving as a cultural gloss. This generalization was made possible because of an implicit (or tacit) claim or assumption: that people's normal lives followed a general teleological path or had an ethical aim. I develop this argument only after a considerable adaptation of Ricoeur's (1992) contrast between ethics and morality.

In summary, this chapter will engage three questions in the following trajectory: beginning with a theoretical overview of the theory of narrative, it will contrast paradigmatic and narrative modes of thought, linking the older generation's narratives to a consideration of ethics and morality. At the same time it will show how the consensibility of narratives in this chapter paints a picture of a 'shared culture', even when accounts concern different aspects of that culture. This consensibility, finally, will be seen as deriving from the non-engagement with the future, and even the absence of the present, in the stories of those who spoke as if their lives were at an end.

Theories of Narrative

Jerome Bruner (1986: 14) writes that there are two modes of thought: the paradigmatic mode of philosophy, mathematics and the physical sciences, and the narrative mode of the human condition, concerned with the landscapes of action and consciousness. The powers of these modes are correspondingly different: 'arguments convince one of their truth, stories of their lifelikeness' (ibid.: 11). As a psychologist interested in the human condition, Bruner considers it more insightful to explore the ways we construct the world and create products of the mind, than to seek to establish the 'ontological status of the products of these processes' (ibid.: 45–46). Narrative, for him, 'deals with the vicissitudes of intention' (ibid.: 17), the intricate and tortuous steps by which we come to endow experience with meaning. An irreducible feature of the story is its joint placement in the space of action and in the subjectivity of the actors; thus the timeless underlying theme of a story – its fabula – is a unity that is achieved between plight, characters and consciousness (ibid.: 20–21). Three features make a narrative act powerful: the triggering of presupposition, subjectification ('the depiction of reality not through an omniscient eye … but through the filter of the consciousness of protagonists in the story' [ibid.: 25]), and multiple perspective ('beholding the world not univocally but simultaneously through a set of prisms each of which catches some part of it' [ibid.: 26]). These three features of narrative discourse make it possible for the reader to 'write' his own 'virtual text' – that is, read into the text a message other than the one the author intended. (For reader and author, substitute listener and speaker of oral narrative.)

These three features together succeed, in Bruner's words, in 'subjunctivizing reality'. Bruner consults the Oxford English Dictionary on the use of the subjunctive, defined there as marking an action or state as expressing 'a wish, command, exhortation, or a contingent, hypothetical or prospective event' (ibid.: 26). This 'as if' trick of the narrative allows the narrator to mean more or less than she says – or, following my own theoretical discussion on elicitation, actively to modify that meaning – so narrative can only work with the active participation of the listener. Several narratives in this book will show how language is used to evoke subjective landscapes and multiple perspectives, by means of what Bruner (ibid.: 29) calls mode, intention, result, manner, aspect and status. These evocations successively transform the story, and permit its discourse 'to acquire a meaning without this meaning becoming pure information' (Todorov 1977: 233. For further discussion of 'story' versus 'information', see chapter 6 and Benjamin 1968). In this chapter, the 'multiple perspective' emerging from the differently positioned narrators results in a 'cultural gloss' which nevertheless portrays individual persons as originators of cultural life, rather than having that cultural life thrust upon them.

Narrative and Paradigmatic Thought

In his major study on culture, Michael Carrithers engages Bruner's formulations through his own ethnographic stories. I will let Carrithers lead us back to the distinction, crucial for the narratives discussed in this chapter, between paradigmatic thought and narrative thought. Narrative thought, as Carrithers expounds it, is the capacity to understand multi-faceted human interactions ('deeds and attitudes') and plots which show, as part of an unfolding story, the 'consequences and evaluations of a multifarious flow of actions' (Carrithers 1992: 82). The three requirements of a story is that it must show the flow of events, display the attitudes, beliefs and intentions of specific characters, and reveal the relationship between those events and attitudes or intentions (ibid.: 98. See p. 170 for a detailed account, especially with reference to the robustness of the story and its independence from its use by the anthropologist).

To demonstrate the difference between paradigmatic thought and narrative thought, Carrithers recounts, from his own fieldwork, two stories that purport to explain true religion or genuine Jainism (ibid.: 95–96). The first story, a cross between a sermon and a catechism and told by an educated man ('Mr P', glossed as 'philosopher'), expounds in general terms on the spiritual quality of *ahiṃsā* as the essence of all religions. The second story, offered almost as a corrective to the first by the less educated 'Mr S' ('storyteller') after the overheard Mr P had left, begins instead with a specific character, whose single act of selflessness exemplifies the quality of *ahiṃsā* which then requires no further explanation. Mr S first negotiates a common understanding with Carrithers – did he speak Marathi? – and proceeds to establish a proper basis for the interpretation of his story by links to prior tellers (his grandfather) and geographic locations. Thus Mr S's account gains force, relevance and coherence by establishing a series of relationships which are laid out as tracks on which to roll the story. As Carrithers puts it, he was '[negotiating] relationships in order to negotiate meanings' (ibid.: 106). From Carrithers' mutualist perspective, 'it is people in relationships who make things happen' (ibid.: 111). Moreover, 'things' are particular events, not general precepts: Jains, we are told, understand Jainism through stories, and stories 'exalt the particular' as gossip (ibid.: 109).

Where do Kewa stories fit in this distinction between Mr P's paradigmatic mode and Mr S's narrative mode? To recapitulate, the narrative mode is concerned with the landscape of action and consciousness, by means of which we construct the world and create products of the mind; it deals with the vicissitudes of intention and how experience comes to be endowed with meaning. The timelessness of the story, being placed at once in the space of action and the subjectivity of the actor, is a unity achieved between plight, character, and consciousness; and the narrative act is made powerful by the triggering of presupposition, subjectification, and multiple perspective. The combination of these traits allows the listener to read into the narrative a message beyond the one intended by the speaker. Storytelling thus subjunctivizes reality, by implicating the listener and making her complicit in the unfolding meaning, but also arousing her desire for the action in the story. Narrative thought, in short, is the capacity to understand multi-faceted human interactions and plots as part of an unfolding story, and works by establishing relations as the proper basis for interpretation of the story.

While the stories in chapters 4 and 5 fit these criteria, the stories of the older generation in this chapter are not narratives in this sense. The minimal narratives of this generation (in this and later chapters) are better fits for this category, as are all portraits of people's engagement in the vicissitudes of current social life. The stories in the present chapter scramble narrative and paradigmatic categories. Though they are told in the first person singular, they are given as authoritative accounts that tacitly and subtly generalize personal experience, yet without forfeiting personal integrity: in elevating the self to the generalized subject of experience, the stories at the same time construct the individual self as a moral person at the centre of life's conventionalized dramas.[2]

Ethics, Morality and the Self in Paradigmatic Accounts

My use of 'moral person' needs qualification, to clarify what meaning of 'morality' is at issue here. Particularly relevant to my approach is the philosophy of Paul Ricoeur, who locates narrative theory at the crossroads between a theory of action and moral theory. Reminding us that narrative was part of life before (in literate cultures) being exiled from life in writing, he asks: 'in what ways does the narrative component of self-understanding call for, at its completion, ethical determinations characteristic of the moral imputation of action to its agent?' (Ricoeur 1992: 163). Ricoeur's linking of ethics with narrative and morality with action gives a good indication of the meanings he attaches to these concepts. The ethical aim is the general teleological aim for the good; it is the narrative moment in which the good life is described or envisaged. Morality, on the other hand, concerns duty and obligation, the deontological moment of action, as Ricoeur describes it, which becomes actualized in a moral norm (Ricoeur 1992: 219). These understandings of ethics and morality are associated, respectively, with Aristotle and Kant. To some extent they represent (and enforce) the tyranny of etymology, to which I am not obliged to submit. (Aristotle, after all, had only the Greek word at his disposal.) When I refer to 'the moral self' or 'the moral person' in this book I shall always mean the Aristotelian understanding of the ethical, and will not normally engage in discussion of specific moral norms as obligations. I hope that this explanation will forestall any confusion over my choice of the word 'moral', despite Ricoeur's distinction. I may still use the word 'ethical' to refer to a kind of life. But in the argument of this book 'moral norm as obligation' is merely the language of rehearsed talk, while the 'deontological moment of action' is part of the negotiation carried out in rehearsing talk.

How do elderly Kewa people's narratives construct a moral self, understood as the person who lives the good life described in the narrative? The concept of the good as the end-aim of the ethical life incorporates not only notions of how to treat others, but also criteria for self-esteem. For my argument here it may suffice to define the good as an end in itself. But it will be more helpful if I substitute 'the good life' for 'a particular way of life' or 'this way of life'. Though the old people's stories may not be what Keesing (1985) has referred to as 'moral texts', they do give accounts of 'normal lives', and normal lives were implicitly good lives. The old people tell their stories with the assurance that this was how lives were lived, and their self-esteem is rooted in their embodiment of such lives. As in Benjamin's (1968) expression, narrators 'sink' the thing (of their stories) in their lives. The ethical, then, is exemplified in the paradigmatic, and Bruner's paradigmatic mode meets Ricoeur's ethical aim. Old people's narratives rest on a shared perception of how life was lived (Carrithers' 'consensibility'), with 'is' replacing 'ought' as the latter has no place in their narrative conceptual categories. In that sense the moral construction of the narrators' lives is a paradigmatic account. Taken together, the accounts simultaneously construct a shared background and reveal the commonalities of people's lives. They scramble Bruner's and Carrithers' categories, being personal stories implicitly oriented to ethical aims embodied in the narrator's life.

The Storytellers

I begin with a short introduction to the storytellers before moving on to the stories themselves. Wapa, Pupula, Ragunanu, Yakiranu and Payanu belong to the oldest generation of Yala villagers. The Kewa suffix *-nu*, meaning net bag as well as womb, denotes a feminine name; thus the last three names belong to women while the first two belong to men.

Wapa
Wapa is my father. When Rimbu made me his sister, his father Wapa became my father too. Wapa seems entirely the product of those other, pre-contact days. Our worlds and experiences are widely different yet we are so cosy together, walking long stretches in companionable silence as he makes gruffly sociable noises. He always did his duty by me, bringing me pork and contributing to my feasts, now solicitously holding an umbrella over my head to protect me from the midday sun. Once, when my visit to the building site of my house dragged into the late afternoon, Wapa suddenly sprang up from among the sitting men, grasped my hand in a firm hold, and said: 'It's getting dark, you will be going now.' His gentleness and solicitousness revealed the charm he would have used on the women he wanted to procure as wives for his sons. As I write about him I catch my lips

Plate 3.1. Wapa drinking Coca-Cola. (8 January 1980)

curling into a smile of affection. His laughter, deep and full, shook a fragile frame still taut and straight with muscle, and ended on a phlegmy, bronchial note. Only Coca-Cola was good for him when he was ill. A snapshot etched in my memory shows him sitting cross-legged, dishevelled, distant-looking and bleary-eyed, a half-drunk bottle of Coca-Cola in his hand. Yet how crusty he is as he struts up and down the settlement, threatening his daughter-in-law with his bow and arrow, flying off the handle when his nephew is passed over in food distributions, tackling Mapi the magistrate with a spear and summoning up warriors in defence of the peace. Wapa considers his irascibility an inalienable part of his personality as a warrior, quite beyond his control.

Plate 3.2. Payanu with granddaugher Wapanu. (April 1980)

Plate 3.3. Ragunanu with cat. (17 May 1980)

Plate 3.4. Pupula (right). (25 November 1982)

Plate 3.5. Yakiranu. (April 1980)

Lari, his daughter-in-law, thought she was too often at the receiving end of this warrior-temper. Once she summoned the magistrate on account of this. She was preparing to go to the garden while Rimbu was sitting outside passing the time of day with Wapa and other men. On her way out she handed Rimbu their little daughter, Lisette, to look after while she was gone. This was a trigger for Wapa's fiery temper: it's the wife's job, he thundered, not the husband's, to look after their children. Lari lashed back at him: she wasn't *his* wife to order about, he was an old man with a bad (evil) eye (*le kolea ali*). It was then that Wapa began to prance up and down with his bow and arrow, and Lari summoned Mapi the magistrate to adjudicate. At the hearing Wapa complained that Lari had left little Lisette with him five times recently, and every time he had to clean up her faeces. She should take her child to the garden with her. Mapi told him that threatening with bow and arrow was against the law, but so were Lari's words to him, so the two offences cancelled each other out. He reminded Wapa of the occasion when he had threatened him, Mapi, with a spear, but he had not taken action then. It was time Wapa mended his ways. Wapa's rejoinder was to accuse Lari of wishing him dead. He claimed that she had said to him, 'Old man, it would be a good thing if you died.' This was a serious offence, Mapi conceded, but as there were no witnesses the matter could not be taken further. Did Rimbu, asked Mapi, like his father's treatment of his wife? Rimbu replied that his father had paid brideprice for the woman and it was his affair what he did, but it did upset him when Wapa quarrelled with his wife repeatedly and never with the wives of his other sons. Mapi turned back to Wapa and asked him to refrain from constant bickering. Wapa's reply blended reasonableness with fatalism: 'I may say anything now, but these are only words. You know my temper. Once I get angry I'll forget these words and behave like I've always done. I can't help it.'

Wapa recorded his life story, at my request, on Sunday 24 August 1980. We were sitting in my house and had just finished eating. Young Sipi and Rimbu were also present, and Rama, a clan brother junior to Wapa, joined us later and added his own observations and recollections to Wapa's. Wapa prefaced his story with an account of his grievances against his sons. It was a peculiarly appropriate venue for this airing; Rimbu was forced to translate to *me*, in many ways the wellspring of his prestige, the story of his own filial failings.

'I moved down to Yakopaita when my sons promised to build me a little house. They didn't keep their promise, so I returned to my home on the mountain. I came back some time later, still hoping to have a house built. When I fell ill they had to take me to Puliminia, to a house belonging to another man's sons. I went to court over this. I told the court how well I spoke to my sons, and how ill they spoke to me. The village magistrate [Mapi] said that he and his brothers had treated their own father [Gapea] differently. They made him comfortable in the porch of the house, but he died just the same. The magistrates were angry with my boys for not looking after me well and said I should demand compensation. But I said just let them build me a little house.' With these words, Wapa turned to me: 'If I lived close to you I would look after your house and sweep the rubbish away, but I am not close.'

The above portrait of Wapa is a 'minimal narrative' which introduces him as an actor. What can we elicit from this portrait? It begins by establishing my relationship with Wapa, then proceeds to set the scene by providing information about the village and its daily practices. Consider this reading of it:

> Men sitting around while women go to work. Wapa picking on Rimbu's wife – he had paid her brideprice. The role of language in everyday life; the power of speaking to bring about an event: Wapa claims he speaks well to his sons while they speak badly to him. His daughter-in-law has 'free speech', indicating the ability of women to use language in this way as a weapon. Anyone can be 'sued' for using such language, but in this case the verbal offences cancelled each other out. The magistrate's judgement was fair, giving no credence to charges relating to exchanges not witnessed by other persons. But even in this fair adjudication Mapi manages to smuggle two covert criticisms of Rimbu: for allowing his father to abuse his wife, which suggests little respect for the son, and for not treating his father right, as Mapi had done for his. Mapi is 'eliciting' a response here, by constructing for himself the persona of a worthy son and prestigious big man on the back of Wapa's defamation of his own son. Wapa himself is engaged in a form of elicitation, about how far he can go in claiming for his temper a natural, even commendable quality of fierceness that cannot be quelled, by appealing to a 'rehearsed talk' about a warrior ethic. He reminds Mapi how he suffered on a previous occasion as a result of his (Wapa's) fiery temper, but this cuts little ice. Undaunted, Wapa uses the platform my presence offered to air, in his son's hearing, his grievance about the house – this is eliciting talk with perlocutionary intent. To make his case even stronger, he contrasts it with Gapea's treatment by his sons.

The rivalry between Mapi and Rimbu makes a double appearance. First, as a jab from Mapi himself, in his covert claim to have scored over Rimbu, then by Wapa, who drives home to Rimbu Mapi's stolen march over him, in an attempt to force Rimbu's hand in the house-building affair (this is the perlocutionary intent). Metonymy makes its appearance when Wapa recounts Mapi's story about Gapea's death, but in fact the metonymic pragmatics here is a statement about Wapa's own prospective death: a warning that though Gapea died peacefully and in the right place, Wapa will die unfulfilled and unhoused. This 'rehearsed talk' about how sons should treat fathers puts perlocutionary pressure on Rimbu in two ways: by suggesting that Mapi will triumph over him as the better son and therefore more prestigious big man, and that he himself will suffer ancestral wrath. (Mapi is pre-empting accusations of unfilial behaviour in his own case by putting it on the record right away that Gapea died despite his sons' doing their duty by him.) Wapa also hints that a larger compensation is his by right, but he would settle for a little house. Finally he turns his charisma on me, but this is another hydra-headed message to Rimbu: that he does not deserve the reputation of hosting a white woman when he cannot even keep her yard clean; that his actions are hindering Wapa from fulfilling this task; and that Wapa is a bigger man than Rimbu, because he would ensure that my house was swept. (Here the anthropologist is used as a source of prestige, like a big pig kill or any other item of wealth.) But Wapa's solicitousness is also reminiscent of the way men look after women whose brideprice they hope to receive.

Ragunanu
In my early fieldnotes I refer to Ragunanu as a 'clown'. I remember my first meeting with her, when she ran up to me laughing and boisterously demanded I give her the pancake I had just bought in the market. It was saturated in pig fat and I was happy to part with it. Our second meeting took place when I was returning home carrying a beautiful net bag Lari had given me. Ragunanu suddenly sprang out of nowhere and made as if to grab the net bag (and me), insisting I give it to her. By now impatient with these sallies, I said in Tok Pisin, 'Lapun i longlong tru' ('the old woman is crazy'). Though Ragunanu did not understand Tok Pisin she picked up the phrase and repeated it, parrot fashion, guffawing loudly. (No old man would have behaved in this way except if he really had been mad, and Ragunanu was certainly not that.) Years later, when I took my barely three-year-old daughter to the field, Ragunanu was to lick the toes of both her feet, slowly and deliberately. By this time Ragunanu and I had developed a joking relationship, by which I mean that I had resigned myself to the liberties she continued to take with me, such as grabbing me, pulling my things, demanding I give her any food I happened to be holding. She called herself my mother, though the mannerisms and liberties I describe were never to be observed between true mothers and daughters. When she heard that I was recording people's stories she offered to tell me hers, and delivered it in a breathless stage whisper. She came to my house with Ainu, whom she introduced as her daughter, demonstrating the relationship by pulling Ainu towards her and proffering her breast to her. Ainu had been an orphan and Ragunanu was her foster mother.

Ragunanu had left home (Puliminia) and husband (Pupula) because of disagreements over his lack of faith, and was living in Yakopaita. She had belonged to the Evangelical Church of Papua until her daughter married the catechist of the Catholic church in Sumbura, when she switched churches. At Christmas I saw her snugly ensconced in her new church, lovingly tending the nativity set and smiling proudly at me.

Pupula
Pupula, Ragunanu's husband, told his story over four sittings. The first time he came with Rimbu, the second time with Rimbu and Michael (his

son), the third time with Michael and two of Michael's clan brothers, Yoka and Yasi. Rika, a younger clan brother, pushed his way in uninvited, while Rimbu joined us later in the evening. The last sitting, concerned mainly with pig kills, appropriately took place at the longhouse, with many people crowding around and embellishing on Pupula's account. Pupula and Wapa are the oldest clan members and have entirely different personalities. While Wapa is the irascible warrior, Pupula is calm and deliberate, weighing each word. No snide remarks, innuendoes or personal agenda from Pupula, who keeps to the point and shoots his arrows straight and home. (See, for instance, how he dishes out Rimbu's come-uppance in chapter 1, and how he deals with an elderly suitor to his young daughter in chapter 7.)

Yakiranu
Yakiranu was a woman in her late sixties who lived in the adjacent settlement of Poiale. For some time she had been giving me gifts of vegetables, which I reciprocated with items she could not grow in her garden, and soon we had established an exchange relationship. She came to tell her story at my invitation. Like other women of her age she spoke no Tok Pisin. Giame, a younger married woman, came with the intention of acting as interpreter, but with her children crawling all over her and clamouring for attention she had to give up all pretence of carrying out this task. Besides, I had little difficulty following Yakiranu's account in Kewa. I noted at the time that it was 'brief and uninformative', and wondered if she had been reluctant to talk to me about the past or whether I simply lacked the dexterity to elicit more interesting responses. Early in the evening she began to grow nervous. 'It's getting dark, I'm on my own and the cemetery is very close … I have nothing else to say, this is my story …' I plied her with questions for a little longer: Why did she join the mission? She didn't know, everybody was being baptized so she thought she'd better do it too. She didn't know if it was a good or bad move and she didn't do it because she hoped to go to heaven. 'That's for God to decide.' She didn't know what people in the old days thought would happen to them when they died, since in those days all they knew was about killing pigs. I pressed on her a lantern to light her home, and though she was too polite to refuse it she sent a young girl back with it just two minutes after she was out of the door.

Payanu
Payanu was not a talkative woman and I had very few exchanges with her. Though she was Wapa's wife, she was not my mother in the sense that he was my father. For one of those unfathomable reasons driving human sympathies, the emotional connection simply did not develop. Rimbu

had some idea that his mother, as the owner of powerful magic potions, might 'correct' accounts given to me by other women, and brought her to me himself for that reason. My most enduring double image of Payanu is of her lamentations over a household pig about to be slaughtered at a pig kill, and her subsequent tearful demands for a share of the pork sufficient to her exchange needs. Rimbu adjudicated in her favour, frustrating his own wife's competing demands, with the words that 'the old woman should be able to pay her debts'.

Kewa Pre-contact Practices and Persons: A Narrative of Many

I weave the ethnographic story which follows from the maximal narratives of these five elderly people (Wapa and Pupula, Payanu, Ragunanu and Yakiranu), which together establish a minimal cultural, historical and traditional basis for the Kewa. Though each person is credited with his or her own contribution, I break the stories up to make one ethnographic account whose particular sources nevertheless remain visible. In this way the integrity of each person's story is retained, despite the story's dispersal within the larger narrative. The narrative itself, while not seamless, is sufficiently coherent, a distilled account being clearly contrary to my objectives. 'Coherence' also refers to 'narrative unity', when a statement which collects one's self together can be made in just one sentence. Coherence does not rely on length, as my use of 'minimal narratives' demonstrates. I anticipate that after a while the reader will pick up the knack of eliciting from the text a reading that will advance the theoretical interests outlined in the previous chapter, and demonstrated in my commentary on Wapa's portrait.

Growing up

'In the old days a girl was given her first digging stick by her father when she was six years old. She would accompany her mother to the garden and by the age of ten she was an adept gardener.' Thus Ragunanu. However, as Pupula's story shows, boys also worked in the garden: 'My mother died when I was young and my father looked after me. I made gardens with my father in Awari and had no thoughts of a wife.' Wapa also talks of the importance of gardening in connection with marriage, but his early childhood reminiscences are dominated by different interests:

'When my mother first bore me I drank her milk and slept in the women's house. I became a true man when I came off the breast, put on a bark belt and slept in the men's house. We young boys used to sharpen *pitpit* [cane] and make spears to play war games. When neighbouring clans killed my father's father for no reason, my clan waged war on them and my father killed men from many different villages. All the clans then turned on us – the Koiari, the Pamerepa, the Tepenarirepa, the Pepeawere, the Subulu, the Kamarepa, the Tiarepa and the Perepe – and killed my father and torched our village. I was still playing war games when we fled to Wapia. The man I called father from then on was Yamola, my mother's firstborn. In Wapia there was a lot of sickness, so we built a spirit house. In the second year of our stay there I started courting women, and in the third I was married. I left off playing at war and engaged in real warfare, killing three men in one war and four in another. I was a proper young man, good at fighting and making bows, arrows and axes. Eventually we returned home and settled in Agema. My father made palisades while I went into the nearby bush, and with my spears and arrows killed marsupials and little birds and brought them to my mother.'

Of Courtship and Marriage

Wapa gave the fullest account of courtship and marriage.

'We held *rome* courting sessions in women's houses. Boys and girls sat round in a circle, with older married women interspersed in between. The young men recited the *rome* verses that filled the girls with desire. The girls used their own love magic [*rakia*] on the men they liked. When I saw a woman I wanted to marry I would ask her father to come and receive brideprice. He would bring a fat pig as a bridal gift and the mother would come with the bride. After sending the mother off with a pig I would show my gardens to my wife. Yamola didn't pay brideprice for me and nor did Areali [another older brother]. I myself provided the brideprice, by giving gifts of bananas and game to my married sisters, whose husbands then sent them to me with pigs, pearlshells, cowry shells, headbands and salt.'

'I had many wives, but they didn't all stay. [Polygynists had to build large houses with separate rooms for their different wives, and one large front room where the men cooked and ate with their friends.] The first was a Perepe woman, Porame, who came to me for nothing because of the power of my *rome*. She stayed for a year and got pregnant. I threw her out because of a very bad thing she said to me when I went to courting sessions with other women. [Wapa told me what her words were only after I enquired: 'Eat while you are uprooting kunai grass. The Purupuri creek (the vagina) you cut, give, and go.'] Then Taliame of Tiarepa, Yagore village, came to me. She stayed for six months, until another girlfriend, Rambuame, assaulted us both. Taliame got scared and left, so I started collecting brideprice for Rambuame, a Waluaparepa from Katiloma. She too became pregnant, but my kinspeople couldn't help with brideprice so she left. [I asked what happened to the children. Both women had daughters, so Wapa didn't bother with them. I know from other accounts that an unmarried man has no rights to his children; Wapa himself had laid claim to his unmarried sister's son.] The fourth was Yalanu, also Waluaparepa, Komalo's mother. I gave brideprice for this one – ten pearlshells, five pigs and five other items including a bushknife [*gepere*] and an axe [*kaipi*]. She had a boy and two girls who were stillborn, then a boy who lived to be Sipi's size [about 16 years old], when Koe Rimbu killed him. [Wapa shrugged his shoulders when I asked why; maybe they had not been propitiating this 'bad' Rimbu spirit sufficiently well.] Only Komalo survived. I also gave brideprice for Payanu of Kuare, Kalopo ruru. Yalanu herself wanted me to marry Payanu – they were cousins and didn't fight. They had powerful magic to chase away all the other women I might have married. The sixth woman was Lari, of Yabolape ruru, near Kuare. She had a daughter too, but Payanu's poison chased her away. Number seven was Puame. I promised to give brideprice for her so she stayed for six or seven months and got pregnant, but when I still hadn't paid her kinspeople took her back and married her to another man.'

In answer to my question informed by practices elsewhere, Rama and Wapa said they did not believe that babies have to be formed by repeated acts of intercourse. Women tell them when they are pregnant and they leave them alone. For a good pregnancy women must lie on their side during intercourse; if they lie on their backs the semen will become dispersed and instead of one healthy baby two or three incompletely formed ones will be born. Yasi, a young man just returned from plantation labour, added that this belief was still held by young people today. Fertility drugs will harm the woman, added Rama, Yasi's elder. 'If a woman has no children, never mind, we prefer her barren than sick.' Again testing out what I had read about practices elsewhere, I asked if warriors avoided sexual contact with their wives the day before a battle. Rama and Wapa almost rolled on the floor with laughter. 'No, we make sure we have sex with them, because if we are wounded we are incapacitated, and *then* we can't have sex!'

Pupula launched straight into an account of his marriages, with no preambles about courting:

'Kaluma, a man from Kuare, had two daughters, Payanu and Wasame. I married Wasame, and Payanu, who was first married to another man, followed her sister and married Wapa. Hapkas and Kale were born at the same time to the sisters, but Kale died in Naguri in his third or fourth year. Then Rimbu and Agema [Michael] were born [to Payanu and Wasame respectively]. I killed a pig in the Koe Rimbu spirit house to placate the bad spirit, then helped Yamola to build a longhouse in preparation for a pig kill in Awari. Areali had died so Yala clanspeople came together to help Areali's brothers, Yamola and Wapa, to build the pig killing longhouse. Ragunanu helped in the thatching of the longhouse, and I took her as my second wife. She was from Kuare and had been married to a Kaluyala man but both her husband and child were dead. When she saw Agema's skin it reminded her of her own child, so she stayed. The two women did not fight because I treated them fairly – there would have been trouble only if I had neglected one of them. Yapinia was born after Agema but she died young, then Wasame gave birth to Kamare.'

Ragunanu's account gives an indication of the multiple marriages women were likely to contract:

'I married my first husband, a Yaberepa man from Kuare who already had a wife, before I began to menstruate. When I saw the blood I was ashamed and went into the menstruation hut. I stayed there for four days, until my husband made me a gift of pearshells and a pig. On the fifth day I came out and cooked my husband's food. I gave birth to one boy who was killed in war. I left my husband and went to marry Waliabuali, a Kaluyala man, who had to compensate my first husband for taking me away. I had another son who died young, then my husband also died. So finally I married Pupula. The first girl and boy I had with him died. The third, a girl called Koipame, is married to a Perepe man from Tiripi.'

Yakiranu, also married more than once, reinforces women's feelings about polygyny. Her account also contributes to the evidence of a high infant mortality rate.

'I first became the second wife of a Perepe man, who gave three pigs and many shells for me. I had three daughters but they died, then my husband also died. I married Kale, a Yala man, who gave two pigs and three shells for me. Kale had been married before but he killed his wife because she played around with other men.' [Peals of laughter from Giame: 'She was just like my husband Yadi, whom I've been beating for the same reason!'] I asked Yakiranu if she hadn't been afraid to marry a man who had killed a previous wife. She laughed boisterously. 'No, I wasn't afraid. He looked into my face, sat close to me and said, "I'll have you for my wife", so we were married. I gave birth to Ipanu. I didn't want him to marry another wife, so I bought magic [*alirakia*] from a Mirupa woman, paying her with salt and cowry shells. But he married Walame, Aisepa's mother. I fought with my co-wife all the time, over firewood and gardens. When I saw my husband taking firewood to her I would grab it off him and attack the woman.'

Of Magic and Gardens

When Payanu was small her mother had 'planted' in her the ability to control three plants from the *rakia* family, known as *paropita*, *rarunama* and *itekumba*. The first two make harmless love potions but the third can kill. Her mother told her they had to be grown in secret places and used only on one man, whom Payanu really liked. Though Payanu courted with many men she used the potions only on Wapa. When he came courting she put leaves from the two harmless plants into his food. The leaves have a distinctive taste which is difficult to disguise when served with sweet potato, so it is best to rub them onto greens and pitpit. If a man realizes that a woman has used love potions she is so shamed she can never marry him.

The odds were against Payanu's marrying Wapa. He preferred other women to her, and her own family wanted to accept the substantial brideprice of pigs and shells offered by another man. But Wapa was Payanu's choice. So the next time he came to eat with her she used the dangerous plant in his food and Wapa became ill. His clanspeople discovered the cause of his sickness and were on their way to get Payanu, when Payanu turned up of her own accord and fell down in tears at Wapa's feet. Wapa was touched, and stopped his kinsmen from attacking her with axes. 'Wait,' he said, 'if I recover I'll marry her, but if I die, kill her.' He recovered and offered brideprice for her. Whenever Wapa was thinking of taking another wife Payanu would rub the first two plants, never the third, on Rimbu's skin and send him to his father. After touching his son Wapa would grow tired of the other woman and send her away. [I learned much later that Payanu had used graver methods to stop Wapa's remarriage, which made sense of my being seen as Rimbu's returned sister: on one occasion she had thrown their newborn baby girl into a pit – a strategy mentioned by many women but admitted to by none.]

For her part, Ragunanu was the mistress of *ambu*, a yellow clay which she applied to her teeth and forehead whenever her husband showed interest in another woman. This had the effect of making the woman run away. Ragunanu also owned *kake*, a small pandanus nut 'with teeth'. As she buried the *kake* into the ground she called out the name of the woman her husband fancied, and once again the woman ran away. Another remedy she had for the same result was to collect leaves from the plants *kabe* and *pepeago* and burn them together on the fire.

Ragunanu and Payanu also owned pig-growing magic [*mena mana pia*, 'to make pigs eat'). This was a white clay, *kamu*, which is rubbed on pigs to fatten them. It was versatile in its efficacy; Ragunanu rubbed it on her own belly when she was pregnant, and asked to have a boy. Payanu described how she held the clay in her hand and whispered a spell on it:

> The belly of this pig will grow as wide as the thick trunk of the Yapelea pine. The neck of this pig will become as thick as the base of the Wapu pine. The flesh of this pig will be layer upon layer of fat, as in the sky there is layer upon layer of white cloud. Men from faraway places will come and look at the fat of this pig, they will marvel and go away again. (Wapu and Yapelea are names of villages. Yapelea, meaning 'daybreak', is Payanu's own village.)

Then she would spit on the clay and rub it on the pig, and proceed to tell the same story to the pig's dinner. Afterwards the pig was kept in the house and not allowed to forage in the bush.

Yakiranu insisted she had no pig magic or garden magic; she simply tilled the soil with her digging stick. Though she herself was spending less time in her gardens now, she did not think that gardening as an activity had changed radically. The major difference was that food ran short in the past, when wars were endemic and gardens were burnt and people chased off their land. But other clans suffered more, the Yala were not too badly off. At times of war women hid in the bush. Yakiranu was never caught, nor were other women of her acquaintance. Raiding warriors did not carry off women and pigs, they just killed and burned and laid waste the land. People were constantly on the move, chased from place to place. 'Then the government came, and there was peace.'

Ragunanu was more forthcoming about gardening. On one occasion she broke into an account being given to me by younger women and delivered the following in her gruff, no-nonsense voice:

'In the old days women had many gardens, about fifteen to twenty-five, but now they have other work such as tending coffee, washing clothes, market-selling and church work, so their gardens are fewer. A married woman left home at about six in the morning and by ten she was working on her second garden. Towards the afternoon she would start digging up sweet potatoes for the family and the pigs. Her husband left home at the same time in the morning, cut down trees for firewood and met his wife at about five in the afternoon, when both returned home. In a net bag on her back the woman carried the pig feed, in another net bag higher up on the back of her neck she carried food for the family, on her head she carried firewood, across her breasts she slung the net bag with the baby, and in her hands she held bamboo containers filled with water. With so many gardens, women produced more food than now, and sold the surplus to the 'hungry men' [those with no access to women or who had had bad harvests] for pigs, tree-oil or pearlshells. They held food markets [*mudumato*], though not on a permanent basis like today. Barter [*ropopata*] also took place there.'

Ragunanu had been a big woman, an *adawenape*. She had pigs, pearlshells, cowry shells. 'But now,' she said, 'I am old and have no pigs.' She had a vision once. When they were living in Agema there was a knock on the door in the middle of the night. 'It's the devil coming to get you,' everyone joked. 'No, it's God, it's Jesus,' Ragunanu retorted. There was nothing but the wind when she went out to look. But it had been Jesus, she insisted.

Spirit Houses

Wapa was most keen to talk about spirit houses and his role in them.

'I first entered the spirit house when I got married. First Areali was put in charge of the spirit house and when he died Yamola took over. Yamola brought the [sacrificial] pigs into the spirit house and painted patterns on round stones which he stood upright. He told me to look in all the corners where these stones were kept. When Yamola retired ['stayed home'] I became a religious elder [*ririna alapisua*, 'first to stand up'], with the task of taking in the sweet potatoes. Sometimes I slept in the spirit house with two or three other 'first men', at other times I left while it was still light and slept in the men's house. I would stamp my feet like this in the spirit house: Stomp! Stomp! I would cut a bamboo [into a flute] and blow on it, making the sound 'pi-ruli, pi-ruli, pi-ruli!' while walking 'stomp! stomp!' around the room. Those who heard me play were afraid. Women would run away if they heard the sound. The others ate pigs while I played the bamboo flute, as Yamola had done, and stomped in this way. We call the spirit Koe Rimbu ['bad Rimbu'] because it eats many pigs when people are sick and dying. At those times pigs are eaten only inside the spirit house. The Kamarepa clan made this spirit house for us, because we were getting sick and dying. The Yala had Adalu ['tall'] Rimbu before, but in my father's [Kogalepa's] time they saw that the Kamarepa Koe Rimbu was much more powerful. They bought the cult from the Kamarepa, paying many pigs and shells for it. There were Koe Rimbu spirit houses at Naguri, Agema and Papolata. Adalu (or Mae) Rimbu houses were at Popa and Naguri, while at Popa there was also a Rombake. The Koe Rimbu spirit house is long, the Adalu Rimbu spirit house is tall, and the Rombake house is round with a conical-shaped roof. I put Rimbu in charge later, but the white people had come by then and there was an end to all that.'

Pig Kills

The first pig kill Pupula remembers was for Ilikoi Rimbu ('bad-nose' Rimbu). The men constructed full body masks (*rimbuedali*, 'spirit arrows'), which they painted and put inside the spirit houses. After the pigs were put in the earth oven, the initiated donned these masks and came out to dance. This was very frightening for the uninitiated. Then they removed the masks and took the pigs out of the earth oven. The second pig kill Pupula remembers is one at which he himself killed a pig, provided by his father. 'We invited Madi and Kewa dancers [from the north and the south respectively, with their distinctive headdresses and style of dancing; their presence added to the prestige of the hosts]. We almost threw the pigs at them, they were so many, not the three or four miserable pigs you see nowadays. We had built eight longhouses and decorated a *rungi*. A *rungi* is a long pole kept in the Adalu Rimbu spirit house, on which we fasten the bones of marsupials and pigs eaten over a long time. At pig killing time the *rungi* was brought out and planted in the open ground [*kama*] in front of the longhouse. The longer the *rungi*, the greater the prestige of the group. Groups competed in *rungi* lengths, and sharing a *rungi* within the group indicated friendship and a sense of common identity. At the pig kill [*yawe*] following the death of Kogalepa [Wapa's father] the Yala used the *rungi* to taunt other groups. They decorated it and sang out to their enemies: 'You killed Kogalepa, see if you can match us in this.' The taunts brought on an attack in which Agema was razed to the ground, and the Yala finished eating their pigs while fleeing to Wapia, another Yala village.'

Yadi the driver, a younger man, broke into Pupula's narrative: 'If this had been the old days we would have erected our *rungi* in front of the longhouse and taunted the Tiarepa [their principal enemies]: 'You Tiarepa, do you think you can match us in this? See if you can find yourselves some white people who will live with you for years on end. See if you can send them off with a pig kill and a *kepa* [long bamboo decorated with gifts, now mainly shells and banknotes] as long as this to carry off.'

These kinds of feasts were coming to an end, Pupula resumed. When last they killed pigs at Awari, Pupula slaughtered four, two from each wife, and Rimbu made a *yaweraguna*, a headdress worn only by a multiple pig killer. Michael put on a *kili ra*, as a pledge that he would become worthy of a *yaweraguna*. But he never got to wear a *yaweraguna* because the government had in the meantime put an end to these practices. (Rimbu and Michael often promised, in hushed tones, to make a *yaweraguna* secretly just to show me, but they never did. It was shameful for a man to make a *yaweraguna* when he had not earned it.)

Warfare and Pacification

Pupula's life story was largely an account of wars punctuated by pig kills (for a full account, see Josephides 1985: 31–36). When he was a youth, two neighbouring clans had invited people from Samberigi in the south to their pig kill. Among the other guests were a husband and wife from the neighbouring Amburupa clan. On their way home these two began to fight when the wife refused to fetch leaves to cook with the pork. In a diversionary tactic, the wife pointed out a group of Samberigi people walking on the other side of the road. 'If you were a man you would kill these Samberigis who have finished off so many of your kinspeople, instead of hitting your wife.' The husband swallowed the bait and felled two Samberigis, thus committing a breach of the rules of hospitality and inviting scornful comments from other clans. As a result, the pig kill hosts were stung into joining the Samberigi and other clans in a war against the Amburupa. Only the Perepe clan helped the Amburupa, while the Yala split themselves in half and fought on both sides. Yala clansmen were careful to avoid killing each other on the battlefield, but contradictory alliances did arise as a result of the split. Yanyali and Sawa were both Yala, but the first fought with the Perepe/Amburupa while the second supported the Koiari who were helping the Samberigi alliance. When Yanyali was killed by the Koiari, Sawa avenged his death by stalking and killing a Koiari man, even though he himself was fighting on the Koiari side.

Another war originated in a pig theft. A pig belonging to the Tiarepa wandered into a Yala settlement and was found by two friends, a Kambia man called Baga and a Yala man called Popo, who tethered it by Yokopo's burying-ground. The pig made a mess and angered Yokopo, who killed it with a single blow. The two friends cooked and ate the pig, and one of Popo's kinsmen (Keleke) sported the pig's trotters in his belt. When the Tiarepa came looking for the pig the Yala pleaded ignorance, but they were ready and waiting the second time, when the Tiarepa came to the Sugu bridge singing the war cry of *eee*. Keleke threw the trotters at them and they indicated they understood the message and would return the following day. Having recruited many clans with grudges against the Yala, the Tiarepa attacked. The Yala had no allies and were consistently beaten back. Every day they erected new palisades behind the lines of the day before, until there was no more room to retreat. So one night they stole to Wapia.

Pupula first saw action in the Bala war. He did not know the cause of the war, as the Yala were merely helping the people of Bala. The Yala were chased to Kanada and became trapped in the men's house, where many of them were killed. A Tepenarirepa man then escorted them to Wata, where the Tepenarirepa were living with the Paisa clan. But then Peawi, a Paisa man, was killed by the Kopayo spirit, and since the neighbouring Eno were the original owners of the Kopayo in the area they were held responsible for the death. This resulted in further fighting which drove the Yala back to Wapia. Eventually they were able to return home to Awari. Another branch of the Yala, from Kalu near Awari, had agreed with the people of Pepeawere to participate in each other's pig kill, but both wanted to go first. The Pepeawere resolved the issue in a radical way by burning down Kalu, and the Yala of Agema went to the assistance of their kinspeople and sacked Pepeawere, whose people fled south of Erave. To celebrate this victory the Yala held pig kills at both Kalu and Awari. (It was in the midst of these celebrations that the 1935 Hides patrol stumbled on them; see Josephides and Schiltz 1991.) The Kopayo Kaluali war broke out following a disagreement over payment for the spirit cult Kopayo, which the Perepe had bought from the Ronali clan. The war spread, but when the Kapona (the government, or white people; also *kadipi*) arrived in Erave everyone was so terrified by their guns that they left off fighting.

Pulupa continued: 'This was a hard time for us. We were made to build the government rest house in Sumbura, where the Sepik policeman in charge terrified us. He took away Gapea and we all mourned, thinking he would be killed, but instead he was made into a *luluai* [government-appointed headman]. He came back and told us there was nothing to fear, he had talked with the Kapona and they treated him well. He was a *luluai* for two years, and in the third year Rama took over. Young men went to the coast and returned with tales of marvellous things, of businesses and so on, so we started to change our ways of thinking and hanker after different things. Rake, who is now village councillor, worked for Isunga, the Sepik policeman who terrorised us. Isunga taught him everything and from cookboy Rake became bossboy, then councillor and finally magistrate. Rake was committed to the government and the new ways, and it was he who finally stopped all the fighting.' Having finished his story, Pulupa then proceeded to give an account of their clan origin (see Josephides 1985: 20–21).

Wapa's account also ends with warfare dovetailing into the pacification of colonization: 'Before I married Payanu I had burned down the Waluaparepa village at Batri as well as settlements belonging to the Kambia, the Adalurupa and the Wabea. After Payanu came to me I sacked the villages of the Pepeawere, Pamerepa, Tiarepa and Laperepa. Hapkas was born in Wapia. Then we came back to Awari and held a pig kill. I killed four pigs at that time. Gapea was our surgeon. He operated when flesh had to be cut away and an arrow removed. Rimbu was born in Agema. When I first heard the sound of an aeroplane Yalanu had not yet given birth, but when Ialibu was born lots of planes came. We sacked Yagore and Wakiapada, and the Tiarepa fled to Turili. Then the white people [*kadipi*] came. We were too afraid to fight them and ran off to the bush, but they tricked us with their soft speaking. We were beaten, handcuffed and put to work. Life before the government [*kadipi*, *kapona* and 'gavman' used interchangeably] came was not good. We lived in the bush, and when it rained we couldn't go out for food or firewood. There was always fighting. It was good when the *kadipi* came because they had lots of money, and even gave some of it to the old people. But when it became Papua New Guinea [i.e., with the advent of self-government and Independence in 1975, opposed in the referendum by a majority of highlanders] we didn't like it. White men made us work and we listened to them, but we are obstinate and won't listen to people of our own skin colour. Look at the state of the roads. Everything is reverting to bush and we can't get anything done.'

'The Catholic mission first came to Agema. The Father came with a patrol officer and the people didn't run away from him. He taught them and they listened, he brought them rice, biscuits, food they'd never seen before. The catechists burnt down the spirit houses and sprinkled holy water on the sacred stones. Churches were built instead, first in Agema, then in Aliwi, and now in Puliminia. When I thought I was dying I had them sprinkle water on me and I was baptized.'

Having finished his story, Wapa launched into the more fluent narrative of a myth.

Conclusions: Moral Constructions of the Self as Paradigmatic Accounts

As opposed to stories in sets 2 and 3 – which as we shall see are metanarratives, critical or reflective accounts that 'say something about something' – the stories in this chapter were descriptive narratives that merely say something; they describe the conditions in which personhood had to be forged, and how the full life was lived. These elderly people's accounts barely confront any other reality than the one that had formed their consciousness in pre-contact days. Men talked about courtship and marriage, spirit houses, war and pig kills at a time when they were not old, irrelevant and powerless, leading at least one young man within earshot to contrast the present with a more manly past. Women talked about what they considered to be the achievements of their lives: marriage, pregnancy, gardening and magic. Strikingly, they described their marriage as the result of their free and powerful action. A statement emerged of women's desires: control over their bodies, power to keep their husbands from taking more wives, and the possession of strong love and garden magic. Both men's and women's accounts of 'strong things' were almost archetypal descriptions from people at the end of their lives.

The older generation of Kewa men and women told the story of how they lived their lives as if they were merely recounting facts; and this way of speaking immediately establishes authenticity. It achieves the 'seriousness' Carrithers talks about because it does not open itself to debate or negotiation. In effect, the old people were giving their own lives as a cultural gloss for how the Kewa in general live, removing all diacritical marks between 'how one ought to live' and how *they* lived. Wapa's story, even though told in the first person singular, sounds like 'an explanation in terms of culture', just the sort of 'abstract schedule of motives ... that anthropologists produce when they fill in the background' (Carrithers 1992: 105). Together with the other stories, it provides a horizon of broad general structures, akin to what Carrithers has referred to as 'cultural goods which preserve cultural values' (ibid.: 107).

But these stories were not the anthropologist's abstraction, because the people recounting them had actually lived them. Personal accounts were offered as if they had been paradigmatic, couched as statements of states of things; yet at the same time they made past events, structures and institutions real and convincing for me. They succeeded in this not only because narrators talked about their young selves and their relationships, their courtship, their wars and pig kills, their magical powers and sexual prowess, but also because they referred to other people I knew and places that I knew, in overlapping and criss-crossing stories which reinforced each other. Listening to the narratives, I learned about the flow of relationships. They demonstrated how, as Carrithers put it, 'in the midst of social life, people's knowledge of the generic and the particular are inextricably mixed' (ibid.: 110). The case of brideprice is a good illustration of this intricate connection. People spoke with pride of the wealth (whether given or received) which established their marriage, thus, as Wardlow (2002: 18) perceptively points out, revealing the institution of brideprice to be also a discourse, or a symbolic production through which they actively constructed their subjectivity.

If these narratives are cultural glosses without being the anthropologist's abstractions, so too are they paradigmatic without being based on logic and abstract reasoning. Carrithers makes the point that if the drama/tragedy of Oedipus the King is unintelligible without mind-reading (or the intersubjective understanding of the intentions and meanings of others), 'it is equally so without the notions of a king and queen, a husband and wife, a mother and son, without the conceptions of a human life-span and its proper stations, and without the notion of what constraints and possibilities govern long-lasting relationships' (1992: 86). Notions and conceptions of this sort are precisely what old Kewa people's stories establish: of statuses and relationships, local understandings of a proper and worthwhile life, ideas of personal powers and duties, the nature of marriage and war, the powers of magic and ritual, the remorseless hardships of the everyday. But because this is done through authoritative personal accounts, personal experience becomes generalized and the self elevated to the moral person living the exemplary life. Rather than being responses to injunctions to make oneself a certain kind of person (Laidlow 2002: 321–22), those telling their stories speak as if they already were such persons. There are analogies here with Young's (1983) description of a 'living myth', where narrators take on the persona of the eponymous hero, with the important difference that in the Kewa case it is the teller's life that is cast in the heroic or exemplary mould and offered as paradigmatic of Kewa life in general. Thus it passes into 'rehearsed talk'.

Perhaps the freedom to arrogate such representativeness to oneself derives from the absence of religious specialists, who elsewhere are responsible for '[elaborating] an edifice of reasoning about the conduct of social life' (as Carrithers [1992: 111] notes for the Ilongot and Kaluli). This absence, and the resulting equalizing effect, has two implications for Kewa practice: first, that any claims about institutions and cultural practices can be made only from an ethical perspective, when the self as a socially appropriate person is placed at the centre of the purported good life; and second, that such claims must always be ready to retreat. Both implications are premised on an important connection between ethics and freedom; and Laidlaw (2002: 311, citing Gellner's comments on Malinowski) luckily releases me from the obligation to defend a seemingly individualistic perspective with his timely reminder that it is possible to be a believer in freedom without subscribing to an atomistic social ontology. He refers us to Foucault's point that while the subject constitutes itself through practices of the self, the practices are 'models that he finds in his culture and are proposed, suggested, imposed on him by his culture, his society, his social group' (Foucault quoted in Laidlaw 2002: 323). When elderly Kewa told their life stories as paradigmatic Kewa lives, their ethical placing of the self described the cultural practices through which it had chosen to constitute itself: the marriages, brideprice exchanges, garden magic and other rituals, pig kills and warfare.

Carrithers points to the power, but also limitation, of paradigmatic thought (and thus also my 'rehearsed talk'): it 'is made up of propositions which can be simply, straightforwardly, true or false (1992: 157–58). Part of the very definition of the paradigmatic is that it presents itself as permanent, therefore static, lodged in an unchanging past and leaving no room to retreat. The old people who gave their stories here were already writing history, and not just for the anthropologist; their own lives were in the past. They engaged the present and negotiated social reality only in everyday exchanges ('minimal narratives'), such as those exemplified by Wapa's attempts to have his sons acknowledge their obligations to him; whereas narrative thought, as I encounter it and describe it in the stories that appear in the following two chapters, is more self-consciously nuanced.

Notes

1. The anthropological tradition in life stories stretches back to Smith's *Baba of Karo* (1954) through to Strathern's *Ongka* (1979) and Shostak's *Nisa* (1981). A spate of works in the 1980s sought to theorize personal narratives (Watson and Watson-Franke 1985, Personal Narratives Group 1989), and Cruikshank's ethnography (1990) successfully combined life-history narratives with traditional tales. Self-account has been at the centre of an experiment in interpretive ethnography by Vincent Crapanzano (1980), while other monographs have considered violence and narrative (Gilsenan 1996) and self-revelation through an informant's narrative (Behar 1994).
2. In a poetic expression, Kavouras refers to narratives as 'metaphors of social existence', in which (and with reference to Crapanzano, among others) 'narrators construct rather than describe their cultural realities, contesting the world-views of other people, as well as their own' (1994: 143). I find myself in complete sympathy with this evaluation. More prosaically, Kavouras goes on to define 'narrative' as 'any temporally framed linguistic expression, especially the practice of relating stories whether they are anecdotal in nature or more meticulous in their attention to consecutive details' (ibid.: 162).

Chapter 4

Narrating the Self II
Metanarratives of Culture, Self, and Change

The narratives in this chapter establish continuity with those in the previous one, by picking up the Kewa story from exactly the same place – in the midst of courtship, marriage and war. But immediately thereafter other features differentiate these narratives sharply from the earlier ones, both as biographical accounts and as philosophical views of the nature of the relationship of the self to its world. Four main features, expanded in the conclusion to this chapter, appear to follow sequentially and may themselves be stated as a narrative. The middle-aged people who tell their stories in this chapter straddle two worlds, linking the past with the present in their lives and their persons; their narratives no longer take for granted a representative moral personhood but strive instead to construct it in a changing world; thus the narratives become attempts to construct coherent selves (Linde 1993) seeking their identity on the scale of an entire life (Ricoeur 1992); and in this endeavour they become metanarratives, consciously critical of the lives and events that are their subject matter.

As opposed to the earlier stories, told as if the narrators simply lived 'the Kewa life', these critical metanarratives are simultaneously accounts of the past and attempts to grasp and shape the future.[1] *One Thousand Years in a Lifetime* is the title of a well known book by a statesman, Kiki (1968), which neatly expresses awareness of this giant stride that links 'traditional times' with present times. While Kiki's book metaphorizes the scale of change as the passage of time, it is difficult to claim that middle-aged Kewa, who were born into or grew up in an already changing world, conceive of economic and political change in terms of 'time travelling'.[2] They do, however, experience it as a radical break from traditional times, 'the time of bananas and sugarcane, when people didn't sit together or eat together', before the advent of the church and the law of the government. Like the Urapmin (Robbins 2005: 51), Kewa carefully distinguish between 'before' and 'now', traditional times and modern times; in the accounts given to me, embarrassed awkwardness hovered over the chasm in between.[3]

I begin with an introduction to the storytellers, then move on to the stories, telling only two in full, and finally return to a discussion of the four features which distinguish these stories from the previous ones.

The Storytellers

The storytellers in this chapter were in their forties and spoke no Tok Pisin. Rumbame, Alirapu and Mayanu were women; Mapi a man. All four came from adjoining Yala settlements: Mayanu from Puliminia, Alirapu from Poreale, Rumbame and Mapi from Aka. For reasons of space and focus I will tell the stories of Rumbame and Mapi in full, Alirapu's in abridged form, and limit Mayanu's story to a relevant addendum.

Rumbame
Rumbame was a strong-speaking woman in her late forties whom I knew fairly well though we never developed an exchange relationship. She herself sought me out and insisted on telling me her story, coming to my house for this purpose and bringing along Ramuame, Mapi's wife, and their respective daughters, Ipa and Kumiya. One incident interrupted our session: Wapa was lying ill in Rimbu's house (Rimbu having failed to build him his own house, as we heard in the previous chapter), and in the middle of the evening dirges (*temali*) began to be sung for him. We rushed over to Rimbu's house, fearing the worst, but finding Wapa's condition unchanged we continued with the recording. Rumbame was voluble and in no need of prompting. She had brought with her a young schoolboy to act as interpreter, but he turned out to be superfluous when I found I could understand her Kewa better than his English. I recorded most of her life story, and later transcribed it with the help of my male assistant Yasi. Not long after recording her story Rumbame was involved in a massive fight, which started with her husband and spread to the rest of the family. It ended with Rumbame knocking her husband out with a blow to the head with a piece of wood, resulting in his hospitalization and her short-term imprisonment.

Plate 4.1. Rumbame (left) with daughter Demanu. (15 January 1981)

Plate 4.2. Alirapu (centre) with husband Yembi. (25 November 1982)

Alirapu

People referred to Alirapu in Tok Pisin as '*meri paia*' (woman-fire) and '*fani meri*' (funny woman), for good reason: she was a sharp and lively woman who often made people laugh. Though I did not have a regular exchange relationship with her, we were friendly and exchanged gifts from time to time. She came to record her life story at my invitation, and her visit gave rise to a transmural discussion not unusual among the Kewa: while Lari accompanied Alirapu into the house, ostensibly to translate, Rarapalu made her contributions from the other side of the wall. Though I had written down an account of this narrative at the time, including the discussion, I transcribed the recorded text eight years later with the help of Lari's daughter Amasi, by then a young woman of eighteen. Amasi could barely hide her impatience with the text, as she cut a swathe through it with the words (in Tok Pisin): 'It's the same thing, all one kind of talk.'

Mayanu

Mayanu, married to Rama (whom Alirapu had also wanted as a husband), told me her story in 1993. Having married into the Paripa lineage, she was closer to my sub-clan than the other two women. I have two vivid memories of Mayanu: as a strident Mary in a Christmas nativity play for her (Catholic) church, and harpy-like at the top of our settlement, hurling abuse at the village men for failing to protect Giame, a pregnant woman,

Plate 4.3. Mayanu. (April 1980)

from the blows of her husband in a fight Giame herself had initiated following his drunken late-night arrival home. Mayanu is the mother of Loma, who has twice given her parents grief by ditching the bridegroom and causing havoc with brideprice distribution and transportation (see chapter 7 for both stories).

Mapi
Mapi is a feisty, sinewy man with humorous, sardonic features and a theatrical mobility that makes a perfect accompaniment to any story he tells. Though weighty in influence, being a village magistrate, he is a light and nimble man with a darting step when (as often) he enacts the scenes of traditional lore. His lightness and agility are more than physical, encompassing every aspect of his personality, especially his quick tongue and mordant wit. I still wince at the memory of his stinging reproach when I returned to the village in the midst of a pig kill which I should have attended but for some misinformation. His words, 'You lied!', sent me reeling like a physical blow. Yet this did not prevent him from making sure I took several photographs of him as he dispensed pork. When he came to my house he was usually accompanied by a younger brother (Kumi) and other agnates. Because Mapi was a Tiarepa Yala living in Aka, the Yakopaita clans (Umba and Paripa) with whom the Tiarepa had a competitive relationship wanted to put on a strong showing, so Rimbu made sure he joined us with several of his clan brothers. Like Pupula, Mapi also set his story against the backdrop of war, but his account ended with what he saw as the triumph of Christianity over heathen habits. By the end of my fieldwork he appeared to be obsessed with Christianity. His persistent and pointed questions about Jesus, pursued with the knowing look of someone trying to catch us out, often made us (the anthropologists) uncomfortable.

Rumbame's Story

'I will tell you of my young days. When I met my first sweetheart my father wanted to receive pigs and shells, and it was my wish also to marry this man. First I gave birth to a boy, Pau, then to a girl, Demanu. Next I had Rodopa, and then Ten. When I had Rodopa I cut the cord but retained the placenta, but still had another child afterwards. Now my body is full of water. I went to Kudjip hospital and to Erave hospital, but nothing could be done. I was baptized and put myself in God's hands. There was sickness in my body, but I didn't tell my father, my brothers or my children; they would have said I had done something wrong to become so ill. All my kinspeople will now be able to hear what I am recording, and they will ask what made me so sick. It's because of the placenta rotting in my body. I

Plate 4.4. Mapi pretending to shoot cassowary. (27 September 1979)

don't know if there is another person in Papua New Guinea with a sickness like mine. There was a woman in the Bible who had a disease of the blood, and God cured her; maybe he will do the same for me. I have a placenta rotting in my body, yet he hasn't allowed me to die. I don't know if it's adultery with another woman's husband that did it [she is referring to the fact that she was her husband's second wife]. My husband does not believe in God. He says he will live and die like his ancestors before him. That's my husband, Ana. I think it's adultery that did it, but he won't listen.

When I married I had children, made gardens and took care of pigs. I told my co-wife we should obey God, but she was only interested in gardens and wealth. One of her pigs bit her and she died, leaving her children, her gardens and all her things to me. I brought up the children, but when the girls (Demanu and Ipa) grew up they wouldn't listen to me. I tell them to go and fetch shells and pigs, but they don't care if their mother dies without eating. I see them receiving gifts and not giving me anything, but I still follow God. I always obeyed my father, my brothers and my mother, but my children won't listen to me. She picks up her net bag and goes to one man after another, that's what Demanu does. Now she wants to go to another man in Ialibu, but I stopped her. We argued and I reminded her what expenses I have to go to every time she or Ipa is sick, but they still won't listen to me.

In the old days my sisters and cousins and I enjoyed going on visits and courting sessions [*rome*], decorating and sleeping in a different woman's house every night. Sometimes they tricked me and went off to courting sessions with my *rome* partner [Roga], and we had tiffs over this all the time. Many of us girls ended up as second wives, but we still obeyed our husbands, even though they were old. My first courting partner was Rera, then came Roga. I really wanted to marry Roga, and I made him sweet potato mounds, while his father gave me sugarcane. But Wapelenu married him instead, and I ended up marrying a man who already had a wife. When we wanted to sing *wena yaisia* [women's courting songs] we put on grass skirts with cane-woven rings and rubbed tree oil [*wambo*] on our bodies. Before going to bed I would pour oil on myself. This is what we did when I was a girl, before we had soap. We old-fashioned ['tumbuna', traditional] people can't think well. I wouldn't know what to put in the tape recorder if God hadn't given me the power.

Gapea, my foster father, killed pigs in Awari when he received brideprice for me. As a young girl I looked after many of my father's pigs, and we killed them in Sumbura, Kalu, Agema and Papolata. My co-wife and I dug the ground for a spirit house and killed pigs in Nagurapo. When the Aka pig kill came up, my brother Mapi [Gapea's son] gave me a room in the longhouse and we killed pigs together. All my brothers gave me pigs, I looked after them and killed them. But now I have no pigs. Geali took my last one after his own pig was killed. Another pig went to Pulupa's wife [as part of brideprice]. Then Pulupa [her stepson] used up all my pigs and now I have none.

When my own clan killed a Yala man, the Yala clansmen wanted to kill me, but my father said, 'She is not a man for you to avenge yourselves on', so they spared me. When I was small I planted a casuarina tree in Awari. We levelled the ground and built a spirit house. The casuarina I planted is still standing there, it's not very old and neither am I dying. I have not lived many years. When I was in Mt Hagen my brothers had a pig kill, but my husband and children had no pigs, so we just sat there looking on while they killed their pigs and feasted. My pig killing days are over. I was in Kudjip [at a plantation] when my mother died, and although she had sent word I didn't have the fare to return. My sister's husband also died at this time. My mother sent a message: 'I'm dying but you can't come, *paitapeeee*, goodbye' [Rumbame often employs *loyota*, long drawn-out vowels word-terminal.] I thought I would die because I did not come to see my mother. My mother never saw my bad belly, and now the big sickness has come out. I sang this *temali* [threnody] for her.'

My mother, at your ground at Kalepenalo
I did not come to drink your breast milk
I tarried in a foreign place.

My mother's clan, my brother's iron roof
the thatch roof at my mother's ground at Korame
I did not come to drink your breast milk
I am a woman and couldn't.

A little girl with face tattoos
in a bush house at Kudjip
a daughter of Malie Sugu clan of Korame
I did not come to drink your breast milk
I am a girl, unable to sit.

Your mother's beads I take off
young trees by Lake Mupi
a muddy grave I dig
I am a girl, and can't do this.

My liver is on fire
tarrying in foreign parts
My mother's kin, my brothers,
traversing Wahgi river
I almost fell
but my heart would not give out.

At my mother's ground at Korame
I burn areca palm twigs
Girl with tattooed face
traversing the Wahgi river
I almost fell
I am a woman and couldn't
She was my mother but she is gone.
(For full analysis, see Josephides 2005a.)

When I was very young my father took me and my brothers, Nade and Koai [the same who, in chapter 1, questioned my payment to my housebuilders], to Batri. Nade's mother and her brothers came with us. Lopia of Batri was killed in battle, so his mother uprooted the stakes of the fence around our house and started throwing them at us. My father Kaluka felt sorry for us children, so he killed a pig and gave it to Lopia's lineage. Nade and Koai stayed with their mother while my mother and I were sent off to join Raketa, Mapi's mother, in Karikari. My father followed us but stopped in Pepeawere. He then sent for us to join him in Paguri, where the Pamerepa clan had given him a garden. My mother and *awa* [mother's brother] had in the meantime developed large ulcers [*kalarere*], which I treated with ashes. When they got better they killed a pig and gave me the fat and the belly. My father heard a Pamarepa woman say that his wife's sores were not like other people's sores, they gave off a very bad odour, so to compensate the Pamarepa [for having to endure the smell] he killed a pig and cooked it for them. Then we moved on to Mapiame near Abouma. My father told me to stay with Mapi's father [Gapea], so I went to Awari. He himself was tired of wandering in other people's land and wanted to till his own soil, so with his wife he went to Bala, where he died. My mother and I went to Agema to live with Gapea. I am about to die, so I am putting all this in the tape recorder. *Agele mada*, my talk is finished.' And with that Rumbame and retinue took off, it being after eleven in the evening.

In my translation of Rumbame's story I use the word 'sweetheart' as a gloss for Tok Pisin *preni* (friend) and Kewa *romeali* (courting partner). To make sweet potato mounds for a man, and receive sugarcane from his father, were early and tentative overtures to marriage negotiations. 'Adultery' is my rendition of Rumbame's way of referring to polygyny: 'I went just like that [not in the proper manner] to another woman's husband'. To 'just' do something meant to do it improperly. Thus in pre-Christian days when people died they 'just went', 'walked off'. To 'die without eating' is a reference to women's fear that they will not enjoy their daughters' brideprice. To be given a room in the longhouse, or a longhouse door, means to be designated a pig killer, someone who will provide pigs for the pig kill. Rumbame's brothers gave her pigs as part of their strategy to farm out pigs and ease their own burden; Rumbame would have received the head in acknowledgement of this service.

Alirapu's Story

'When I was a young girl my courting partner was Rama, but he was already married to Mayanu and my kinspeople wouldn't let me marry him. I married Kengeai instead, but I didn't like him and left him within a month, and brideprice had to be returned. Then I married Yembi, though he hadn't been my courting partner. When I wanted to go courting I made a net bag and put it on, but the men looked at my breasts and wanted to touch them, so I used to do this [folding her arms across her breasts].

When my mother married my father she made gardens and worked well. In the time of our ancestors we didn't wear clothes or trousers. The men wore bark aprons and belts, removing them at night to sleep naked on the ground. But now we have good clothes and money and we are really happy. My father never saw any money; he died just like that, eating sugarcane and bananas and killing pigs. When they killed pigs for Rimbu [the spirit house] we women didn't eat the meat, we just looked after the pigs and gave them to the men. We stayed away in the gardens when they took the pigs and put on their decorations, so we didn't see anything, we just heard what was going on. Then the government came and I tied up bananas; we ate them and we had a family. [Binding the fruit speeds up ripening and protects it from fruit bats. The expression is also a euphemism for intercourse, hence the family follows.] We did not live like a family before, we just slept together. At the time of bananas and sugarcane people did not sit together and eat. It's only now, since we've seen white people, that men and women sit together and eat together.

This government hadn't yet come when I married Yembi, and he was still taking bananas and sugarcane to the spirit house. But now we have received the church and the law of the government. At the time of Rimbu's father, of Yadi and Yembi, they made a different kind of spirit house, but now we have the church and we all sit inside together. [Turning to me and speaking more excitedly:] I said then we shouldn't let the white people leave; Councillor Mombe of Yagore heard me and he agreed. Everybody heard me, but still they sent the white people away. [She is referring to Independence, opposed at the time by many Highlanders.]

When I had Yonenu [her first daughter], my clan [Tiarepa] and my husband's clan [Yala] were preparing to fight. I was nursing Yonenu when this war was raging. I saw my kinsmen beaten further and further back, so I threw the baby into the Sugu river and returned to my natal village. My people shot their arrows and were routed, so they settled in the village of Turire.

The war stopped when the government came, and we returned to Yagore and lived in peace. Before this, we women would hide in the bush when wars broke out. Now I am safe, I am happy. When we were still in the bush and making houses wherever we could, the government came and tricked us. The interpreters came carrying guns, and the headmen told them to attack my clan, so they raped the women and plundered our food. We were afraid of the fighting and ran into the bush, where we slept in caves and tree hollows. They lied to the women about marrying them, they just took them, married and unmarried ones. We thought it was white people, but it was the interpreters [Papua New Guineans] who did this. We were terrified. This happened to all the women, but I escaped because I left my nice house and went into the bush.'

At this stage I began to ask Alirapu direct questions, and participation in the discussion became more generalized. Wars, Alirapu explained, were men's affairs and she didn't know the reasons for them. Women enjoyed preparing food when the warriors returned, and they were angry only if their husbands were killed or if they fought with their fathers' clan. Even if a sister was married in an enemy village, in no circumstances would a man kill his sister's child and take the sister away. The *awa* relationship (between mother's brother and sister's child) was a special one. Nor had she ever heard of a man killing his wife's brother (*pali*).

When I asked about Yala big men, Alirapu was careful to say that Rimbu was our big man in Yakopaita, but Mapi, as the village magistrate with 'talk', was the big man of all the Yala. A woman could become big too, and is acknowledged to be so when she gives wealth to her husband's clan when he is sick or depressed. Alirapu had done this and was known as a strong woman. She and Yembi decide together how their pigs are to be distributed. (At one pig kill I photographed her holding up pork ceremonially, unusual for a woman, and calling out the recipients' names.) Nevertheless, arrangements for pig kills are not women's work. Their mothers hadn't done this, so how can they? They build longhouses and kill pigs because their ancestors did it before them; it's a celebration to be enjoyed. Women look after the pigs and the men kill them. Men exult in the prestige of the name; women enjoy the pigs. Now the Christian missions have condemned and proscribed this enjoyment of pigs. But other things have improved: 'In the old days we women worked so hard. We would leave for the garden at six in the morning and not return before five in the afternoon, even in heavy rain.'

Alirapu had eight children, five of whom survived. She described how women always went to the *rameda*, a special house, when they were menstruating or close to giving birth. Her account of conception echoed that of the older generation. It was never believed, as in other areas, that repeated intercourse was needed to form the child.

Lari butted in here: she knew of many couples who continued to sleep together even though the woman was pregnant. 'Mmm,' Rarapalu corroborated from the other side of the pitpit wall. Alirapu continued: some women used contraception, and she herself knew about ways to induce miscarriage, such as rubbing the belly with water-soaked *rara* leaves, though she never used them herself. If husbands found out that their wives were using contraception, they would beat them. Alirapu herself was fitted with a coil three years ago in Erave Health Centre, and has had it changed once since then. Rorea's and Kumi's wives also use the coil. Noko, Kumi's wife, had it removed a little while ago and had a baby boy the other day, while Wareame, Yadi Tupase's wife, conceived while using it. Ramuame (Mapi's first wife) used to take oral contraceptives but stopped, and yesterday she had a son. Liame also used to take the pill, though now she is pregnant. Lari said she would like to use contraception herself but is reluctant, because 'everybody makes fun of ['tok pilai'] a woman without children' – not only a childless woman, but a woman of child-bearing age without a baby at the breast. From the other side of the window, Rarapalu, childless herself and presumably a good judge of the matter, assented.[4]

Mayanu's Story (Excerpt)

'In the old days we had no clothes. When our breasts developed we didn't cover them, we simply folded our arms over them. We were not really interested in courting, but we did it because it was the custom. Many women came to Rama's [her husband's] house, but I chased them all away. I put a stop to his courting and marrying. Well, I couldn't really stop him, but he didn't like it either. This wicked custom of marrying two or three women, and of Rimbu cults, is finished now. I wouldn't go back to those old days; the stream has carried them away. Working on the airstrip was hard; the long walk there carrying our sweet potatoes with us was gruelling. But then the government came, the highway was built, and we had clothes and tinned fish.'

This excerpt is worth quoting for its underlying commentary on two topics, gender relations and attitudes to traditional practices. The claim that women were 'not really interested in courting' is blatantly untrue when taken at face value, for many reasons: courting gave women the opportunity to find a husband, it enabled them to exercise some control over whom they married, and it allowed them to feel the power of their sexuality. Not only was courting fun, but its objective – marriage – was the life-aim of all men and women (see chapter 7). But as with other claims, Mayanu's statement works by means of metonymy. While it provides an example of 'embarrassed awkwardness' vis-à-vis custom, as mentioned in the introduction, its meaning expands when taken together with the preceding sentence, about young women folding their arms over their naked breasts. What this comment hints at is women's oft-expressed feeling, that the power of their sexuality was matched by their sexual vulnerability. On the one hand, young women's sexual availability, signalled by high breasts unspoiled by child-nursing, empowered them (while also leaving them exposed to rape); on the other (and as taken up in chapter 7), once married, these same women had to put up with husbands who continued to enjoy the sexual availability of other nubile women, thus putting the marital relationship in jeopardy.

Mapi's Story

'All the tribes around here were fighting against the Yala. In those days we lived in Aka. Every night a man was put on guard duty, and one night the guard overheard the enemy discussing them: "If all these Yala people lived up in Agema instead of down here in Aka, we wouldn't be able to kill them off so easily." So they all moved up to Agema and started making gardens and building houses there. From Agema they hurled down rocks and killed the enemy. This was not ages ago; it was in Mara's and Yawi's grandfathers' time. Gapea [Mapi's father] went to Agema too. Sawa killed Rudu of Koiari tribe on the road just outside your house here. The Yala were not at war with the Koiari, but Sawa was helping the Perepe, who were. At that time the Tiarepa of Yago came to fight the Yala, and the battle took place near your house. So when the Koiari went to Agema to avenge Rudu they found nothing but empty houses, women and children, and they burned the village down. As a result, the Yala were dispersed to Wapia and elsewhere. Before this war my father Gapea had gone to the Perepe and got a bride from there. Then the Kamarepa, having chased the Koiari out of Roga, invited us back under their protection. I was eight or ten years old when we returned to Agema. When I was fifteen we moved down to Modopu. Then everybody started talking about the coming of the Amali. This was the name we gave in those days to the government patrols. The patrols first came from Erave [in the south]. People were afraid to come down to Aka and tend their gardens when Amali's clan came. We were all rounded up and taken to build the airstrip in Kagua, and then the patrol post in Puliminia, while we were still living up in the mountains. My father became a *luluai* [government-appointed headman – see Pupula's story] when we started work on the Sumbura patrol post. The work was hard. Every day at six in the morning we had to come down from the mountain and report for work. [Mapi repeated this several times with indignation.] My father said, "Let's leave the mountains and return to the open valley." So we came down to Aka in 1963 and built a *tapada* [men's house] there. Umba clansmen like Hapkas and Rimbu were too young to help, but the rest of us worked very hard to build it. [Mapi is insinuating that his lineage should take credit for these feats to which the Umba, being too young and insignificant, would have contributed minimally if at all.] The mission came in 1966. When I was younger I wanted to wear lots of decorations and be like my father, but when the government and the mission came all this was finished. It was not really the government, but learning about Jesus that changed it all. I put aside my body decorations, because they led women to temptation [caused them to have bad thoughts].' (Mapi is not being entirely truthful; he wore decorations at his 1980 pig kill.)

Next, Mapi wanted to talk about traditional cults and beliefs. 'The Rimbu Rombake was a spirit house in which the Rimbunu was kept. The Rimbunu was a stone that represented Rimbu [in female form, -nu being a feminine suffix]. If any woman went inside this spirit house or heard what was going on, she would instantly be struck dead. The men dipped tanget leaves in tree oil and rubbed them on the Rimbunu. When somebody fell ill they rubbed the spiky *rara* leaf on the patient, whispering this spell:

Nainakina Rugurupa nakina pala
kulimi pagueyo ki kulimi pagueyo
egeme pagueyo nareme pagueyo egeme pagueyo.

[This clan's name], [that clan's name],
rub on the skin and bone, on the bone of the arm [hand],
rub the tongue, rub in the sun, rub the tongue.

Rimbu's older brother died because his father failed to do this, and that was how Rimbu got his name. At the time of the Rimbu festival, pig's blood was poured on the Rimbunu.

When people died they were laid in a hammock suspended from two trees. In order to discover the identity of a child's killer, the father tied a piece of string around the child's right wrist and another around the little finger of its left hand. The left side of the child's body belonged to the father's lineage, the right side to the mother's line. Then he would take a spear and lay it lightly on the child's body, pronouncing the following incantation: '*Koma lali pulu apo lotada opalao adolama*' ['The spear will speak about the death and we shall see']. If a speck of blood appeared on the dead child's right cheek, responsibility lay with the mother's lineage. If it appeared on the left, it lay with the father's. If the matrikin were responsible, the patrikin would go to them and demand to be compensated with pigs. The matrikin would prevaricate. If they were strong they would prepare to fight, but if they were weak they would equivocate for as long as they dared. But when the father's people came armed and spoiling for a fight, they would accede to their demands and reluctantly give up their pigs.' [The *pulu* divination method was carried out as recently as 1979 at Rake's death – see chapter 8.]

These confrontations were graphically re-enacted by Mapi, Kumi, Rimbu, Hapkas, Waliya, Papola, Rama, and Mapi's and Kumi's young sons. Yapa, my cat, stood in for the pig. Only men were present. Mapi laid a stick on his son's breast, and stood up, enraged to see the speck of blood appear on the child's right cheek. The men immediately sorted themselves into two hostile camps. Mapi threatened the matrikin with flexed muscles. They cowered, offering excuses and self-deprecations, holding Yapa behind them. Mapi grew more and more threatening, eventually pulling himself up to his full height, stretching his bow string and taking aim. The matrikin immediately proffered Yapa; Mapi grabbed her roughly and stalked off. There was relish in this enactment, and they all fell about laughing helplessly. But there was also embarrassment on the part of some, defiant and amused incredulity on the part of others, that they should have held such beliefs. Mapi said, 'This Rimbunu was nothing but a stone, 'Ol ston pinis. Nem bilong Dsisas istap tasol [Just a stone, only Jesus' name really exists].' Perhaps Mapi's son, the one who played dead, had taken the play too seriously, for in what I can only interpret as a symbolic or perhaps metonymic gesture, he took Yapa's feeding dishes as he left.

Mapi showed off his dramatic flair on another occasion. We had gone to Aka with my sister Sasha (who was rounding off her own fieldwork in Madang), and Mapi, half-painted, showed us how he would creep up on a cassowary and kill it. It was so convincing that his little son, this time standing in for the cassowary, sprinted a few metres when Mapi pretended to release his arrow. We also jumped, to the amusement of onlookers. On yet another occasion Mapi had returned from a big compensation payment and recounted how certain groups had plastered themselves with white clay and cried piteously, in an attempt to secure a share of the redistribution being made by the kin of the deceased, and how they came away in a huff when they were not compensated. Mapi imitated their whining and cringing – yet he himself had been involved in a less than dignified episode on this occasion, when he got hold of a pig rope and tried to claim it for the Yala.

Following the little divination drama at my house, I learned that the tensions and aggressiveness expressed there were not entirely the histrionics of good play-acting. It was no coincidence that Mapi's lineage was in one camp and Rimbu's in another. Rimbu came to see me the day after, together with Hapkas and his little son, Wapa and Nadisua (the father of Liame, who was married to Kiru, another clan brother). The pretext was to tell me stories of origin, but other motives were more pressing. What I learned only now was that a couple of times during the previous evening, Mapi, who spoke no Tok Pisin, had asked Rimbu to find out from me if I intended to follow the example of the 'white man in Kuare', an anthropologist who did fieldwork before me and was in the habit of paying informants K2 each for their stories. Rimbu refused to translate and told Kumi he could do so if he wished, but in the circumstances this was not a real option, as such an action would have constituted a serious breach of etiquette. Papola walked out in anger, while Hapkas and Waliya hung their heads and withdrew to their respective corners. To top it all, Rimbu said, this village magistrate had got his stories of wars and rituals all wrong, that's why he brought Wapa to straighten them out. Hapkas felt I shouldn't invite the Aka crowd here again, and Rimbu suggested I should get all the information from Yakopaita first and go outside only if gaps remained. I explained that I couldn't break off relations with Aka.

Some days later, as we were sitting on the village green after the church service in Aka, I told Mapi (with Ipa interpreting) that I had heard rumours of researchers paying K2 per story, but that I had no intention of emulating them, though of course I would continue to give food and gifts. Mapi made the following response: 'Before, in the time of our ancestors, we lived and slept in bad places. Then the *kadipi* [white people/government] came; they taught us to clear away all the dirt and sit down in open, clean spaces. And then you came to live among us and learn our traditions and language. In our traditions we have no precedent for charging for conversation. There is no charge for mere talk, and if a man has spread such a false rumour you must give me his name and he will have me to deal with.' We had a large audience during this exchange. Mapi finished by assuring me that when his father was well again they would come and eat with me and tell me more stories.

But many significant events intervened before Mapi's next visit. I had been away from the village for two or three weeks, during which time there had been trouble over the death of Rake, a local Councillor and member of the Perepe clan from which Rimbu's mother hailed (see chapter 8). On the very day of our departure, the land dispute between Mapi and the Perepe of Rake's lineage developed into a dispute between the Tiarepa and Umba clans of the Yala tribe. It was not only friendship with the Perepe that accounted for Umba responses; the Umba themselves, especially Rimbu and his brothers, feared Mapi's tactics of land expansion. Mapi wanted to open up the land to the north of the Sugu river, hitherto kept clear of human habitation and used for pig grazing and firewood, build a men's house there and cultivate land for coffee. But the Umba and Paripa clans complained that Mapi had constricted them enough by having a ban put on fishing in the stretch of the river between Yakopaita and Wilimi. (The Forests and Lands Commission had recently stocked that stretch and the ban on fishing was intended to allow the fish to breed, but the Umba believed that Mapi had instigated this move.) They brought up the story of Riesi and Popanu, the original Tiarepa to whom Yawi had granted some land when they married into the Paripa clan. Taking advantage of this initial act of generosity, the Umba complained, the Tiarepa now wanted to spread out and take everything, despite having the weakest hereditary rights.

With this backdrop, I told Rimbu that Marc and I intended to invite Mapi round one day to 'finish his story'. Rimbu acquiesced, but with the proviso that we make it clear to Mapi that if the Tiarepa attacked Yakopaita we would be on Rimbu's side. I said that we could not condone any violence. To Rimbu's further request that we 'talk strong' to Mapi so as to 'turn his liver' (scare him), I responded that we could not act as police. Rimbu made a last-ditch attempt to manipulate my guest list, but when Mapi and Ipa did come, he, Hapkas and Waliya mixed freely with them and no mention was made of the trouble between the two lineages. Mapi talked about cults, the forthcoming pig kill, and dreaming. In Mendi, he said, there is a mountain where people go to dream of the future. The dreamer must pay a fee to the owner of the mountain. Each clan also has a 'home' dreamer, and Mapi had taken this role over from Wapa. In a dream Mapi had seen decorated men dancing and singing a *temali* (a dirge) in Rake's men's house. Dreams such as these presage the death of a man. Waking, Mapi put a curse on Rake: 'If this is not your land you will die.' Now that Rake has died, Mapi is made answerable for this speech.

Mapi came to see us again after the pig kill was over, Ipa in tow. Two children also came, becoming three and then four when Marc was serving the food. Mapi quickly apologized, seeing Marc's confusion; he couldn't stop these children from following him around, he explained.

I tackled Mapi on women's roles in pig kills. Remembering the fracas with his wife Noeme at the time of the pig kill – when in a tearful rage she had hit out at him and he had run off, staying away for a few days until her temper had cooled – I asked why she had been so angry, and not accepted the two legs of pork he had given her. I ignored Ipa's answer that this was just an example of women's nasty ways, and pressed Mapi for his response. He said he had taken K100 from Noeme to buy a pig, but at the pig kill she thought he had given too much pork to his own kin and not enough to hers. She was unreasonable, Mapi said; if he had given her what she demanded he would have neglected others. Men can't accede to all their wives' requests because they have other obligations to fulfil; everything is distributed, the man himself doesn't get to keep anything. 'The brother [patrilateral relative] will come from down here, the cousin [matrilateral relative] from over there, and they must all be satisfied.' Mapi and Ipa conceded that in preparation for the pig kill women helped in the building of the men's house and the longhouse by digging the ground and fetching grass for thatching, but dismissed the idea of any further contribution. (Some women cite this contribution as conferring rights of residence on them.) 'How on earth can women climb poles or ladders? Women can't talk at public meetings, or even privately about certain matters. Well, they didn't in my father's time, but now …'

Marital relations are different in Papua New Guinea from Europe, Mapi mused, because here men pay for their wives. This line of musing moved from claiming that Papua New Guinean women's mental capacities were inferior to men's, to subordinating both to European thought: 'Women can't think well like men; they are all rubbish. Men change their wives in desperate hopes of getting something better, but it's no use, they are all the same rubbish. Both men and women in Papua New Guinea are rubbish. You Europeans think clearly, but we can't think straight. We can't change our ways now, but we hope our children will grow up to be like Europeans.' Mapi concluded, in a bitter tone: 'Are your children disobedient, your wives unhelpful? What can we do in these conditions? It's very difficult to get help from anyone, whether it's our clan brothers, our wives or our children.' Over the years that I knew him Mapi became increasingly preoccupied with Christianity, and this preoccupation culminated in his visions and life-changing experiences. The last part of his story, which stretches from 1980 to 1993, focuses on this topic.

Mapi: Visionary and Dreamer

In Aka in 1980, counting pig stakes for the forthcoming pig kill, Mapi asked if I thought Jesus would return in the year 2000. The question was one of faith, I replied, not of knowledge, and I was not a believer. The church, Mapi continued, preached that in that year Christ would come and punish the sinners, putting to death all those who did not come into church but sat chatting outside, or came in but did not close their eyes to pray. I said I would be included in the list, since people often hissed at me 'Close your eyes!' while I sat wide-eyed during prayers in church. He nodded laughing and asked why I did not believe. I attempted two lame answers: everything in the Bible had taken place very long ago if it happened at all and I had not been there to see it; and I had never witnessed God's power or his miracles.

But Mapi sees God's hand in everything. When he plants a banana tree and it grows and bears fruit, it's because God has had a hand in it. The men's house he is building could not be completed without God's assistance. There is no need to point to miracles when humanity is seen as powerless and its successful actions are attributed to an omniscient and omnipotent God. Mapi believed in God and prayed to him because this life was hard, and exacting labour was required to achieve anything. His body may rot on earth when he dies, but he wants his soul to go to heaven and enjoy eternal comfort and peace. In the days of his ancestors people died completely, but in these days of faith they can go to heaven. I asked Mapi if the coming pig kill was not a heathen practice? Mapi smartly outwitted me: the Bible says that people shall eat the fruits of the earth. Finally, I asked why he had chosen Evangelism when the Catholic mission was already established in Agema. Because the Catholics were too lax and liberal, he replied, failing to prohibit traditional practices, such as decorating, singing and dancing, and instead allowing drinking and smoking. [Yet as noted earlier, he himself wore decorations at his pig kill.] But he was disconcerted by the presence of so many denominations in Papua New Guinea. Why could the missions not amalgamate and present a common front? He asked sententiously if I thought there were many roads to Jesus. I laughed and said there probably were. He laughed in turn and said he thought I was lying. We shook hands and I took my leave.

Mapi was no longer village magistrate on our return trip in 1985, having failed to be re-elected in March 1983. This was not on account of his prison sentence following his part in the fight with the Perepe over Ipa's pig, but because the Yala tribe is much smaller than the one whose candidate was appointed. In 1984 Mapi had his vision. We invited him to eat with us in spite of Rimbu's strongly expressed opinion that we should not entertain in our diminished house (Rimbu having sectioned off the front half which he used as a trade store). We pressed a reluctant Rimbu to join us, stressing how much we depended on him to keep Mapi's talk short and to the point. We served rice and tinned fish to Rimbu, Mapi and later Kumi.

Mapi had received three 'signs' (he used the Tok Pisin word '*piksa*') of what I shall call his election. The first was when he was a small boy in Modopu. He had called to his father '*Apa!*', but his father heard the voice of a grown man. The second was in 1982, when he had a child that never crawled but moved straight to walking. The third sign had many stages. The Perepe had stolen eight of his pigs, so Mapi collected his spears and went out to shoot some of theirs. He came across Rake's dog first, shot it and shoved it under a rock. Then he returned home and tried to sit down, but his knees would not bend. For two or three hours he stood there with rigid knees, until he vowed to pay compensation for the dog, and God softened his knees so he could bend them.

The next stage concerned his polygynous marriage. Some time before, he had left Noeme in Aka and went to live with his first wife Ramuame in Wilimi. But he felt sorry for Noeme, and asked her to join them. Early the following morning, as he lay asleep in bed, there was a knock on the door and he heard Ramuame's voice, saying, 'You won't go to heaven. You like Noeme and her fat pig too much.' Later that day (it was a Saturday) he went to the market, leaving K200 in two-kina notes at home. He wanted to buy a hundred kina's worth of pork, and asked the Tiarepa seller to accompany him home for the payment. But after counting out K100, he came across a strange two-kina note which he was sure had not been there before. It was stamped PAID in red ink. (Kumi, who joined us at this stage, showed me the exhibit. Earlier we had to say grace for Mapi and Rimbu to eat, now we had to do it again for Kumi.) On Sunday he asked Pastor Rorea to bring all his clan along, and he showed them the marked note, saying, 'It's my bone that made this mark.'

The following Saturday Ramuame told him their child was sick, and asked for money to go home to Tiripi. He gave her K40, keeping K180 for himself. (The arithmetic does not add up here.) She said, 'I'll throw your money down a water hole, your mouth is fire, you'll go to hell.' He was so angered by her words that he put all the money in one wad and tried to tear it up, but it was too thick. So instead he threw the money in her face, with the words, 'You take the money and the sow and go home, I am finished with you.' Instead of going, she gathered up the money and gave it back to him, and with a gentle voice entreated him not to be angry. They shook hands (that is, made up), washed and went to the market. On the way back Mapi stopped in Poiale to play basketball, staying until six in the afternoon and then going to wash in the river. All of a sudden he felt the breath leaving his body, he had no power, he was finished. He hugged his arms round his body and slowly made his way home. Once there, he asked for a large dish of sweet potatoes and some water. His wives were surprised; it was not his habit to eat out of large dishes.

But no matter how much Mapi ate he was not sated. He didn't feel that it was really going into his belly; he felt weak and his skin was slack. So everybody said he had died. Three weeks passed like this, until on the Friday of the fourth week he felt stronger and rose up. His soul (*remo*, 'satan' in Tok Pisin) had returned to him. They thought he had been poisoned (ensorcelled) and came with leaves (that is, antidotes) to cure him; he saw the leaves though they were inside net bags and asked for them to be taken away. By Saturday he was strong again.

Many strange things now happened. While he was lying in bed there was a loud knock on the door, and his wives asked him not to push the door so violently. 'It's not me pushing, I'm lying here in bed,' he protested. His soul had left his body and walked out. He saw a stone wall and a good road alongside it, at the far end of which was a large hole, and when he looked inside there was nothing but darkness. He turned back and the stone wall was now hidden by clouds. There was thunder and lightning. Right at the top there he saw beautiful houses in many colours and lovely open spaces. [This image comes straight out of a Kewa myth; see Josephides 1982.] He always thinks of this place now and wants to return there soon. He has lost interest in earthly things, such as gardens, good food, his wives, his home, but longs instead for that tranquil, beautiful place in the sky. The lightning had struck down a fine elm tree (*yare*) in Paipada (I saw the scorched tree myself), and five cockatoos (*koke*) came and sat on the blackened *yare*, dancing with the sun, the moon and the stars. The Yala, the Tiarepa and the Perepe saw them, and made a song of this.

He travelled all over, in Wapi, in Sumi, talking about the signs he had seen. He heard the prayers of the Catholics but they didn't go to heaven; they stopped in holes in the ground. Others prayed and their prayers went to the sheep stalls (Kewa don't keep sheep). Only one woman's prayer went to heaven. His soul is now in heaven; he thanks Jesus. He composed a song about this. He can't get angry with anyone any more. If he feels he is getting angry the breath leaves his body and he becomes weak. Hapkas was in Popa and dreamt that God had got Mapi. 'How this could have happened I don't know,' Mapi said, 'for I'm a man with two wives. But it's true.'

During our 1993 fieldtrip Mapi had more to tell. 'The day after we buried Roga [a clan brother] I was asleep with my body in bed, but my devil [his word for *remo* this time] was wandering about. I came to a big lake, in the middle of which stood all the dead people – my father, Roga – and their clothes did not get wet. I am the man who says prayers in our village [that is, he heals through prayer], so when I saw all these people standing in the water I put my hand on their heads and prayed. While doing this I heard the sound of a soft threnody. I looked up to see the singer, but it was just the wind. Whenever I sleep I hear this threnody again, and now I sing it myself in church.' Now God even shows him, in dreams, which candidate will win in the local elections.

Four Features Revisited and Expanded

On the basis of the stories just told, I return to a discussion of the four features mentioned at the beginning of this chapter. To restate them in brief: the narratives straddle two worlds; they strive to construct moral personhood; they present coherent selves seeking their identity on the scale of an entire life; and they are critical metanarratives. The first feature is too self-evident to require separate elaboration: the stories straddle two radically different worlds, and in telling them the narrators link the past with the present in their own lives and persons. The linguistic conventions used to illustrate this position were mentioned in the introduction and demonstrated in the stories: 'before' and 'after', 'then' and 'now'. Evaluations of the two worlds, and the strategies followed by those who straddle them, are the subject of the remaining three features, taken up in more detail below. Their discussion leads to some final comments linking to the whole project of the book.

Creating Moral Personhood

The narrators in this chapter, in contrast to their elders in the previous one, cannot take for granted their own moral representativeness as Kewa, living normal Kewa lives. For what is a 'normal life' in a changing world? Their narratives thus strive to construct a moral personhood for themselves, while the question of 'representativeness' remains open. The two principal stories, Mapi's and Rumbame's, are more about innovation, creative action, personal revelation, about being different and being singled out, than about representativeness and the norm. Individual desire for a particular lifestyle surfaces in the two other women's stories. In constructing a new personhood, from big man with political office to religious visionary, Mapi's account is of a man chosen to lead a people through a transition. Having lost one avenue for prestige and influence, Mapi had found another. Since the new morality was bound up with Christianity, he needed to create a pioneer's niche for himself in this new religion, where his moral personhood would be unassailable. This is not to cast aspersions on the nature of his belief, but simply to recognize how he placed himself in the world, as all human beings do, both personally and as a politically ambitious man.

In his major work on Christianity in Papua New Guinea, based on fieldwork among the Urapmin of the Telefomin area in West Sepik, Robbins describes the anguish of revivalist 'second-stage conversion' Christians as they strive to achieve a moral personhood 'while existing in the midst of a social world that routinely draws one into sin' (2004: 254). 'Most Urapmin are troubled', Robbins (ibid.: 313–14) observes, not because their traditional world has collapsed, but because its thriving state also supplies the grounds for another culture – a Christian one, whose values they experience as incompatible with their traditional ones yet also recognize as their inescapable fate. What they find troubling is the clash of those two cultures, with a dissonance that wrenches them apart. In chapter 8 I describe how the Kewa are also painfully aware of the passing of an old order, seen as radically different from the new one. But they experience the change as the end of an era and a moving on, almost like the inevitable march of time. The comparative lack of anguish may be due in part to the persistence of well-known 'technologies of self-formation'; though like the Urapmin they also put much energy into 'moral self- and social reconstruction' (ibid.: 316), unlike the Urapmin their stories show the continuing use of elicitation and rehearsing talk, rather than the 'creation of an elaborate new set of ritual technologies' (ibid.).

Almost expressly in order to make this point, Rumbame right away presents circumstances in which she might be misunderstood as being morally unworthy, and deftly tweaks the picture, without over-defensiveness, to reveal herself as morally worthy – why else would God not let her die? Through an alternative explanation she constructs a different social knowledge from what may at first be deduced on the basis of the events she herself describes. She claims to be led by the higher authority of God, while her husband – who is not even her first choice of spouse – 'will not listen'. She has behaved properly and aimed for the good life as well as encouraging it in others (her co-wife, her husband, her daughters), but they won't listen no matter how much she tries to get them to change their ways. Rumbame talks about what is good and proper and what is due to one in general terms, while she constantly contrasts times and behaviours. The ethical aim that emerges is an attempt to construct propriety in changed circumstances – precisely what Mapi is also engaged in.

Constructing Coherent Selves

In their endeavours to construct moral persons (as mentioned in this chapter's opening paragraph), narratives as life stories must also construct coherent selves (Linde 1993) seeking their identity on the scale of an entire life (MacIntyre 1981; Ricoeur 1992). This suggests that, notionally, a life is coherent in so far as it is complete. Any addition, especially when 'not in character', momentarily destabilizes that integrity until it is interpreted in a coherent fashion, even if (as in this case) the outcome is the redrawing of the picture. I offer these comments as an alternative reading of those features that led Linde (1993: 16) to the conclusion that a life story, and even more so the narrator's evaluation of it, must remain discontinuous and incomplete while its subject still lived. I argue instead that a judgement about discontinuity and incompleteness can only be made outside local time and space; when the stories are told it is always in the context of a decision concerning both of these, which gives them a certain finitude and coherence, and when on a later occasion the story is lengthened and modified the stitching will not show. As seen above, Rumbame's story has a narrative unity in that she has gathered herself together to present an account of her life, from its beginning to its projected end, without allowing the radical disruptions she has suffered to dissipate her identity. Though earlier in her story she says she has not lived many years and is not yet close to death, she closes with the words that she is about to die. What she means by this is that she has lived a full life from beginning to end, and any extension of it now will not make a significant difference to its actual achievements or activities (she has no pigs, her daughters go from man to man and do not listen, and she has given herself to God; although Rumbame is trying to talk of her own youth, she is unable to stop herself from interjecting these grievances against her daughter). From the perspective of a life narrative, her life is over. But she wants to be the one to give it its meaning.

For his part, Mapi puts together a story whose coherence is achieved by one main constant, himself.[5] Through a series of disruptions Mapi retains a coherent self by remaining flexible, rising to the occasion and ushering in the future by seizing hold of the present as a major protagonist. The transition tells his whole life, and whatever else may follow will only be another anecdote of a story whose general contours are known. To sum up my argument in this section, I do not claim that disruptions never dissipate identity, only that narratives represent attempts to overcome such disruptions.

So far I have emphasized the ability of the narrator to construct a coherent narrative by imagining the unity and completeness of her or his life, but Linde (1993: 16) reminds us that coherence is not an inherent property of texts; it is a product of the interaction between speaker and addressee. For her, oral accounts are 'units of discourse' which demonstrate our understanding of and adherence to the moral standards of the community (ibid.: 3–4). A life story, expressed in these units of discourse, becomes coherent only when it has been negotiated and accepted. The components of negotiation and acceptance are crucial in Kewa stories, as I discuss below and throughout this book; but negotiability begins even earlier, with the 'moral standards of the community' themselves. These standards are especially open to negotiation at times of radical social change.

Constructing Critical Metanarratives

As opposed to the earlier stories, told as if the narrators simply lived 'the Kewa life', the stories in this chapter are critical metanarratives that 'say something about something'. Told by people in the midst of negotiating change, they are simultaneously metanarratives of the past and attempts to grasp and shape the future. A salient feature is their implicit and often explicit critical commentary on local practices, lives and events. They are part of a quest for the full life and worthy personhood, a forge for the fashioning of a new social reality out of the debris of the old.[6] Mapi sifts through this debris in his accounts of wars, which men of his generation had not fought, and ruminates on the social and moral basis of pig kills and body decoration. He weighs these old practices against the new routes to knowledge and power, and though he abandons them as 'heathen', he still pursues their ultimate objective: prestige in the new world.

All female narrators constantly contrast 'government time' with 'traditional time', old times with new. As in the narratives of women from the older generation, a statement emerges of women's desires to control their bodies and prevent their husbands from taking additional wives. Mayanu and Alirapu dwell on the vulnerability experienced by young women who had to go 'naked' (that is, bare-breasted), feeling that they were at the mercy of men's desires, and how much safer and protected they feel now. They are tireless in their praise of modern times, seen as the advent of clothes, Christianity and family life, trade-store food and money, and the demise of polygyny, war, and religious practices that excluded them. Alirapu is proud of the political acumen evident in her public support of the continued presence of white people in Papua New Guinea (which is how she describes her opposition to PNG's independence). Traditional beliefs and values are contested by Rumbame's reinterpretation of the reasons for her illness: not secret fornication, but open adultery as a result of polygyny. Thus she redefines adultery and outlaws polygyny. Yet despite the strong Christian belief that leads her to claim God as the source of all her powers (as Mapi does), Rumbame also wants to 'eat' brideprice, and considers herself cashiered because she has no pigs.

Nonetheless, women's accounts can be seen as most critical in their attitudes to traditional understandings of political power. While

Rumbame's story describes amazingly peripatetic lives, she makes scant reference to the wars punctuating these moves, being more interested in the relations and the kinship ties forged in them. Alirapu mentions war and big men only in response to my direct queries. Even then she deals with bigmanship in a peremptory manner, as something quite uninteresting and even irrelevant, or, at best, relevant in so far as it services the local community; for which reason she is more careful to point out that each small settlement has its own man of influence.

Facing Modernity and Christianity

It is clear from the above that a critical stance towards traditional practices goes hand in hand with perceptions of Christianity and the experience of modernity. For both men and women, modernity is bound up with Christianity, but each gender nonetheless has a different way of becoming modern and a different relationship to Christianity.[7] As illustrated by their stories, women see modern changes as giving them control over their bodies and persons, facilitating mobility, and, for younger women, offering new opportunities through education. (See Josephides 1999 and 2005b for a fuller discussion.) Their perceptions of modernity are not, of course, scholarly analyses that take into account its deleterious effects elsewhere in PNG. Because Christianity seems to them an integral part of the new way of life, they talk about it incidentally, without recounting the spectacular dreams and visions experienced by Mapi or (as shown in the next chapter) Hapkas. For Mapi, Christianity became an obsession which took over the whole of his intellectual life. During our fieldtrip in 1993, he plied us with searching questions about Jesus. Here is a sample:

> Mapi: 'Have you seen Jesus?'
> Me, taken aback: 'Jesus lived long ago, if he existed at all, I couldn't have seen him.'
> Mapi, testily: 'There are so many pictures of him, where would artists have got their likenesses from if he hadn't existed?'
> Me: 'They draw him the way they imagine him; you can draw him the way you imagine him.'
> Mapi, shortly, exasperated: 'I can't draw him at all, I have no way of knowing what he looks like apart from the pictures I get from your country.'

From a perception that Jesus is white, Mapi concludes that all their own traditional things are bad. Despite this comment, Kewa ethnography will not permit an understanding of Kewa attitudes to their traditional practices in terms of Sahlins' humiliation hypothesis. Sahlins argued that in order to modernize, 'people must first learn to hate what they already have', they must experience a 'certain humiliation' and a 'global inferiority complex' (Sahlins 1992, cited in Josephides 2005b: 115). Elaborating on Sahlins' thesis in a volume of papers that apply it to cultural change in Melanesia, Robbins (2005: 47) observes that Christianity taught Urapmin 'to be open to the idea of human worthlessness, but more pointedly to use it to humiliate themselves', since debasement is necessary to salvation. I argue in the same volume that though Kewa may laugh at old practices or recall them with embarrassment, 'wry self-deprecation is an old Kewa trait' (Josephides 2005b: 116). Concerning modernity, I add, 'what defines each modernizing strategy is not whether it is an attempt to localize modernity or embrace it in an alienating foreign form, but whether it is undertaken in the spirit of an active, bold self-externalization, or a desperately anxious submission' (that is, humiliation as a fully-fledged pathology) (ibid.: 123–24).

Judging by the stories in this book, Kewa people favour the spirit of active, bold self-externalization. Mapi expresses no feeling of humiliation as he recounts how, despite having two wives, he had been chosen by God. Both he and Hapkas exploit their experiences to the full, suggesting in their self-presentation that God chose them in an election that somehow singled them out; whereas women themselves chose God. The different ways men and women view modernity will become more apparent in chapter 5. At this stage I merely observe, in conclusion, that though in their negotiations between the old and the new both sexes place themselves at the centre of their changing universe, men continue to be more concerned than women about their stature in the local community, and their ranking in relation to other men.

Conclusion

The narratives in this chapter enrich Kewa ethnography by contributing several emic accounts, resulting in the insights and perspectives discussed in the previous section. In this conclusion I consider the major ways in which the stories and their analyses advance the whole project of the book. I focus on two points: the extent to which narratives are used as 'eliciting talk', and how they act, in Ricoeur's words, as 'the first laboratory of moral judgement'.

As discussed in chapter 2, 'elicitation' denotes the contestability and negotiability of meanings and intentions. Eliciting talk serves two functions, to draw out the meaning of others, which is generally assumed to require interpretation, and to test, bit by bit, the acceptability, coherence, and intelligibility of one's own claim before staking it outright. Mapi's narrative is replete with innuendoes; he makes several tacit claims, and elicits responses through messages to other interlocutors. He begins by challenging the Umba clan to convey to me his request for payment for information; my generosity, pitted against an earlier anthropologist, is at stake, and any suspicion of meanness will reflect on my host clan. When I take up the subject with him, also in an indirect way, Mapi smoothly turns the incident round, defying me to say that he had been the one to broach it in the first place. His manner is not defensive or apologetic, but confident and suave, as if it had truly not been him. His 'eliciting talk' had achieved at least its fall-back objective: he had let me and the others know that he was aware of the possible value of his services, in a form of communication which is never free of a whiff of menace. In other respects his accounts, purportedly to me, also spoke to the Umba, making claims and eliciting their response. By stressing that the Umba were too young to help build the men's house, he created the impression that they were not as substantial as his own clan. The enactment itself of traditional practices played out these rivalries. (As was seen in Wapa's story, Mapi insinuated much of this rivalry into his adjudication of Wapa's court prehearing, as he will again in discussions at Payanu's funeral in chapter 8.)

The women's narratives in this chapter illustrate less obviously the use of eliciting talk. Rumbame's story sends out messages to several people, her daughter in particular being constantly apostrophized and her kin informed that she is blameless and enjoys God's favour, while Alirapu's comments about her political acumen seek to establish as 'rehearsed talk' a claim about the value and influence of women's political opinions. But eliciting strategies are more clearly exemplified in interactive, 'minimal narratives' (further described in part II), or when the narrative conditions, as in Mapi's case, specifically invite such elicitation.

What these narratives show in general is that elicitation may not be separated from moral self-construction, the two being part of the same action: one *elicits* acknowledgment of one's moral self-construction. Concerning the last operation, Ricoeur's work (1992: 113–14) offers support for the general argument of this book, by clarifying how the subject designates itself in utterances that signify the world. This act of designation thus renders personal identity a form of historical narrative, which constitutes both the self and the world. The narratives of the elderly Kewa, offered as paradigmatic accounts of Kewa lives in general, best exemplify this activity. In this respect they bear out Ricoeur's definition of narrative theory, as combining a descriptive viewpoint of action with the prescriptive viewpoint of a normative attitude (ibid.: 114). This historical dimension of narratives works both ways: while it makes human lives 'more readable', it also enhances historical understandings. Thus, life stories perforce implicate the world in breadth and length, bringing together the subject or the self, its social milieu, history, and morality.

In the present case, when narratives straddle two worlds, establishing permanence in time becomes the most pressing requirement in the construction of personal identity. But how to establish such continuity at times of radical change? In chapter 2, having translated Ricoeur's terms into my own conceptual vocabulary, I took up the discussion of innovation in closed systems. The process of innovation, I wrote there, is one in which the agent elicits the possibilities of the system to be influenced by the agent's abilities. I now look at the temporal significance of that passage, always with recourse to Ricoeur. The 'closed system' can be seen as an already acquired habit or disposition. Habit, though giving a history to character ('character' being understood as immutable condition, 'the set of lasting dispositions by which a person is recognized', reidentified as the same [ibid.: 121]), also covers over 'the innovation which preceded it' (ibid.). Translating back to my own conceptual vocabulary, habit is 'rehearsed talk', which covers over its origins as 'rehearsing talk' (a claim that may at any moment be overthrown), yet is unable to escape the challenge posed by the ambiguity (in Kewa practice) of all talk – as both ampliative and defeasible, able to spread or to withdraw (or be modified) when challenged, without loss of speaker-credibility. When Ricoeur (ibid.: 121) states that it is through this sameness that the self is announced, the constancy thus claimed, in so far as it is made up of 'values, norms, ideals, models, and heroes *in* which the person or the community recognizes itself', is mainly (just like the immutable condition which was really a past act of innovation) the achievement of the actions and narratives of particular persons, who must take their lives and futures in their own hands and push them over the chasm to a new terrain. Rumbame, Alirapu, Mapi, as well as the narrators in the next chapter, are all engaged in this dangerous and courageous activity, which is the lot of all human beings who want to live.

Narrative is 'the first laboratory of moral judgement', Ricoeur declares (ibid.: 140, emphasis removed); thus no narrative can be ethically neutral (ibid.: 115). This simple declaration can be treated as a profound insight into ethics and morality as living systems. If, as I believe, Dilthey (cited in Ricoeur 1990: 115) is right to see the 'connectedness of life' as a pre-understanding of narrative theory, it follows that 'connectedness' is somehow a moral attribute; and to see narratives as accounts in which 'the self seeks its identity on the scale of an entire life' immediately introduces the moral/ethical dimension, as it ties the narrating self into a social and historical context. Moreover, narratives understood in this way also clarify how particular moral understandings can be reversed, and the narrators' lives and worlds still retain their moral force in terms of 'connectedness'. In his discourse on narrative composition, Ricoeur discusses the roles of concordance (Aristotle's 'arrangement of facts') and discordance (the reversal of fortune that transforms the initial situation). I poach this model of transformation for the case of people telling their stories, but avoid falling into a Lévi-Straussian structuralism by adding a dynamic dimension. The concordance can be seen as the aforementioned 'identifications with values, norms, ideals, models, and heroes' that people claim to share (my 'rehearsed talk') – which is a set not concretely specified. The discordance will be the various individual interpretations of this set, made in the form of placing oneself and one's life at their centre ('rehearsing talk'). Just as the narrative plot transforms contingency into necessity (when what might look like a chance occurrence is understood retroactively as necessary for the plot's denouement), so does successful elicitation – the action that reverses a situation – claim to be stating a fact (as when Rumbame's conversion to Christianity reveals her polygynous marriage to be adultery). Though for Ricoeur discordance originates in the 'disruptive effect of unforeseeable events' (ibid.: 147), these events must have had a cause and certainly an agent. To use an example from the classics (Sophocles, not Freud), though Oedipus killed his father 'accidentally', he actually killed Laios in a deliberate act. He did not know Laios was his father, but the act of killing seemed excessive and unnecessary. It was a chance event that brought about the meeting, but the killing itself was not a chance event.

My argument here, in summing up, is to point to the labile nature of the initial situation and the importance of the agent. The initial situation (concordance), in being reversed, is also exposed as improvised or open to contestation. The lability is covered up when the agent of change hails the novelty as self-evident truth. Concerning the causal relationship between the storyteller and the story, it is mutual, as Ricoeur so well expressed it: 'The person, understood as a character in a story, is not an entity distinct from his or her "experiences." Quite the opposite: the person shares the condition of dynamic identity peculiar to the story recounted. The narrative constructs the identity of the character, what can be called his or her narrative identity, in constructing that of the story told. It is the identity of the story that makes the identity of the character' (ibid.: 147–48).

Notes

1. It is possible that these differences derive from the stories being told to me at a particular time; I am not arguing that stories with these four characteristics were never told in the old days, only that the older and younger people told me their stories in particular styles that enabled me to make this deduction about how they saw their own lives and themselves as historically placed.
2. The phraseology is the anonymous reader's, whom I must thank for bringing the issue to my attention.
3. My analysis here is in accord with Jackson's (1998: 154) perspicacious observation – that what is important is not so much whether beliefs are 'traditional' or 'modern', but what people do with them and what follows from their use.
4. The PNG government permits access to contraceptives only to married women. Pregnancy in unmarried girls usually results in marriage or the adoption of the baby by the girl's parents, as seen in some accounts.
5. Mapi can be seen here to be pursuing a 'life project' as described in Rapport 2003.
6. I am grateful to Marc Schiltz for bringing to my attention the similarity between this sentence and one cited by Lévi-Strauss from Boas. In his discussion of bricolage, Lévi-Strauss alludes to Boas' comment that '"it would seem that mythological worlds have been built up, only to be shattered again, and that new worlds were built from the fragments"' (1966: 21). Lévi-Strauss concedes the point, but adds what he thinks Boas has overlooked: that in this reconstruction from the same materials, 'it is always the earlier ends which are called upon to play the part of means: the signified changes into the signifying and vice verse' (ibid.). It also needs to be said that the 'materials' are not always 'the same'; two sentences after the one reminiscent of Boas, I show Mapi weighing old practices against new routes to knowledge and power.
7. In 1993, we found that Seventh-Day Adventists, resisted in earlier days, were now making inroads in the Kewa area. For an account of the SDA converts' view on Christianity and modernity, see Jebens 1995.

Chapter 5

Narrating the Self III
The Heroic, the Epic and the Picaresque in a Changed World

The narratives in chapters 4 and 5 draw their vitality and very life from the landscape painted in the chapter preceding each of them. Then, sometimes tentatively but always inevitably, they proceed to paint over it, creating a palimpsest of culture, traditions, practices, ethics, persons. By now the landscape painted by the earliest narratives is completely written over, and the experiences of the narrators are based on a transformed reality. The younger adults in this chapter are all involved in the new spheres of life; instead of wars, spirit houses, courting and magic, they talk of road-building work, plantation labour, business and cash cropping, church and Christianity. Beyond the transformative visions of dreamers, the routinization of Christianity is also glimpsed. Ways to marriage remain a central feature of the narratives, but here also there have been re-routings.

How was the landscape transformed? Let me count the ways. Ever more nuclear family houses have sprung up, with woven pitpit walls and even some roofs of corrugated iron; motorable roads have cut into valleys, forests and mountains; skeletons and future fossils of motor vehicles litter the countryside, others still belch out their poison as they clang and screech their way; helicopters or light aircraft hover overhead; trees are felled to feed sawmills; tradestores abound, erratically stocked; cash crops encroach on subsistence farming; oil prospecting company shares are floated to local buyers; plantation work plays the role of rites of passage; bread baked in drums has joined other market wares; parliamentary candidates tour in motorcades promising trucks for votes; rascals have replaced warriors as the purveyors of violence, and knives and guns have overtaken spears and arrows as weapons of choice; health clinics have sprung up, though sparsely stocked and understaffed; schools and

Narrating the Self III   113

churches have proliferated, the latter better attended than the former; card-playing continues in the open, beer-drinking on the sly; volleyball and basketball are pursued with passion, especially in the one-house hamlet with the humorous banner proclaiming it 'The Republic of Central Paipada'; young people wear flashy shoes and colourful clothing, turning to tape-recorders, guitars and church songs for their music.

In this chapter, as in previous ones, the narratives are preceded by an introduction to the storytellers. I follow their accounts with analyses at two different levels: of the content of the stories and their political and social claims, and their function as means of communication and modes of organizing experience.

The Storytellers

The narrators who had grown up in these changed times all came from Yakopaita, the Yala settlement in which I lived throughout my fieldwork. Rimbu is my patron-brother; Lari, his only long-term wife; Hapkas, his unassuming full brother; Papola, their father's sister's son brought up as a brother. They all started telling me their stories in 1979, when Lari, Rimbu and Hapkas were in their early to mid thirties, Papola in his late twenties.

Plate 5.1. Hapkas with son and paintings of his dreams. (December 1985)

Plate 5.2. Hapkas with son. (December 1981)

Hapkas
Hapkas is a shy and mild man. Although Rimbu's elder, he makes no claim to seniority. His name was Nasupeli, but he appeared very light skinned to the Australian District Officer, who gave him the nickname 'hapkas', Tok Pisin for 'half-caste'. The name stuck, even becoming Kewanised into 'Apokasi'. When Hapkas found his vocation as a visionary, he was transformed into an articulate dream-teller, songster and symbolic artist. In 1993 Pastor Ore said of him: 'This man can laugh for twenty minutes at a time, you should see him in church.' In 1979 Hapkas and Papola came together to tell me their life stories, accompanied by Rimbu and Waliya. Though I communicate well with Hapkas, when Rimbu is present he prefers to have him translate, almost as a show of deference. I did not use a tape recorder but took the account down in longhand, mostly in reported speech. The same recording mode was used in 1985 and 1993, when Hapkas gave me updates on his life story.

Papola
Papola is Wapa's sister's son living matrilocally. His mother, Wareame, first married a man of Wapia clan, with whom she had no surviving children. When the Kambia clanspeople were chased out of their home and living in neighbouring Puri, she had an affair with a Kambia man and became pregnant. Though the man paid compensation, she had to wean

the baby and leave it with Wapa before they could be married. The husband soon died, and Wareame became his brother's wife in another short-lived marriage. Later in life she married a Yala man, but had no children by him. Papola, her only child, grew up under Wapa's care, ignorant of his father's identity until after Wapa's death. Rimbu, some seven years older, resented Papola as a child. When Wapa wiped the snot

Plate 5.3. Papola with daughter. (1 January 1980)

off Papola's nose and gave Rimbu food with the same hand, he refused to take it, demanding food from his mother instead. Wapa treated the boys fairly, but Rimbu thought he should get everything because Wapa was *his* father and not Papola's. He bullied Papola, pushing him into latrines, which in those days were shallow ditches. But Papola was a survivor. His distinguishing feature, to my mind, is a droll humour. He personified the wry, self-mocking, self-deprecating humour of the Kewa – which made his transformation in 1993 into a pastor all the more unexpected. But he took to his calling with a seriousness that no residual pragmatism and droll humour could disguise. In 1979 he told me his story in Tok Pisin.

Rimbu
Rimbu is my brother. Hapkas and Papola are my brothers too, but more by extension. Over the years I watched his influence grow and his leadership qualities become more marked. From the beginning he was my gatekeeper, my mentor and my go-between, without whom my work would have been an entirely different work, like a child by a different father. He came on his own initiative to tell me his story, with Waliya and then Lari and the children on his heels. As usual, he talked in Tok Pisin, giving a blow-by-blow account of his adventures, until Lari, sensing my ennui, told him he was stringing it out and 'Lisette was tired of writing'. To my feeble suggestion that he *could* shorten it a bit, he responded indignantly that he was doing all the shortening possible. We adjourned at ten, to continue the following day.

Plate 5.4. Rimbu (right) with Councillor Mara. (26 September 1979)

Lari

In the evening Lari came to tell me her story, with Ipa and Rimbu in tow, I cooked a large pot of stew. When they had all eaten I asked the men to leave me alone with Lari. Ipa thought that as the Public Service salaried 'tanim tok' or interpreter (a sinecure which would be terminated some years later) he should stay to make sure Lari didn't get her Tok Pisin wrong, but I insisted we could manage. So they toddled off, and I was face to face with a very shy Lari. She was soon at ease, however, bemoaning the delay in this tête-à-tête of ours. Between Tok Pisin and Kewa we communicated very well. I took notes as we talked, having decided not to record.

I recorded early on the extent of Lari's outspokenness in large companies of men. In fights with her father-in-law over childcare, or with her brother-in-law over a banana tree, she had no problem holding her own, and was not slow to tell Rimbu off when he was slack in building my chicken house. When once I made the mistake of thinking that Rimbu controlled her exchanges and assumed that she had given me a certain item at his request, and asked him if I could pass this gift on to my sister, Rimbu quickly put me right: I would have to ask Lari. Before I could do so, Lari turned up with a replica of the gift (a netbag) for my sister. My mistake was especially egregious as netbags were women's articles and men could not control them.

Plate 5.5. Lari. (11 May 1980)

The saga of the Kalalo sweet potatoes also illustrated Lari's independent decision-making powers in everyday matters. When our settlement was preparing a feast to mark mine and Marc's departure, I offered to pay for the purchase of sweet potatoes. Rimbu suggested that Lari should buy some mounds in the fairly close settlement of Kalolo, dig up the tubers, stay overnight and be picked up in the car the following day on our way back from another errand. Lari refused to go, offering one half-hearted excuse after another: she couldn't be bothered, it was too much work for one person, it was too wet and muddy, Ruma (her youngest child) was sick. She made her way to Kalalo in her own good time, recruiting the help of her brother and daughter to dig up the tubers. Rimbu fully accepted her right to make her own decisions.

The Stories: Third Set

The stories are primarily people's narratives, written down in longhand at my house, where I entertained the narrators. They appear mostly in reported speech for three reasons. First, this is how I wrote them down at the time. Second, when I tried to turn them back into direct speech I felt I was perpetrating a fraud, passing myself off as Lari, Rimbu or Hapkas. I kept them in reported speech so that my intervention would not be forgotten. Third, other stories are implied in these stories and in my analysis of them, spanning the period from 1979 to 1993. These stories 'in the shadows' are a mix of events, actions and talk that make up my everyday knowledge of people.[1] As 'minimal narratives', they move to centre stage in part II of the book.

Hapkas's (Nasupeli's) Story

When the Erave and Kagua stations were established (around 1935), the 'kanakas' [indigenous people] were still living high up on the mountain. They ran and hid at the sight of the 'redskin' – the engineer who came from Erave to map the road – but were soon lured down to provide labour. Hapkas was Sipi's age (about eighteen) when he started to work on the Kagua road. They worked four days a week, with pairs of clans rotating each fortnight: the Yala and the Perepe, the Koiari and the Kamarepa, the Miripa and the Tiarepa, and so on. They were paid K3 to K5 a fortnight each for their labour.

Kambenu's clan was working on the same road, and Wapa, Hapkas's father, befriended her with gifts of food. Hapkas was Mala's age (about twenty) when Wapa made the match for him with Kambenu. It was raining heavily when Rimbu and Wapa went to her village carrying a netbag containing twenty pearshells. The river was high and difficult to ford, and Wapa, pulling Rimbu with a rope after him, swore the woman would not escape. Hapkas did not go to see the bride at this time ('We are too ashamed', Papola quipped). Two days later the bride, with her parents and two sisters, returned the call and the brideprice was supplemented with five pigs. Wapa prepared a feast of possum with sweet potatoes, taro, bananas, greens and pitpit. After helping Kambenu to start a garden, the women left, carrying gifts from Wapa and Hapkas: an axe, a bailer shell, pearshells. Four or five months later they all moved down from Popa to Genoa, where Kambenu gave birth to a daughter who did not survive. Then they came to Yakopaita with Kiru and built houses here; they made gardens and planted chillies. Kambenu gave birth to Yamunu (1969), Yamola (1973), Lari (1976), then to boy and girl twins (1980), of whom the boy died. (Kambenu herself died of breast cancer in 1986.)

In 1970 Hapkas worked on a coffee plantation in Erave for two months, earning 28 toea per drum of coffee, plus board and lodging. He was so slow that while other people made K5 a month he scraped only K3. Soon after he had planted his own coffee garden, his son Yamola was born, and Hapkas, following the common practice of leaving a post-partum wife, joined Koipe on a tea plantation in Mt Hagen for three months. Once again, other people earned K10 to K20 a fortnight but Hapkas managed only K5. Fed up and afraid of trouble, he scrounged his fare money from Waliya and Papola and returned home. He had managed to avoid the spears of a local man bent on killing him, and didn't want to die on foreign soil. Now Hapkas has 400 coffee trees, but couldn't say what revenue they brought in. When one bag of coffee is full he sells it for K20, they 'eat' the money, then they fill another bag, and the process is repeated until the coffee runs out. Hapkas's narrative also ran out at this point.

On our visit in 1985–86 we found a transformed Hapkas, seized by the spirit and turned into a 'dreamer'. He showed off his chalk drawings depicting his dreams, in white, yellow and red colours on black slates. There were human figures (pin people), the sweet potato shoot, some flowers, a cockatoo (*yako*, the emblem of our village, Yakopaita, whose name means 'where the cockatoo sits/sleeps'), and a very large cross overshadowing everything. Hapkas's dreams always came true, said Rimbu. Before giving an account of how he 'received life', Hapkas recited the *temali* (dirge, 'cry singsing') he had sung in church the other day.

Everywhere in Papua New Guinea
They say Jesus is on the way
I think he will come

Everywhere we go
They sing his name, high and low
Now he will come

This ground I lived on with my dirty skin
until I saw the good place Jesus lives in
And I have no pleasure in this ground any more

God our father, you gave good and powerful things
to Moses in the tablets
Now all of us can share your gifts.

Hapkas had 'received life' before Mapi, and it was he who had dreamt that Mapi would also be chosen. He first found Jesus in Kagua, where he was imprisoned following the fight with the Perepe clan. It happened like this. In Sumbura market the police took down the names of all the men who had taken part in the fight, checking them through twice, and both times Hapkas's name had been on the list. But when Rimbu came to pay the fines and set his brothers free, Hapkas's name could not be found on the list, so Hapkas was released without having to pay a fine. 'God removed my name,' he said.

As a born-again Christian Hapkas campaigned against polygyny, and in protest went to stay on Yamora hill when Rimbu, Kiru and Waliya all took second wives and Komalo committed incest with his sister (Rimbu's second wife). He was in Yamora for two months, and on the third month he had a dream. He saw the stony ground on which he sat, with all its trees and vegetation, move out of the frame as in a movie-picture, swaying as if drunk, to be replaced by a nice clean place. A white man stood there, who said to him: 'This bad place, where the pitpit cuts people's skin and they live in suffering, will disappear, and you will find yourself in another place. You must pray to God and Jesus and thank them for bringing you to this good place.' The man taught Hapkas how to pray, and praying while still dreaming he opened his eyes and saw that his skin had turned white. Mapi stood next to him, and his skin also was white. The white man said, 'This land which is full of noxious things, where you can think only of gardens and pigs, has gone now, and these thoughts [of temporal things] have gone with it. Now you will think only of one thing.'

In this new place there was an abundance of good food. A wheelbarrow overladen with food rolled in all by itself, and Hapkas took and ate. He was about to eat some more when he woke up and saw that he was back on the stony ground. He tried to sleep again but couldn't. He wept over this, then went to church in Poiale and described his vision. Now he has this dream every other night. Another time the white man was sitting on a chair atop a tree. He held a white shirt which he gave to Hapkas, saying, 'This uniform is for Rimbu.' Then, taking a wooden cross, he put it on Hapkas's shoulder, with the words: 'They hanged Jesus on this; you carry it.' That was when Hapkas made his first drawing. He told Rimbu about the uniform [symbolizing that Rimbu too could 'receive life' and become white] and warned him of the evils of polygyny, of smoking and drinking and playing cards. Another time he dreamt he was in a garden in Awari, when a white woman arrived in a car. She gave him the blossom of the sweet potato and asked him to pray. When he opened his eyes after finishing his prayer, he saw a black *aladi* bird and a white *yako* bird. The woman said to him, 'You must leave the black and take the white.' He took this to mean that their old customs were embodied in the black bird and Bible teaching in the white, and the two could not be mixed. The message was clear: they had to throw away those bad traditional things before they could embrace the good teachings of the Bible.

At this time his son Adawi fell sick, and his wife also was ill. Adawi languished in Sumbura health centre for four months, and after receiving twenty-five injections he still showed no signs of recovery. So Hapkas went to Yamora to dream. He dreamt of a large wooden cross and a voice saying to him, 'Shake the hand on the cross.' But there was no hand there. So he put his own hand on the cross and sang the following dirge:

> God our father, it was you who gave me
> this little marsupial on Yamore place
> Yet you want to take its breath
> back again.

Then he turned to see who had ordered him to shake the hand on the cross, and saw the face of his own dead father. The following day he removed his son from the health centre against the advice of the medical staff, and the boy recovered.

Another time he dreamt of the white man telling him that soon Lisette would arrive on an aeroplane. He looked up – and the aeroplane landed on his head! He shook hands with me, but when he awoke in the morning he found he had been dreaming. Yet he had a sore head. He told this dream in church, and the following day my letter arrived with the news that Marc and I would be visiting. He was overjoyed. Another time he dreamt that his wife Kambenu would fall ill and remain ill for a long time. (Rimbu told me later that the arrival of my letter, together with the dreams, were interpreted as signs that Kambenu would die soon after our departure. She did indeed die, but one did not need to be a dreamer to see that by this stage her death was inevitable.)

Papola's Story

Papola hadn't yet started shaving when he went to Rabaul with Rimbu. He stayed for two years, working in copra and cocoa plantations and earning K1.50 a month as well as a lump sum of K70 on completion of contract. Back home, he killed a pig and distributed pork, money, clothes and other goods he had brought with him, receiving pearlshells in return. A week later he set off for Mt Hagen with four clan brothers. The journey, on foot, took two and a half days, and they were often afraid. On the third night they reached Kaguli, where a Pangia man billeted them among his 'wantoks' (people of 'one talk', or relatives) at the plantation. The following day they went to Kagamuga airport, to enlist for coastal work, but the clerk couldn't find their home village on the map, so he pronounced it nonexistent. 'Come back when you can tell me where you are really from', he said. So they kicked their heels at Kagamuga for a few days, when the brother of one of them turned up. This man was dressed in a showy manner, thinking it would attract women, but he was quite penniless. He suggested work on another plantation in Mt Hagen, and they all set out on foot. After some hungry times Papola got work at the Sugiri tea and coffee plantation. On the eleventh month he was transferred to the job of caring for the black boss's pigs, earning K2 a fortnight. Then a fight broke out, leading to their arrest, and after their acquittal Papola and his clan brother Michael signed a two-year contract at a rubber plantation in Port Moresby. There he earned K2 a fortnight, returned to Mt Hagen with K50 in his pocket and another K70 waiting for him on contract completion.

Back home he had an argument with his mother's brother, Wapa. Papola wanted to give brideprice for Kambenu's younger sister, but Wapa wanted to hold a pig kill first. (This is a reversal of positions from Rimbu's case, when Rimbu pushed for a pig kill while Wapa wanted to get him a wife.) Disappointed and resentful, Papola started for Mt Hagen on his own. He picked tea on a plantation with Waliya for three months, then the two of them decided to go to Madang. At the airport in Kagamuga Waliya wasn't quick enough to get his name on the list, so Papola had to leave him behind and board with another two clan brothers. In Madang he worked on a copra plantation for two years (1973–35), earning K20 a fortnight. But board was not included, so most of his pay went on food and beer. One by one his relatives broke contract; only he stayed on. He returned when he had K100 saved up for brideprice, but found that the girl he had fixed on was no longer free. Nevertheless, married he would be, as the following transaction shows.

'Kambenu's younger sister, is she still single?'
'Oh sorry, she is already married too.'
'What about the youngest, is she free?'
'Yes, she is still single.'
'All right, go and fetch that one.'

Three pigs, ten pearlshells and K50 comprised brideprice. Papola's mother, for whom he felt profound admiration ('she was a very strong woman') died after his first child was born. Papola wanted to return to the coast (post-partum blues again), but he saw Roga and others distributing money (Papola made a sweeping gesture) and thought to himself, while I've been slaving away on the coast these people have been making fortunes. So he stayed home, and in 1975–76 planted his own coffee trees. By 1993, however, he was a pastor.

Rimbu's Story

Rimbu was about eighteen years old when he went with an older kinsman to work on the road construction project. It was a big team, consisting of seventy carriers (thirty-five from Erave, ten from Kagua, twenty-five from Samberigi), four Papua New Guinean clerks and four expatriates. His kinsman, who knew some Tok Pisin, was made 'bossboy' (foreman). On their first walk to Samberigi they had to carry their food, but later a helicopter would air-drop supplies, with one white man in the helicopter taking pictures. Food was so plentiful, it got wasted. Their work was to cut the grass to the specification of the white men. They walked to Ialibu and to Muli, then on to Karada and Kalu. Kalu was just bush, not even a helicopter could land there. In Erave they did nothing, they just ate. They were given shirts, trousers, cigarettes, matches. Then from Erave back to Kalu and Karanda, again doing nothing, wondering if the white men knew what they were about. Over many months they went back and forth, cutting some grass here and there. They covered Muli, Samberigi, Angolo, Erave, Tipake (Mt Murray). When the patrol stood down they were loaded with food, in addition to the wages they collected from the office in Kagua. Hapkas got married about this time. Rimbu squandered his money, contributing to Hapkas's brideprice, buying food and treating his girlfriends.

A year later a recruiting truck came to Kagua, bringing an affine ('Tambu') who had been working on a plantation in East New Britain. Rimbu, Waliya, Koipe, Koke and Papola signed on. The Highlands Highway had not yet been built and the journey to Mt Hagen was long and hard. Waliya was horribly sick and vomited all over Rimbu. At Kagamuga airport they were put to work for two months, to test their mettle. They knew they were ready to go when they received their second set of vaccinations. In Rabaul (East New Britain) Rimbu was given his kit and put into a dormitory with nineteen other men, sleeping in an upper bunk. (At this stage of the story Waliya, Lari and the children joined us.) When they were first given bushknives they didn't know what to do with them, they were mere boys from the bush ('bus kanaka'). The big fat white boss threw the bushknives at the Tambu to test him, but he was adept at catching them. At first Rimbu's job was to cut the grass, but when his Tambu showed him how to break open the coconut he was promoted to copra work. Soon they had a big fight with men from Tari in which the Yala were outnumbered and thrashed, but the Tari men ended up with long prison sentences. (This is where Lari admonishes Rimbu: Lisette is getting tired, cut it short!)

At Christmas-time they put on their decorations for a singsing. Rimbu recalled the Tambu's story of how he and a younger relative were taking a break when they spotted a man walking into the bush. 'Let's go after him and kill him,' said the Tambu. ('Why kill him?', I asked. 'Just kill him, for no reason,' Waliya quipped, while an uncertain smile played on Rimbu's lips.) They followed him until they arrived at a deserted spot by a lake, darkened by a clump of bamboo. As prearranged, the younger relative engaged the man in conversation while the Tambu waited at the other side of the bamboo cluster, where he jumped him, hitting him on the neck with his axe. The younger relative, scared of the blood, made a pretence of hitting at the man's legs with his axe. After taking his bag (containing K70) they pushed him into the marshy ground and covered him with bamboo. The body was never discovered. The man was a migrant like themselves and his kin were far away. The Tambu and the younger relative shared the loot, telling their kinsfolk: 'While you were dancing we two took a break and found a wallaby. We killed it for its fur and threw it in the water, but it had very little fur. You will see it next time we decorate.'

After two years in Rabaul, Rimbu returned home. His brothers told him that Lari had just left, having spent some time with his parents in Popa. He understood what they meant: his parents had been entertaining and observing a prospective bride for him. But he didn't want a wife, he told them, he wanted to eat pork. The response was customary, as were his brothers' prejudices: 'She is not a local girl, who knows what she's been up to; she might be the sort who sleeps around.' But on another occasion Rimbu gave me a different reason for his reluctance: he had wanted to marry Giame, of whom his father initially approved, but subsequently Rake (the local big man) pronounced the match incestuous, for no good reason. Giame and her younger sister were very pretty, the sort of women, Rimbu said, who 'turned men on'. The two of them begged Rake to change his mind, but he was adamant. For a long time Rimbu thought he would not marry at all, and Giame waited until Lari had a child before she herself got married. Now that Giame married a brother (Yadi) and lives close by, it's not so bad, Rimbu said.

So while Wapa insisted on the marriage with Lari, Rimbu insisted that he was hungry for pork; and since his clan brothers (Hapkas, Kiru and Roga) also wanted to have a pig kill, Wapa had to accept the situation, but he invited Lari to the celebrations. Except for K40, Rimbu distributed all his wealth, even asking Wapa for the twenty pearlshells he was keeping for him. Wapa would give him only ten, keeping the rest for brideprice. When Rimbu attempted to give Lari K6, Wapa would not allow it, saying she wasn't his sister that he should give her money. Rimbu killed two pigs, while Roga, Wapa, Papola, Kiru and Koke killed one each. Pigs' heads belong to caretakers, so Rimbu gave one to his mother, asking her quietly to give the neck to Lari. Wapa himself would not take anything from Rimbu, so Rimbu gave his share of pork and money to Pisa, Wapa's agemate

On the night of the pig kill Wapa came crying to Koke's door, where Rimbu was lodging, complaining that he had a wife all lined up for this rubbish man, who was about to send her packing and waste his father's efforts. Rimbu, now fearing that his disobedience may make Wapa sick or even kill him, agreed to the match, provided that Wapa paid the brideprice. This was a ruse, Rimbu said; he didn't think his father had the wealth. The following morning Rimbu sent Koke's wife to eavesdrop on Lari and his parents. She reported back that Wapa was on his way to finalize the matter with him, and soon Wapa came, singing Lari's praises. He confiscated Rimbu's remaining K40, added the ten pearlshells, and put ten sticks in the ground (representing ten pigs). This offering he showed to Lari. Kiru, Roga and Rake all contributed one shell each and Hapkas threw in a pig as well. Rimbu was sorry to see the pigs go, especially the big boar Kegemena. When Lari's people came to collect the brideprice, this pig broke loose and ran into the bush. Rimbu said to leave it for the time being; they could collect it when they were ready to hold their pig kill. They had to be satisfied with this, though Wapa was dismayed. He never intended, Rimbu told me, to let them have the Kegemena. For her part, Lari undertook to feed the pig, but vowed that she would go if he killed it, sold it or gave it away. When eventually he sold the pig in Yago for K450, he challenged her to leave him, but Lari changed her tune, saying it was his business what he did with his pigs.

Rimbu didn't stay with his wife at first but slept at friends' houses, flirting with other girls. When finally he went to her he saw that she was a good worker, so he stayed with her and was happy. He had been home for six months when he began to hear about coffee. Extension officers visited Aka and planted Mapi's coffee gardens, as a demonstration for other villagers. Rimbu uprooted sugar cane and other vegetables and cleared a garden site, then Lari planted pineapples and chillies all around. Rimbu bought coffee saplings in Erave, and he and Lari planted them with the help of Hapkas, Waliya, Koke, Roga and Wapa.

When their firstborn, Wapanu, was just two weeks old, Rimbu left Lari in charge of the coffee garden and went off to Kurumul tea plantation in Mt Hagen. He was there for only a week when Kiru had a fight with the white boss and ran off to Sukiri. The following week, when Rimbu received his pay, Mapi came to visit with his sister, bringing garden produce. A big fight broke out later in the day, over a woman from Banz who was married to a man from Erave. (Banz is in the Western Highlands but Erave is in the Southern Highlands, and Rimbu's clan, the Yala, have kinship connections there.) A little boy had overheard the woman arranging a tryst with an old flame, a man from Banz, and Rimbu's clan brothers – Pombo, Koipe and Waliya – took it upon themselves to intervene. Despite arguing that it was not their affair, and attempting to stop them from fighting, Rimbu became involved in the generalized fight that resulted from the attack on the man from Banz. The police arrived and locked everyone in their houses, and the following morning moved them into prison cells, so small they had to sleep standing. When they asked to be let out to the toilet they were told to do their business on the spot. The married couple got off, after the husband testified that he was on the way to the police station with his wife when Pombo began to champion his cause and embroil the others. The Yala champions were given a two month prison sentence, but Rimbu was told that he had bigger assizes coming up.

This was a manslaughter charge. While defending the Kagua bossboy, Rimbu knocked out a man who apparently subsequently died. The Tambu had brought him a piece of tree bark (*yada repena yogale*, fight-tree-skin) to keep in his mouth while he answered the magistrate's questions, and a kinswoman gave him leaves for his ears and forehead and to rub on his teeth. The magistrate, a man from Simbu Province, asked where he was from and if he was a troublemaker. Rimbu glanced at the two white men sitting in the aisle, but they told him that his judge ('kiap') was up there and he should fix his eyes on him. The magistrate asked Rimbu twice if he had killed the man, and each time Rimbu answered 'Yes.' He explained the circumstances several times over. Then Mapi's sister and her husband testified.

[While Rimbu is telling me his story, there is a ruckus from Aka: Ipa is summoning all men to Aka. Hapkas goes to investigate.]

Hearing that Rimbu was given two months for his part in the fight, the magistrate said: 'I'll add twenty years to that.' Rimbu felt faint and sick. 'Yes, I see you feel it,' said the magistrate. 'All right, I'll give you two months. Is that all right with you?' 'It's all right,' said Rimbu, deeply relieved.

He thought prison would be a holiday but he was wrong. Food was short and he had a miserable time of it. After serving his sentence Rimbu stayed with friends, who gave him food and K20 in cash. In the market one day he was accosted by a white man named Bill, who offered him a job on road construction. Bill drove around with him for a fortnight, teaching him the duties of a bossboy, and Rimbu worked his way from the Kuman river to Kudjip, earning K15 a week. But Wapa kept writing that he was about to die, so after eleven months Rimbu returned home. He had spent sixteen months altogether in Mt Hagen. Bill gave him a testimonial, and Rimbu said he would return if he could, but he never did.

Back home, Wapa was far from dying. After spending two years in Popa, Rimbu was off again in 1974. Lu, a Yala man from Erave, invited him to accompany him on a visit to his sons who were working in a hospital in Port Moresby. One day, after Rimbu had been in Port Moresby for two weeks, the two sons came home drunk with some friends from other parts of the Highlands – Pangia, Samberigi and Mendi. These people spoke in Motu, and Lu, who understood something of the language, said they were plotting to kill them. He was proved right when one of the 'friends' suddenly hit his second son on the head with a bottle. Lu and Rimbu then picked up their spears and pursued the assailants outside. Rimbu lost Lu, and after spearing one man he was too scared to return home in the night, so he slept inside a drum. At first light he stole out and crept back to the house, where Lu had given him up for dead. Having speared two men himself, Lu was keen to return to the village double quick. The sons bought them clothes and aeroplane tickets and gave them K40 each in cash. With exhortations to the sons not to go out drinking with strangers, but instead buy liquor and drink in the safety of their home, the two flew to Erave, where, playing it safe, they lay low for a fortnight.

In 1975, Rimbu married a woman from Erave. He paid only K150 for her, but (he said) she would have come for nothing. Soon after her arrival, she attacked Lari, Lari in retaliation trashed the house (they were still living up in Agema), Rimbu joined the fray, and their daughter Wapanu (then five years old) went for him like a wildcat in her defence of Lari. Lari had to spend some time in hospital, and as soon as she was out she went to a store and bought a knife. She wounded the other woman, the police became involved, and when the two wives had recovered all three of them set out together for the village court and presented a united front.

They had suffered enough, they said, and didn't want to have to serve prison sentences as well. The magistrates agreed to let them straighten things out among themselves. But the two women were still unhappy, and their work suffered. Rimbu responded with the usual male strategy for escaping marital problems – he took off for a few months, staying with relatives in Mt Hagen, living off their gifts and his own capital of K100 from coffee revenue. When he returned he sent the other woman back to Erave, and has remained in the village ever since. At our return trip in 1993, Rimbu's political importance was of a different order, but this will be evident in subsequent chapters.

Lari's Story

Lari's parents died when she was a baby. The man she refers to as father is Ili, her father's brother, and the woman she calls mother is his wife Rumbame. (The proper Kewa kinship terms are *mai* and *papa* respectively, but when these relatives act as parents they are called *apa* and *ama*, out of courtesy, or '*waspapa*' and '*wasmama*' in Tok Pisin, because they 'watch' over the child.) Ili had had two wives before Rumbame, one of whom was still living at the time. Lari was born around 1950 and grew up in Alomani near Kuare, where she attended a Catholic mission school for three years. All she retains from the lessons, where pupils had no pen or paper but simply listened to the teacher and looked at the writing on the blackboard, is the ability to recite the alphabet. In spite of these early lessons Lari is not fluent in Tok Pisin, but is now learning the language.

[An argument flares up outside: Kiru is complaining that Yadi never paid back the K10 he borrowed. Lari quips: 'This man never pays his debts, he owes us money too.']

When Lari was Loma's age (about sixteen) her father pulled her out of school to 'sell' her ('salim' means to sell in the market, but also 'to send off', especially in marriage). '*Ipu mena rekere meaniala*', 'go and fetch pigs and shells', he said. But Lari had other plans. A priest from the Karia mission in Kagua was baptizing people in the area at the time, and she joined them in the hope that baptism would enable her to stay on in school. Her father and brother, fearing that it would scupper any marriage plans, prevailed on the priest to advise her to put it off until after she was married. Feeling frustrated and let down by everyone, Lari broke in two the cross the priest had given her. In a dramatic gesture she put one half of the broken cross in her father's hand and the other in her brother's, and went off to live with her aunt (*papa*, the wife of another father's brother). Her mother brought her food until she started her own garden, and a few months later her father turned up. He pressed her again to marry, this time a much older man from Pangia. Lari refused, not out of dislike for the man or because of the age difference, but because she resented her father's action in frustrating her desire to become baptized. The Committee member and the Councillor (both modern offices) took her part and gave her father a good talking to. 'You can't force her. Only if the woman herself wants to marry can you collect brideprice.' But he was adamant and threatened her with an axe. Lari too was stubborn, daring him to kill her and face prison.

Next he tried gentle persuasion. He killed a pig for her, saying she could marry after eating it. Without her consent he accepted brideprice, and Lari, together with her sister, their mother and mother's sister, was sent to the house of the bridegroom's mother. The man killed a pig despite Lari's protestations. Taking advantage of a full moon, Lari absconded with her sister. Her mother defended her to her father. 'The girl doesn't like the man; there will be plenty of time for marriage later.' Rumbame waited until the man had taken back the brideprice, then met Lari in the garden and told her it was safe to return home.

But it did not prove so safe. Ignoring intercessions by the Committee member and the Councillor, Ili, in a rage, made for the longhouse where Rumbame and Lari were sleeping. Torrential rain was falling. Rumbame, afraid Ili would kill them both, took to the bush and called for Lari to follow. But Lari was sick of running. In a typical, bluff-calling tone, far from resignation, she said, 'Let him kill me, I don't care.' Nevertheless, she went to an adjoining longhouse room, where an elderly couple hid her. Later, still in the pouring rain, she went in search of her mother. Did she have a sister with whom she could stay? Rumbame did have a sister, but Lari had to retrieve her netbag first. Gingerly they stole back to the house. To their dismay Ili had left his young son as a sentry outside, and this child now called out to his father. But Rumbame was a strong woman; she pushed down the door, they grabbed the netbag and fled. They walked for two hours through bush and up hill until they arrived at Alepea near Puli, the home of Rumbame's sister. The rain was pelting down and they were drenched. When the sister's husband heard their story, he said, 'This man is a pig. If he comes here I'll tell him so to his face.' He called to his wife to bring food, and mother and daughter stayed with them.

Rumbame's brother-in-law's clan was building a longhouse in preparation for a pig kill. In two days Ili turned up, grabbed hold of Rumbame's hand and started to pull her away. All her siblings reviled him: '*Nere ke ali*' (You madman), '*Nere kapapara ai ali*' (You wild pig), '*Nere kone naya ali ya na*' (You have no sense), '*Nere kalu naya*' (You have no head), '*Nere yala napeada epapili*' (You have no shame). But Ili responded, 'I am holding my wife's hand, why should I be ashamed? The girl I leave with you, she is too headstrong, but my wife I'm taking home.' Rumbame's brothers hit him and spat at him while the Councillor tried to restrain them. Eventually Ili left, and Rumbame followed two days later, accompanied by two of her brothers. (Here certain reparations would have been made, the brothers ensuring their sister was not made to pay the penalty for the fracas.) Before leaving, Rumbame advised Lari to stay with her siblings, where this 'bad man' could not molest her, and promised to send food treats whenever she could.

Lari had been living with her aunt and uncle and their son Wamili for two months, when the Councillor warned her that she could be charged with evading community work. So she joined her kinspeople on the roadbuilding roster in Sumbura. Wapa and his first wife Yalanu, who was Rumbame's sister, also worked on the road. On the third month of her stay there they held their pig kill. Wamili gave her a piece of pork back, his brother and his uncle gave her sides of pork. (Thus establishing rights to her disposal in marriage and share in the brideprice. Wamili being Lari's father's brother's wife's sister's son, *papasi* in Kewa kinship terminology, was not an obvious brideprice recipient.) As Rumbame's brother-in-law Wapa was invited to the feast, and he vied with her hosts for Lari's favours. She declined an invitation to go and live with him and Yalanu, but accepted food from them while they worked on the road. Wapa brought her bananas, pandanus fruits and tobacco. He and Yalanu were so kind to her that she thought of them as 'wasmama' and 'waspapa', to whom she would give a share of the brideprice when she married. Wapa visited her many times at home in Puli, bringing vegetables and tobacco. While working in Sumbura one day Lari and other Puli clanspeople were overtaken by a storm, and stayed overnight with Rika, whose sister had married a Puli man. Wapa reproached Lari for not staying with him instead.

Immediately on Rimbu's return from migrant labour, Wapa told him he had been giving food to a woman. Lari professed she felt betrayed on hearing of Wapa's motives: 'I accepted food from you thinking you were my father. One day I'll reciprocate.' This is the way parents go about getting wives for their sons, but it is also customary for the girls not to 'understand' their intentions. Wapa was set on the match, and his forcefulness frightened her. 'I gave you food only because of my son', he said. 'If you marry another man you will die.'

Some days later Yalanu visited Lari in Puli and invited her to the feast to be held for Rimbu. Lari came reluctantly, accompanied by Wamili and his wife and child. At this time Komalo (Yalanu's son and Rimbu's younger half-brother) rolled a cigarette for her, which she later realised had been a love-drug intended to induce her to marry Rimbu. Yalanu and Wapa gave her sides of pork, Rimbu the pig's neck, and Koke some other cut. As she was about to leave the following morning, Wapa sounded her out: 'He (Rimbu) has already disposed of his money, will you accept partial payment (of brideprice)?' 'I thought you were my father and I ate your food,' Lari reiterated indignantly; 'Now I will go.' Wapa retorted: 'You can't go. I gave you food for this reason.' Some of her relatives said that Wapa was a bad man who would beat or poison her, but Wamili defended him. 'He is a good man; he has given me shells and other things. We can accept partial payment, it's not a problem.' Lari had a bitter response: 'I didn't accept when my father was forcing me, and came to live with you instead. When my brothers come I can accept partial payment, but not before.' 'Your brothers won't come in a hurry,' was Wamili's response.

Two days later, Wapa visited with Rimbu and Koke, bringing gifts of tinned fish, tobacco and cigarette-rolling paper. The following morning Wapa proposed to fetch the brideprice, but Lari demurred. 'Who will take care of me? I am losing mother, father, brothers.' Wapa responded: 'I will make your gardens, I will look after your pigs. What do you have to worry about?' 'He speaks the truth, let's go,' Wamili urged. So off they went to Popa, where Wamili received partial brideprice. When Lari's brothers (Miniapa and Koai, Ili's sons) returned from migrant labour, they would claim the rest. Lari was vague about how much was given altogether (not so Rimbu in his account).

At first Lari lived with Yalanu. Rimbu's own mother, Payanu, had not wanted him to marry Lari and she had little to do with her before Yalanu's death. Lari said she accepted the brideprice because she had been afraid of Wapa, and she was afraid again when she saw Rimbu's face. 'You needn't be afraid,' Yalanu reassured her, 'that's just men's way. We'll work together in our garden.' After the brideprice was paid Lari stayed with Wapa in the men's house, where he cooked food for the newlyweds. Payanu allocated her a garden, and Wapa helped with the preparation and planting. She stayed with Wapa for four months.

A week after brideprice was paid Rimbu came to her in the garden. '*Modo meda kusa*,' 'you cook my sweet potatoes', he said, and added, to put her at her ease, 'All right, get on with your work.' The garden was still bush. He said to her, 'Will you stay or go?', and she replied, 'Never mind, I can't go back now. When my two brothers come you can give them the rest of the brideprice.'

[At that precise moment, about nine in the evening, Rimbu called out from the longhouse: is she going to cook some food? Apparently the large helpings of dinner I had provided earlier were not enough. Of course, Rimbu was 'eliciting', trying to find out about our talk or just put an end to it. But Lari ignored him and stayed on until almost eleven o'clock.]

She was high up on the mountain and working in her garden when labour pains started for Wapanu. She came down to Yakopaita, where Hapkas and Kiru were making houses for their wives. Rimbu was working in Sumbura. When he heard that Lari was in labour he came and erected a strong post in the ground for her. Crouching on her knees, she bent forward and held onto this post with both hands. Wapanu slipped out and Lari cut the cord (*moko*) with a piece of sharpened bamboo. Two days later Rimbu gave her a little pig.

It was another five months before Lari could continue her story. One day I heard her singing and asked her to come and record her song. She didn't want to tell me what she had been singing with the men present, and when she came into the house she insisted she no longer remembered, so we talked of other things instead. Lari told me how hard a woman's life was, punctuated by childbearing. Children had to be fed and infants had to be carried about everywhere. (While speaking, Lari shared out among her children the chicken I had cooked for her. They ate everything, including the bones, and licked the plate.) Women's fear of having children vitiates enjoyment of sex. In the old days women used banana fibres when they had their periods. Lari remembers how the blood would run down her mother's legs and smell awful. They were confined to the *rameda* (menstrual hut) at these times, unable to go about freely as they do today, when they use lengths of cloth to soak up the discharge. Lari expressed mild surprise on hearing that white women also have periods, but this may have been out of a natural delicacy.

Lari was about eighteen years old when she got married. After the birth of her youngest daughter (renamed Lisette after me) Lari menstruated for eighteen months, but now she has not had a period for two months. Rimbu told her that after giving birth to a boy she may start using birth control. Many women were using contraceptives, and some of them had caesarean sections before. Some women have intercourse while they are still breast feeding, but this means they lose a lot of blood and will probably die. This is all because men are selfish and don't think of their wives. Three women in the settlement are pregnant, despite having babies at the breast. The question of a son weighs heavily on Lari. Wapa wants Rimbu to take another wife for this reason, and Rimbu himself is concerned about it. Lari gets on her high horse and tells Rimbu he can get himself another wife if he wants, but Rimbu responds sagely that he remembers too well what happened the last time he did so. 'If Rimbu sends me away,' Lari says, 'I won't cry or grieve, I'll just go.' She'll take whichever child he gives her and return to her natal village. Lari admitted to me that she would not put up with a co-wife, as there would be trouble over coffee and gardens. What about sexual jealousy, I asked. 'The man will sleep with the new wife for two to three months until she is pregnant, and then come back to the old wife. That's men's way.'

Eleven days later, when Marc had joined me in the field, we accompanied Lari to her garden, where she was about to plant peanuts. Lari goes to her gardens early in the morning if she is not working on coffee; otherwise she goes in the afternoon. She has four gardens (in Popa, Kaimaneka and Rombea) planted mainly with sweet potatoes, but also with taro, pitpit (grasses such as *padi* and *alamu*), greens, corn, peanuts, pineapples, beans, sugarcane and bananas. She visits Popa very rarely, because it's such hard work, and is about to relinquish one garden that's not doing well and replace it with a new one lower down, halfway between Yakopaita and Puliminia. In addition to the sweet potato gardens (*modomapu*) Lari also has a taro garden (*yamanu*) close to my house, and a mixed-crop garden (*emapu*) in Kolepada. She was given the Rombea garden when she was first married, when Wapa had cleared the primary growth for her. She had done the woman's work of setting fire to the cut grass with a burning log from the hearth, clearing away the charred grass and preparing little square mounds of about 36 sq. ft (the garden itself measured 400 sq. yds; I dutifully measured all this). The *modomapu* are used for as long as they give good yield. No fertilizers are put on indigenous crops (though mounding is a form of composting), but coffee cherries (the outer pulp removed from coffee beans) are strewn on some introduced crops. The *emapu*, one-season mixed-crop forest swidden gardens, are left to fallow for two years and then burnt. Gardens are burnt in the dry season and planted in the rainy season [but since 'rainy season' denotes any (unpredictable) time of the year when it rains for a long period, planting in fact takes place throughout the year]. The subsequent clearing after gardens have reverted to bush is women's work, and Lari did this last year, when she burned the grass and turned the soil for a new garden. The Department of Primary Industry was at the time encouraging the planting of maize corn, and Biru, as extension officer, had asked villagers to clear gardens in preparation for maize corn planting. Rimbu espoused the project enthusiastically three weeks ago, going as far as to hang up some cobs to dry in my house, but there he stopped.

Lari resumed her complaints against Rimbu: he doesn't make new gardens for her, that's why they have so little food. The soil is dry and hard; the vines she planted in the new mounds are not bearing good tubers because they are poor vines. First Rimbu was busy with the longhouse (in preparation for the pig kill), then with my house, now with his own house and his coffee garden. He has also been paying lengthy visits away from home. From Tuesday to Thursday he was in Batri, half of the Saturday before last he spent in Puri, and the whole of last Saturday he was in Katiloma, where he expected to receive the red pandanus *marita*. The whole of next Sunday he will spend in Roga and Puli. But it's not only Rimbu, Lari continued:

'Men here don't work. Except for Waliya and Kiru, they are all lazy. The garden situation is so bad, I have to buy sweet potatoes in the market to feed the pigs.' She hired Yaupas ('ears closed', an unmarried deaf man) to prepare a garden for her, and for the last few days she has been picking coffee to raise the K10 she promised to pay him, but the cherries are not ready. Rimbu told her she could stay home and not work, but how are they to eat then? Wapanu used to look after little Lisette while Lari went to the garden, but now Wapanu is at school. 'Rimbu has been staying on in the village only because of you, when you go he'll also leave and take up wage labour.'

After the last pig kill, she and Rimbu felt anxious about the children. What if one of them fell ill and they had no pig to slaughter? So they bought two pigs for K40 each, one from Waliya and another from Koai. Lari would be angry if Rimbu gave these pigs away without consulting her, though she understood that at the pig kill he would distribute pigs to his partners, just as she would distribute to her own kin what he gave her. The pigs belonged to both of them, Lari said, but when I pressed her to explain why Rimbu can do what he likes with them she explained that pigs are men's things while sweet potatoes and pitpit are women's things. The pig kill is men's affair and they decide how to distribute the pork, though women consider the head and belly their due. Pearlshells belong to men but money and coffee belong to both sexes. (At the time I considered this an example of a woman's succumbing to the idiom or ideology of men's superior powers and control, an acknowledgment of inescapable material and structural conditions. But now I wonder if Lari was not speaking under duress. I had forced her to be unequivocal and unsubtle, a strategy unerringly successful in producing 'rehearsed talk'.)[2]

On the day of our farewell feast Rimbu ran out of pork early in the afternoon, and Lari was sobbing because she could not fulfil her obligations to a woman who had given her K10. She protested when Rimbu took the head I had given her and quickly cut it up, but he told her curtly to shut up. This was not the tone of a man doing what is given to men to do, but the shortness of someone feverishly trying to accomplish what he wants before someone stops him. Watching him I was reminded of Mapi, whose only option after his pig kill was over was to run away to Kagua, to escape the fury of his cheated wife. Rimbu used half of the head for his own exchanges and Lari distributed the other half to her kin. When I suggested giving some pork to Lari's people, who had made some of my *yagi* (going away gifts), Rimbu said no; too many of them had come and eaten and received pearshells and money. If I wanted to help Lari I should give her some pork so that she could discharge her obligations to the woman mentioned before. I agreed, and Rimbu put aside the best and most generously cut leg.

In 1985 a church had been built in Yakopaita and Rimbu and Lari were becoming literate in Kewa, with the help of primers produced by the Evangelical Church of Papua some ten years before. They were now on Book 2; on completion of Book 6 they will receive a Bible. A teacher from the adult literacy programme visited from time to time to test them on each book before they could progress to the next. Rimbu and Lari started their learning in June and hope to be on Book 3 by January next year. After that they will learn to read and write in Tok Pisin. This is the sum total of Pastor Rorea's learning too, Rimbu said. He read out a passage from the book, with obvious pride. Lari was too shy.

Seizing the New World: Narrative, Consciousness and Communication

Without exception, the narratives in this chapter show people grappling with a changed world. They are metanarratives in which men portray their heroic taking over of the new world, and women attempt to establish a worthy and independent self through practical as well as symbolic acts, some no less heroic than men's. (Though only one woman's account is reproduced here, my analysis draws on a larger corpus of collected accounts and observations, some of which will be found in chapter 7.) In the discussion below I begin with a summary of the face-value content of the stories, including their political and social claims, drawing on the earlier narratives for a more complete picture of changed and persisting conditions; then I move on to an examination of the narratives' deeper levels, as means of communication and modes of organizing experience.

The Heroic, the Epic, the Picaresque and the Symbolic

Men's Narratives
All the self-accounts in this book construct experiences in people's own social worlds. Thus, while older men talk of wars, pig kills, spirit houses, gardening, courtship and marriage as a cycle of interrelated activities,

younger men recount picaresque journeys of migrant labour on plantations in transient but repeated episodes that replace the displacements of war but retain some of the violence of its warrior ethic. Their narratives follow a similar trajectory, opening directly on a transformed world when the storytellers are already adolescents, the trauma of first contact having driven a permanent wedge between their childhood and the rest of their lives (for details of Kewa contact, see Josephides and Schiltz 1991). Their earliest recollections are of forced labour on roadbuilding, where first contact is also made with their future spouses. Another rite of passage, plantation labour, will be undergone before marriage is successfully established.

Travel to plantations combined the possibility of radical action (if not rebellion) with conventional rites of passage that reproduce a society, both in normative and physical terms. It started off as simply what was available to young men, in place of the old paths to manhood, but ended up transforming the basis of relations of power back home, by giving young men insights into the new regime which their elders lacked. The decision itself to travel was the young men's own radical initiative, not mediated by traditional leaders. Physical travel on this scale was unknown in the past, even in the context of warfare, and the experiences it offered added new dimensions to old practices and expectations. Humorous events combine with sobering ones, as if the narrators were in a constant state of bemused mockery, a self-mockery that also saw with searing clarity the foolish flaws of others. Some aspiring travellers are out of rhythm, unable to get the timing right; Papola is told his hometown does not exist, Waliya's volatile stomach will not permit him to travel in a motorcar. Most fights are seen as silly, confused brawls into which people are drawn willy-nilly. The Port Moresby fight involving Rimbu was worthy of a Charlie Chaplin or Laurel and Hardy film, whereas the plantation ambush involved a traditional theme minus the risk of payback. Rimbu's story in particular is highly dramatic and action-packed, with a substantial expenditure of emotion as well as physical activity. He pokes fun at white men's perceived naiveté: did they know what they were about, feeding their idle 'workers'?

What Rimbu does especially well in his account of his travels is to place himself at the centre of his changing universe. He resists the personally alienating effect of the encroaching legal system by professing an understanding, even complicity, between himself and the court personnel, to the degree that he is consulted on his sentence.[3] Although Rimbu's accounts involve 'modern' personages in active interaction with himself, what he stresses is not so much his own active agency as the manner in which these personages respond to him, somehow acknowledging his humanity (if not his importance) as a participant in life's dramas. The white man who singled him out with the intent to train him as a 'bossboy' is one example. (Hapkas is likewise singled out in his dreams.) Rimbu may have agency, but it is others who select him, things *happen* to him on his travels. He acts and suffers, but the acting is his response to what situations throw him into. He really 'acts' (as do Hapkas and Papola) when he returns home, as a man does when he emerges from a passage to adulthood.

Plantation work is more than a rite of passage, however.[4] As well as furnishing young men with knowledge and skills unavailable to traditional leaders, it also serves as an impersonal source of wealth, independent of village relations. Young men return to the village with the means to provide their own brideprice, escaping reliance on local big men. Once married, they proceed to establish themselves as mature men, complete with coffee gardens and other gainful enterprises. But unlike earlier rites of passage, plantation labour continues to provide refuge for men running away from marital troubles or taking time out after the birth of a child. Despite this, the incidence of polygyny is notably reduced.

The storytellers were baptized Christians, some more ardent than others but all of them seeing the new religion and its accompanying virtues as inseparable from the new order. Hapkas's visions likened the old order to the transience of temporal things, equating Western ways and persons with divine goodness and everlasting life. His accounts of visions, which idealized white people as standing for the new world order and even the Kingdom of God, were in sharp contrast to Kewa experiences of actual white people, whom they did not hold in particularly high esteem. But the visions were a sign of prophetic abilities, and making them public was the visionaries' way of seizing the present by predicting their own futures.

Hapkas, Papola and Rimbu are all men seeking a particular route to a prestigious life in a changing world. To be 'heroic' in this context is to place oneself at the centre of the world as one experiences it and attempt to take charge. All the stories in this chapter are to some extent heroic in this sense. They describe adventures in the *Bildungsroman* mode, undertaken in conditions of such radical change that the term 'odysseys' seems entirely appropriate. Rimbu's picaresque tale depicts the hero as a young man who sets forth into the world, has adventures, passes through times and places and emerges transformed, to chart new political territory on his return home, beyond the frame of the story told here. Papola eventually finds his feet as a pastor and Hapkas as a visionary, the first exerting influence locally through ministering and the second by interpreting life's meanings. The past, though spoken of disparagingly as a time of ignorance and discomfort, is also half-regretted as an era of prestige, large gestures, self-sufficiency without overlordship, abundance of pigs, game and garden produce.

Women's Narratives

Throughout this book women have talked of courtship and its excitement, marriage and the trials of polygyny, childbearing and the importance of having children (and how to avoid having them), gardening, magic and pig raising, and finally Christianity and a new way of life. Bigmanship was peripheral to their accounts, war a nuisance and a disruption – a scourge whose causes they had no interest in fathoming. Strung together in a seamless narrative, the women's accounts, spanning three generations, provide a rich biography of women's work, their lives and endeavours, their self-perceptions and cultural agency. Yakiranu's simple observation in chapter 3, that garden work has not changed much other than becoming free of the disruptions of warfare, is expanded by Ragunanu's comments that women have fewer vegetable gardens than previously because of calls on their time by the claims of new cash crops, new standards of hygiene requiring laundering, and a new religion that involves lengthy church attendance. For these older women, the idiom of pig ownership defined the boundary between mature, active, socially effective life and marginal old age ('I have no pigs, I am old and cashiered', Ragunanu bewailed). An old-style big woman had pigs, pearlshells, cowry shells, and considered herself the provider of these items of wealth to her husband's clan. She would occupy longhouse doors as a recognized pig killer and have pigs killed in her name. Older men readily acknowledged women's contributions to pig killing activities and their rights to pigs.

Marriage continues to occupy a central place in the narratives of both sexes. Many women considered brideprice an acknowledgement of their value. Older men in particular described marriage as achieved through women's power, using love potions to attract men and other magic to keep away potential co-wives. (By contrast, Lari saw herself as the victim of love magic.) Older women fought with prospective co-wives, just as their younger sisters do today. Yakiranu's account of attacking her co-wife whenever she caught her husband doing anything for her can be put alongside Rarapalu's complaint in chapter 7, that her husband showed unfair preference for another wife. It suggests that a woman may interpret any relations her husband has with her co-wife as 'unfair preference', and underscores the oft-noted perception that this complaint may be a covert rejection of polygyny in any form.

A striking difference between Lari's account in this chapter and the accounts of older women in previous ones is their point of departure. Where they begin with courtship and marriage, Lari's young life opens on a landscape of exciting promise, which the threat of marriage cruelly shatters. She recalls the events surrounding this period with doom-laden precision. Forlorn and frustrated, she escapes into the dark, elemental bush, lashed by torrential rain, her every return to the domestic sphere endangering her anew. She breaks the cross in an act of defiance, but also to symbolize her cloven self – being promised one life and delivered into another. Rather than being chosen by God, she is abandoned by his priest. Rimbu's narrative also describes emotions around marriage arrangements, but how different the emotions in each case. Wapa's 'crying' over Rimbu's churlish defiance did not so much denote emotion as a strategy of sentimentality calculated to scare Rimbu into submission. But Lari had undoubtedly suffered a genuine emotional shock akin to trauma. This is not contradicted by any hope she may have entertained that her frustration, even her fatalistic resignation to the possibility of her death, might convince her father of the depth of her despair, and cause him to relent and allow her baptism to go ahead.

MacIntyre (1984: 213) observes that the true genre of the life story is 'neither hagiography nor saga, but tragedy', and Lari certainly gives her early story in this form. As Aristotle requires tragic heroes to have fatal flaws, we may even wish to draw a parallel with Sophocles' Antigone, the daughter of Oedipus who buried her brother in defiance of her uncle Creon, the King of Thebes. Antigone, whom her sister accuses of being 'in love/with the impossible' (Grene and Lattimore 1991: 184/104–5), personifies the eternal conflict between private conscience and public authority, pitting one duty against another. Though her brother died dishonourably as a traitor, she cites the law under which she gave her brother precedence: both her parents being dead, 'no brother's life would bloom for me again' (ibid.: 216/968–70). While Creon fulminates that '[t]here is nothing worse/than disobedience to authority' (ibid.: 207/726–27), his equation of authority with *his* authority, in his statement that 'he that breaches the law or does it violence/or thinks to dictate to those who govern him/shall never have my good word' (ibid.: 207/717–19), reveals the sleight of hand of his rehearsed talk. Indeed, his son Haemon, betrothed to Antigone, in just a short sentence justifies the act which his father has proclaimed incendiary: 'There is no reverence in trampling on God's honor' (ibid.: 210/807). With these words, Haemon (switching to my vocabulary) regularizes Antigone's action within a body of shared practices, establishing it as a holy duty beyond mere private conscience. At the same time, Creon's expostulations that '[w]hen I am alive no woman shall rule' (ibid.: 201/578), and 'we must not let people say that a woman beat us' (ibid.: 207/734) reveal his cause to have other motives, closer to hubris than good order. He is appropriately punished by the double suicide of his wife and son.

While Lari's case is undoubtedly different from Antigone's, 'private conscience' is the key to my argument. Lari's wish to be baptized was not a ploy for avoiding marriage, but a desire to stay on in school and discover what else life may afford. I call this curiosity 'a life of the soul'. Lari's retort that she wanted to be a nun was fired by this curiosity, an interest in something beyond the mundane, hinting perhaps at an inner life. It was not a statement about religious vocation or a concern with a Christian immortal soul. This is precisely the area where women differed from men. Mapi and Hapkas may have talked about their immortal souls, but not the women and certainly not Lari. In their relations with missionaries and the church, women attempted to avail themselves of opportunities beyond the confines of marriage, childbearing and gardening, expressly to develop different kinds of understandings and find different sorts of fulfilment (see Josephides 1999). Though I was predisposed to see Highlanders as pragmatists using the missionaries and religion for their own ends, I soon realised that it was not easy to distinguish between sensible, practical, logical explanations and emotional ones (see, for instance, my initial readiness to accept economistic reasons over psychological or emotional ones, or rehearsed talk over rehearsing).

What light does Lari's story shed on women's changed lives? In material ways the lives of women of Lari's generation have changed less than men's, though younger women are making greater strides (see Josephides 1999). These are not modern women in the sense of being educated seekers of economic self-sufficiency and political reforms, but they live in a world transformed by education and political and economic change.[5] Many aspects of their behaviour are not new: their mothers also refused to be forced into marriage and were vociferous in their defence of encroachments on what they considered was due to them (myths also attest to this aspect of women's independence; see Josephides 1982, 1995). They saw their interests as being threatened by polygyny, and went to great lengths to sabotage their husbands' remarriages. Again, as before, women are concerned that no blame be attached to them because of failure to reciprocate a gift, a service or an obligation. But instead of treating this as a question of prestige, they think of it as maintaining relations and an acknowledged worthy personhood. When Lari speaks of exchanges she does not describe a strategy of 'pulling' money or pigs, as Rimbu does, but instead refers to the personal relations they forge, and the requirements of maintaining them as meaningful social activities, indicative of moral worth. The requirements are simple: obligations must be discharged, and earned rewards must be advanced.

Whenever I try to identify a quality or behaviour that characterizes women's transformed lives, the same quality leaps out of the accounts of older women. Maybe what I am looking for is not so much a new quality or behaviour, as the expanded potential of external opportunity. In Lari's case this was evident in her glimpse of a life before marriage. Perhaps in all societies what determines social status and prestige is not so much a quality (which is not visible), as the product of its social externalization. Pigs were such a product for Kewa women in the past, and they continue to be necessary for social life, but they no longer provide the idiom of the prestigious and socially effective woman. Money, education, and an important position in government are becoming the new idioms. Like pigs before them, they are seen as the external products of a personal quality, which I can describe only by its pursuits: a striving for personal agency, creativeness, integrity, unimpeachability, and the demand for practical recognition of the value of one's contributions and recognition of oneself as inferior to none. Mayanu's and Alirapu's accounts (chapter 4) express their difficulty with maintaining a certain integrity and control over their bodies and persons in the past, and their stories can be seen as attempts to achieve such control. What is new is the expanded horizon of opportunities that Lari glimpsed before her marriage, making her aware that not all of a woman's life is contained by marriage, but that other forms of fulfilment can be aspired to.

Do men's stories blend in more with current events and move them forward, while women's stories tend to be concerned with redefining practices, institutions, their own personhood and their place within the moral universe? It is certainly the case that men's narratives concern their taking over of the new social and political world, while women's are attempts to prove worthy personhood, claim more space for themselves, establish some independence and a life of the soul, as described above. These are radical pursuits.

Narrative as Form of Consciousness and Organization of Experience

The preceding sections considered the narratives from a double perspective: as personal texts describing the world as perceived or wistfully imagined by the narrators, and as face-value claims about the narrators' own worth and position in that world. In the remainder of this chapter I consider how the narratives work at a metanarrative level, as modes of communication and a form of organizing experience as part of our consciousness.

Experience and Consciousness

Cohen and Rapport (1995: 8) cite Stephen Crites' observation that narrative is the form of consciousness, 'the form in which we organize experience', and draw on Augustine's work ('consciousness *anticipates, attends and remembers*') to identify the three modalities of our conscious experience: 'an orientation to the past, present and future' (ibid.). From these premises they offer a definition of narrative as 'a lasting if selective chronicle of the temporal course of experience, fixed in memory' (ibid.). In Kewa narratives the diachronic aspect of experience is most pronounced, because in people's lifetimes, *time* appears so starkly as *change*. From this perspective it is not difficult to demonstrate the ways in which Kewa narratives, as 'the individual's acts of orientation' (ibid.: 7), organize experience. Rimbu coaxes potentially alienating events, associated with a system that could be seen as imposed on him, to the level of his own relations and active interaction with himself, as a participant in life's dramas; Lari imputes a particular significance to her own premarital experience that ties it in forever with how she views her whole life. Selection accompanies evaluation in this narrative action of organizing experience, as 'experiences' become incorporated into 'consciousness'. Lari's narrative may also provide catharsis, like a session with an analyst. Edelman (1992: 170) defines consciousness as 'a habitat ultimately beyond the physical'; for my present purposes it suffices to see it as the evaluative integration of experience into memory. Experiences, then, become part of consciousness as they are evaluated.

What this discussion makes clear is that, for narrative to have the organizing function envisaged by Crites, the unity of the self whose life is narrated must also be presupposed; it is one self's experience that consciousness thus organizes. As already argued, the unity of a life is constructed in all Kewa narratives. Lari's story makes sense when we see her later actions informed by earlier ones, which have made her the woman she now is, but also the woman she was at each juncture of her narrative. Hapkas's story has no centre without its climax in a teleological aim. But this unity, as Ricoeur (1992: 162) points out, is an unstable mixture of fabulation and experience; 'It is precisely because of the elusive character of real life that we need the help of fiction to organize life retrospectively.' This elusiveness has both temporal and spatial aspects: at no particular time can we see the whole world (synchronic totality) or the whole of time (diachronic temporality). The discontinuities of social change, in addition to the normal elusiveness of the endings and meanings of a situated life that cannot glimpse totality, accentuate the need to supplement experience. Thus all Kewa men borrow plots from myths of picaresque lives, full of non-sequiturs or unexpected sequences. Rimbu also borrowed from his experience back home, across worlds, to fill in the gaps and give meaning to the actions of the magistrate and the white people in court. When Ricoeur concludes that literary narratives and life histories are complementary, people borrowing emplotment from fiction or history to tell their life stories, he invites the question: where do people in non-literate societies borrow from? 'From their myths' is an obvious but timid response; a bolder claim would be that they are also creating fiction in their narratives. An example of this activity is Hapkas's (and Mapi's) story, in which the meaning of Hapkas's life was provided by a vision, a 'fabulation' that was not locally available for cross-checking. While it is true that traditional Kewa 'dreamers' were part of Kewa culture, it was never their remit to have visions of such radically changed lives.

To sum up the argument so far: narrative organizes experience, and thus consciousness; the unity of a life is presupposed in such an organization; but this unity is a mixture of fabulation and experience, because life is elusive; and because life is elusive, we need to organize its experiences retrospectively. As a corollary, self-understanding is attained in such organization, thus self-understanding is an interpretation.

A final point in this argument concerns our entangled histories ('The narrative of any one life is part of an interlocking set of narratives' [MacIntyre 1985: 218]), which imply that the 'whole world' of the narrative includes relations with others (as well as with the past). Carrithers (1992: 82) has this in mind when he defines narrative thought as 'a capacity to cognize not merely immediate relations between oneself and another, but many-sided human interactions carried out over a considerable period'. Lari presents a psychological portrait of herself as created through those interactions with the priest, her father, mother, brother, father-in-law and husband. Rimbu appears to come to the knowledge of his own persona through other people's responses to him – but always, of course, through his own eyes. Self-understanding can be seen here as an interpretation (Ricoeur 1992: 114, fn 1). The entanglement of other lives in our narratives also provides a link with morality, as I discuss below. But from this section I carry forward two working definitions of narrative: as a chronicle of temporal experience, organized and reintegrated into consciousness; and as the capacity to cognize many-sided human interactions over time.

The last two points bring me back to the palimpsest analogy used in the opening lines of this chapter. Each set of stories recounted in this book writes over the landscape in several ways, as it chronicles the changes (physical, architectural, social, political, and so on) as experienced by the narrators – leading to a transformation of consciousness. On one level, then, the book can be seen as a history of consciousness and cultural change.[6] From their stories, we can see that people now think of themselves differently in relation to their culture (no longer taking for granted a representative moral personhood or giving their own lives as a cultural gloss for how the Kewa in general live), but also in relation to what is a human being and its powers in a broader world. The palimpsest analogy does not imply erasure of the past, but rather a condensation and embedding. Nevertheless, each story is a claim, painting over other claims. This observation applies to the whole of the book.

Morality

The link between narrative and morality can be seen in several ways; here I discuss only four. One concerns the content of the stories and the narrators' own moral stand vis-à-vis the 'good life'; the other three, with which I begin, can be seen as structural requirements of the narrative form itself. The first, mentioned in the previous section, arises from the mutual entanglement of human lives, which necessitates that not only oneself but also other selves be gathered together, in a 'narrative unity' that effectively organizes, retrospectively, the life of the whole moral community. An ethical notion of the good life is inevitable in a narrative which draws in the lives of all the people in the narrator's community. The second structural requirement arises from a view of narrative as analogous to a form of action – which, in another sense, pervades this book. To paraphrase Ricoeur (1992: 163), since the agent as a matter of course is attributed with the moral connotations of her actions (as action ascribes its moral character to the agent, or, differently put, action is always attached to agent by moral bonds), it follows that narrative is linked in like manner to narrator. This leads Ricoeur (as discussed in chapter 3) to place narrative theory at the crossroads between a theory of action and moral theory. The third requirement follows from the first and concerns accountability. These stories are told in the thick of everyday activities, so that in each narrative the narrator gathers several selves together, but at the same time each of these 'selves' has her or his own narrative, and the multiplicity of narratives inevitably leads to comparison and accountability. The narratives of Mapi, Rimbu, Lari and the others are given in a form and tone that acknowledge both this contestability and the obligation of narrators to be accountable – in the sense of displaying a readiness to elucidate, elaborate on and argue for their accounts. For these reasons, MacIntyre (1984: 218–19) concludes that there is no narrative without accountability, intelligibility, and personal identity. A narrative quest, like life itself, can founder if the narrator fails to maintain the unity of the narrative; a telos or end-aim is a necessary part of unity; and is always bound up with some conception of the good for man (ibid.); which leads straight into the final question of this part of the debate.

Several reasons have been adduced, in chapter 4 and above, for the claim that narratives are not ethically neutral. Below I focus on the argument, put forward by MacIntyre and Ricoeur alike, that 'the idea of gathering together one's life in the form of a narrative is destined to serve as a basis for the aim of a "good" life' (Ricoeur 1992: 158). For Ricoeur, ethical intention is defined as 'aiming at the "good life" with and for others, in just institutions' [ibid: 172]). Three points from Kewa ethnography provide support for this perspective. First, claims made in narratives are presented as socially established, true understandings of cultural norms (this will be seen especially in chapter 6). In this regard Ricoeur (1992: 176) writes, following MacIntyre, that practices are 'cooperative activities whose constitutive rules are established socially'; and points out that this character 'does not exclude controversy but provokes it'. Second, there is good evidence that Kewa narratives subordinate the ought (deontological compulsion) to the aim (teleological good). For Lari, the 'ought' required that she obey her father and accede to the proposed match; but the 'aim' was to seek a 'better' life for herself, with self-esteem, even at the risk of losing the respect and goodwill of others. Lari wanted to be allowed to stay on in school, not be forced to marry, but be treated as a person with free will. Thus her praxis – of crossing her father – had an end in itself, but it and all her other actions had the ultimate end of the good life for herself. With this example, I can 'maintain at the same time that each praxis has an "end in itself" and that all action tends towards an "ultimate end"' (Ricoeur 1992: 178).

But – and this is the third point – while attempts to construct the moral self in a full, active life are clearly visible here, can it be argued that a concern for the good life of others is also part of the narratives? I have presented the Kewa as striving for self-esteem; can I also take on Ricoeur's (ibid.: 180) proposition that solicitude or regard for others 'unfolds the dialogic dimension of self-esteem'? A response to this loops back to the earlier point concerning interlocking histories, lives, and selves. Ricoeur (ibid.: 187) cites Levinas in a sentiment and a sentence that sums up the approach to the self taken in this book: 'no self without another who summons it to responsibility'.[7]

It may be objected that a face-value reading of Rimbu's story does not immediately reveal how solicitude or regard for others 'unfolds the dialogic dimension of self-esteem', nor, in Carrithers' formulation, how it demonstrates the 'capacity to cognize ... many-sided human interactions carried out over a considerable period' (1992: 82). In so far as this objection is justified (and it is not entirely, as I discuss below), it is an effect of the organization of the narratives in this book, which places an account of Rimbu's early life in this chapter. Rimbu attempts no justification for the killing in Rabaul, because to search for a motive was futile and any explanation irrelevant, as the event belonged to a different era, when the Kewa were not yet 'modernized' and he himself was still a callow youth. This is how I interpret his 'uncertain smile', using the principles of the pragmatics of speaking (discussed in chapter 2), which reveal the contextual implications of the awkwardness and embarrassment so frequently appearing in this book.

But the objection is not entirely justified. Though his self-placing and intentionality are still inchoate, in Mt Hagen Rimbu describes himself as trying to take control, counselling against unwarranted violence and putting himself in the picture as someone who affects the outcome of life's dramas. His solicitude for his clan brothers is evident, as are his attempts to make fair judgements about responsibility. This is a background to the man he becomes, as seen is subsequent chapters (and in Josephides 1998b) after a longer period of many-sided interactions with a larger number of people.

Narratives as Communication

In conclusion, I indicate three ways in which the narratives in this chapter function as means of communication. First, they exchange experiences of practical wisdom, as Benjamin (1968) has put it. They were narrated in my house, on these occasions serving as a public forum for the externalization and intermingling of memories and judgements. The sessions thus became part of village events, interrupted by other happenings which wove in and out of the narrative, making them the carriers of messages in more ways than one. At times people engaged in consultations about events and practices, at other times they listened as if they were learning something new. Men exchanged memories of migrant labour; women offered their opinions and experiences of gardening, childbearing, birth control and polygyny. Hapkas's narrative was a plug for Christianity as well as a proclamation of his own newly-attained status.

Second, the narratives make claims, seek approval, and try out particular understandings for more general agreement. 'Telling a story', Ricoeur (1992: 170) observes, 'is deploying an imaginary space for thought experiments in which moral judgement operates in a hypothetical mode'. This mode of suspended judgement allows for the possibility of constructing new understandings, but also of withdrawing unsuccessful claims. In different parts of this book, women, as heroines of their stories, stress their moral nature, their political astuteness, their spiritual and intellectual independence. Lari is in turn thwarted, betrayed, besieged and beseeched by her father, whose attempts to enforce patriarchal authority trigger (in Batesonian fashion of symmetric schismogenesis) her own acts of defiance and set in motion a series of dramatic adventures. But her story in its entirety makes claims about the sort of person she is, moulded by experience for pre-emptive defiance towards Rimbu.

The third point is an extension of the previous one: narratives seek feedback. This characteristic belies any claim or assumption that narratives merely impart self-contained information. The feedback may be of a moral nature, as when the moral core of the story is sought in the telling rather than – as in the case of a morality play – assumed as self-evident. Most of Rimbu's narrative is constructed in a world full of strangers and enemies, to whom he had to give moral designation which he was then obliged to negotiate in the context of the story, retrospectively, with me and with others. His listeners, differentiated in terms of authority, would receive his story and assign moral status to the hero's actions and judgements.

Finally, the narratives were accounts of communications as well as means of communication. For something to act as a means of communication, it is not always necessary for it to take place in a public forum.

Notes

1. Stories 'in the shadows' is an allusion to Behar's story of Esperanza (1994). Behar uses another memorable phrase to describe how she feels when she edits people's accounts: that she is cutting off their tongues.
2. In response to my questions, Lari gave me accounts of other aspects of her activities. Sometimes she sells sweet potatoes, sometimes she buys them. A few weeks ago she had to spend K12 on buying some for pig fodder, but then she had a good harvest and sold a mound to a Koiari man for K10. Bananas and sugarcane belong to men, though women may plant them. Wives must always ask their husbands' permission before cutting them, said Lari, as she cut two generous lengths of sugarcane and offered them to us for our refreshment. Lari usually 'eats' one third of her market earnings and saves two thirds. She will give her current savings of K20 to Rimbu 'for the store' or for any other need he may have. She made an initial contribution of K40 to stock the tradestore, and now gave another K15, using money earned from selling vegetables and pancakes. When they were about to sing *tupale* (pig killing songs) in Ora, Rimbu needed money to

'open the door' and he came crying to Lari, who contributed K20. 'His brothers don't help, so who is to help him?', she reasoned. Lari recalled some of her other exchanges for my benefit. She gives money to a younger sister, but her visits are infrequent. Last week she gave K4 to her mother (*papa*, or aunt, Alomari) when she came to visit, and K20 to Rimbu's clan sister (married in Tiripi) who had promised her a pig. But the pig was too small and the money was returned. Even before Ragunanu came to live here Lari gave her money when she brought vegetables, and Ragunanu reciprocates by helping with pig care. Noko gave her pig feed a few times, so she will reciprocate with K2. Sometimes she gives young people a few toea when they are playing cards, but she never expects a return. When I gave her K6 three weeks ago she added it to the K10 I had given her when Wapa was sick and bought a large parcel of indigenous salt (*aipa*). Waliya's brother was selling it for K20 but Lari 'cut' the price to K16 and deferred payment of K2. She will dry the salt, cut it into bars and sell it. As for assisting with childbirth, when Kambenu (Hapkas's wife) gave birth to Rimbanu Lari helped with the delivery by cutting the cord (*mogo*), burying the placenta (*nu yapara*), washing the baby and putting K1 on it. She had given another kina for the twin who died. She also buys clothes for Yamola, Kambenu's son, but Kambenu has not reciprocated. She washed Rorepame's baby and put K4 on it and Rorepame (Papola's wife) reciprocated with K8. She helped Liame (Kiru's wife) when she had Mumuare, washing the child and bringing food, but there was no return. So she will stop helping women in childbirth in this settlement. Giame (Yadi's wife) has her babies in hospital, and Lari herself does not require assistance, though Ainu helps her because she comes from Lewa, near Lari's natal home. Ainu helped with Lisette, though she did not wash her, and once gave forty toea for her. Lari would give Ainu small amounts of money, fifty or twenty toea, and after a long time Ainu gave her a little pig. But since the feast for Lisette's second birthday Lari has given no money to Ainu. In conclusion, Lari said that only I give her money.

3. In his refusal to accept the given framing of the situation, Rimbu behaves like Gilsenan's informants in *Lords of the Lebanese Marches*, a book also focusing on 'narrative structures of social life and enacted stories in a changing society' (1996: 57).
4. A powerful narrative of a different kind of rite of passage in contemporary Papua New Guinea is offered by Adam Reed (2003), in his harrowing account of prison life.
5. I am painfully aware of the deleterious effects on women's lives of developments in other parts of Papua New Guinea, especially in the mining industry (e.g. Polier 1998, Wardlow 2002), but I am telling a different story here.
6. I never thought of the book in quite these terms – as a history of consciousness revealing Kewa people's conscious understandings of their stories as a structuring of their lives – before the first reader raised the question and elicited the insight.
7. Does this view describe a pursuit of the general or universal 'good'? I engage this question elsewhere (Josephides 2003a), by providing ethnographic illustrations of Aristotle's 'grounding experiences' through which it can be shown that people's decisions about action are based on a desire to 'seek the good' rather than the way of the ancestors.

Part II
Portraits (Several Weddings, Some Divorces and Three Funerals)

Chapter 6

Portraits and Minimal Narratives
Elicitations of Social Reality

It is one thing to tell a story and quite another to engage in theoretical debate. To imbue narrative with theory is always a small miracle, even when the theory was extracted from the narrative in a barely conscious process of distillation, until it emerged fully-formed, both explicans and explicandum.[1] But once theory has taken on that separate existence – clean, concise and economical, unencumbered by the messiness of multi-stranded life which nevertheless is congealed in it – it passes as pure understanding and wrong-foots narrative, as being excessive to its needs. In the following chapters as in previous ones I shall be doing two things: telling a story (an ethnography) and making theoretical points about the narratives and actions through which the story is told. If the stories unfolding seem excessive to the analysis, it is because the ethnographic narrative, no less than theoretical analysis, must retain its integrity. In its theoretical contribution, this chapter should be read in conjunction with the debate on narratives in chapters 3 and 4.

Part II is concerned with explicit knowledge: how a social group comes to acknowledge the interpretative actions of persons as part of the accepted conventions of its common world, and how persons strive for such acceptance, making personal claims in the process of creating explicit knowledge. It puts together a narrative that brings Kewa people to life through their own words and actions, as they communicate active attempts to construct a social self with its relations. The demonstration of how knowledge of social arrangements is made explicit also enables the elaboration of an epistemological point about the effectiveness of social action, which implicitly questions a conventional theoretical orientation towards some key concepts that we use to describe social determination. As discussed in chapters 2 and 7, for the Kewa at least, 'institutions' (such as mediated conflict settlement and local court hearings) do not operate as essentially different cultural forms from everyday strivings to achieve specific social ends.

Part II is also marked by a methodological shift. Whereas chapters 3 to 5 contained self accounts of people's own stories told from memory in more or less coherent narratives, chapters 7 and 8 follow events as they unfold, pulling together materials from various sources: accounts from many individuals at first, second, third hand and hearsay; my own observations of events unfolding, enhanced by the commentary of others; my recordings of actual verbal and non-verbal exchanges, equally assisted. What I refer to as 'talk' (Tok Pisin 'toktok', Kewa *agele*) is an amalgam of those statements and verbal exchanges which operate as 'elicitations' in real-life situations, negotiating general understandings of social realities by making them explicit in the public domain. As explained in chapter 2, elicitation is a discourse strategy whereby variously aggressive claims test the degree of their acceptability through the use of a judicious mix of contradictory tactics: while pushing for a favourable response by presenting their standpoint as a true interpretation of cultural norms and proper practice and therefore unassailable, they also evince a readiness to negotiate a mutually agreed position. (Only in one sphere of life is this flexibility entirely absent: in the fierce confrontations of co-wives, where every inch conceded to the other is an inch torn from one's own flesh.) 'Talk' is thus poised between concealment and explicitness: while it must hide the desire from which it sprang, its ultimate success will be measured by what it manages to make explicit, what *real* effects is creates, in the form of agreed-upon knowledge, at least for that occasion.

To sum up, in this part of the book I consider people's talk-and-action in the context of how it becomes operational in real-life situations as they negotiate their positions.[2] My aim is to elicit the strategies by means of which Kewa create the discourses of their world. Thus I record a local discourse as it arises from the unfolding of everyday activities in which the ethnographer barely has a role; even when I am the conduit for their elicitations, other responses than mine determine whether their constructions are successful. As mentioned in chapter 2, my intention is to bring to view the social processes by which explicit knowledge is constituted and disclosed in social action; not to discover what action hides or mystifies. To some extent, my findings interface with Marilyn Strathern's in *The Gender of the Gift* (1988). While she engaged an extensive body of comparative ethnographic materials to develop a theory of action that discovered the mechanisms which create Melanesian sociality, I turn instead to the strategies that make knowledge of that sociality explicit. This exercise requires intensive and localized rather than extensive and comparative materials. Once released in public space the accounts develop their own impetus, filling the pages with interconnected persons whose talk and actions, as performed and recounted, create their social world.

The ethnographic content of part II is organized in two chapters, under the headings of marriage and death. For the Kewa these are privileged arenas for elicitation and negotiation, being concerned with the enactment and precipitation of tensions in the community, and chosen for the differences they illustrate. I omit discussion of the other major event around which people gather (the pig kill), as this was the subject of a previous work (Josephides 1985).

The rest of this chapter focuses on the key methodological concepts used in the analysis of the practices and strategies in the two ethnographic chapters that follow. From the notion of elicitation elaborated in chapter 2, I develop the twin concepts of rehearsed and rehearsing talk and action, already put to use in chapter 4, and minimal narratives as counterparts to the maximal narratives in chapters 3 to 5.

Portraits, Stories and Minimal Narratives

As discussed in chapter 3, narrative thought is the capacity to understand multi-faceted human interactions and plots as part of an unfolding story. It works by establishing relations as the proper basis for the interpretation of the story. In his discussion of the distinction between narrative thought and paradigmatic thought, Carrithers (1995: 265) identifies two modes of inference: explicit inference based on logic and impersonal abstraction, and implicit inference which refers to the background knowledge required for any slices of talk to be intelligible. While explicit inference belongs to the paradigmatic mode, implicit inference is necessary for all narratives.

The 'minimal narratives' engaged in part II are Carrithers' 'un-story-like invocations' or 'compact utterances'; they evoke stories rather than telling them, by '[orienting] people to events and intentions in a flow of action' (ibid.: 268).[3] Evincing narrative thought without having narrative form, they depend on both types of inference, implicit and explicit, and link past to present and future, 'from showing what has happened to what people now feel, and from what people now feel to what should happen' (ibid.). Minimal narratives best show how narrative thought is bound up with action: 'Their speech had a cognitive and an emotive or evaluative element, but also a connative element, an element of will and determination' (ibid.: 273). In Carrithers' ethnographic examples (taken from Schieffelin 1976), each speaker invites others to join him or her in a process of 'confabulation', a term denoting both consensus and fabrication of a shared world (ibid.: 275). These strategies are evident in the Kewa case, but the slices of talk and action cited here show more indeterminacy of meaning and more openness, and thus also more agonistic interaction. Rather than confabulation, I see negotiation, claim-staking and the Kewa slant of aggressive elicitation.[4]

If Carrithers' storyteller is right to imply that narratives are superior to reasoning (Carrithers 1992: 92, 107), they must be 'consensible' across cultures (ibid.: 159), that is, understood as resting on shared perception. We recognize signs of being upset, Carrithers argues, because 'being upset' is not an abstract state; in the Tikopean example given (ibid.), Firth's friend was upset *with* someone, and his mental state could be grasped only through interaction. As Jackson points out, narrative redescription, unlike theoretical explanation, 'is a crucial and constitutive part of the ongoing activity of the lifeworld', 'a form of Being as much as a way of Saying' (Jackson 1996: 39). In this vein, I observed that 'Kewa stories bring together in continuous accounts various daily interactions as they are made socially visible' (Josephides 1998a: 138): narratives of self and other, eliciting strategies and responses, fights, disputes, jokes and gossip. I coined the term 'portraits' to refer to these collages, made up of my re-presentations of people's accounts and my observations of their talk and actions.[5]

But most importantly, I do not see Kewa stories as culture-bound; when I retell them I expect them to communicate as stories in Benjamin's sense (see below). I contextualize them to make them clearer, not to restrict their sense to the Kewa or to Kewa culture. Away from their cultural context their content will still touch us, even in unwieldy ethnographies that threaten to slip from the ethnographer's grasp. In 'The Storyteller' Walter Benjamin (1968: 89) distinguishes between stories and information: while the latter is already 'shot through with explanation', the art of the former is not to explain the story but to let it unfold in the telling. Though Benjamin is dealing with the more conventional narratives of storytellers, his insights into how stories are constructed and how they communicate have a relevance for my Kewa portraits. Benjamin reminds us that storytelling is a web, one story tied to another, as in the tradition of *A Thousand and One Nights*. (For a similar purpose, Lévi-Strauss [1963] stresses the importance of different versions of myths for an adequate analysis, while LeRoy's (1985) study of Kewa tales emphasizes 'intertextuality'.)

The portraits in my accounts snake through events and relations, and are refracted through different illuminations and perspectives. Though they derive from *my* observations of people's everyday interactions, their fights, their disputes and their gossip, my writing strategy is to reproduce them as closely as possible in people's own words, including verbatim tape recordings.[6] I select accounts but then let them dialogue, without contextualizing them within a hierarchy of values drawn from another sphere, whether local or foreign. On this plane they communicate as lived narratives, retaining some of the redundancies and non-sequiturs that cram life, since life as activity does not require that everything have a point or be carried to a conclusion (Josephides 1998a: 142). Paralleling the appropriation of the storyteller, who 'sinks the thing into [his life], in order to bring it out of him again' (Benjamin 1968: 91–2), the Kewa actor interprets other people's actions and shows their causal relation to her or his own actions.

Elicitation and Explicitness

Portraits bring out the meaning of 'eliciting talk' as elaborated in chapter 2. No matter how frequently Kewa people may claim never to know what is inside somebody else's head, it is everyone's constant endeavour to discover the intentions of others. Talk and action elicit and probe, make claims and seek approval; they try out particular understandings for general agreement, always ready to retract unsuccessful claims and construct new understandings. Thus elicitation is the sort of activity that seeks feedback.[7] It operates by making one understanding explicit by placing it in public space, the space of disclosure. One example will demonstrate the point.

A young boy, Busi, accounted for an altercation in the settlement with a story about serious disagreements that were likely to lead to the failure of the impending pig kill. He told me that Rimbu, the organizer of the pig kill, had taunted and given marching orders to matrilocally resident men, spurred on by a revelation (Busi claimed) about the true paternity of one of his brothers. Busi's claim was experimental, a line and a bait, 'placing in public space' his reading of the social implications of matrilocal residence and biological paternity. He was learning to play at the game of constructing his social reality, but elicited and provoked more than he had anticipated. He received a public arraignment that reduced him to tears. However, for a while there was an uncertainty in the air, as if everything may be other than it appeared. But a certain social confidence was also exhibited: that what may be covered up is not necessarily more powerful, or more real, than the social arrangements that are made visible (for a full account, see Josephides 1998a).

Language, Talk and Action

My analysis in this study does not treat language only as performance (Chomsky 1965) or even only as action (Austin 1962), but makes it part of a theory of action which incorporates speech. In an overview of linguistic anthropology, Duranti (2003) identifies three paradigms that have characterized the sub-discipline. The second paradigm views language as 'a culturally organized and culturally organizing domain', and promotes the study of its use across speakers and activities, thus effectively divorcing language study from psychology (ibid.: 329). Closer to Duranti's third paradigm (ibid.: 333), I view language as 'an interactional achievement filled with indexical values', since context is key; I use linguistic practices 'to document and analyse the reproduction and transformation of persons, institutions, and communities across space and time', and investigate the theoretical issues of 'formation and negotiation of identity/self, narrativity'. My method of data collection documents 'temporally unfolding human encounters, with special attention to the inherently fluid and moment-by-moment negotiated nature of identities, institutions, communities' (ibid.).

Given this view of language, I must take issue with Bourdieu's contention, and Bloch's elaboration of it, that speech is 'after the fact'. Their assertion is that people act first, then systematize with talk. Bloch (1998a) argues that agency is tacit and embodied, not linguistic, and that anthropology, following its mistrust of structures and words, has shifted its interests to practice. Perhaps not entirely refuting this assessment, I describe people as using language (and action) as a tool for finding out, not as a structure that contains meaning.[8] The crucial distinction of course is between speech and language. It is speech, in the Kewa case, that constructs by finding out, in the sense of getting agreement on what is put in the public domain. Thus I am making speech part of action, but this is not the same as what Bourdieu or Bloch means by practice. The practices of language use, rather than its grammatical structure, are responsible for the openness and ambiguity in communicative practices which find their meaning in interaction, forcing an openness in less fluid social practices (see Josephides 1999; also chapter 2, section on 'Strategies').

Norms and Claims: Rehearsed and Rehearsing Talk and Action

The connection and interdependence of the Kewa stories, as seamless webs of life, reveal the commonalities in people's lives, despite my emphasis on personal agency. We see how people are 'bricoleurs in the same spare parts yard', engaged in constructing definitions of institutions while defending their interpretations of the social meaning of action in specific situations.[9] Though people's constant negotiations and claims construct a picture of social life and social knowledge as improvised, their improvised arguments are stated as redefinitions or true definitions of rules. Even if a particular case is based on extenuating circumstances (as discussed in chapter 2), the person advancing it will generalize the argument in terms that regularize the exception within a body of common practices, making explicit a common understanding on which to operate. This stance has the effect of scrambling Carrithers' 'paradigmatic thought' by revealing that the relationship between the explicit inference of logic on the one hand, and experimental claims on the other, may be merely tactical: as outlined in chapter 4, 'rehearsed talk' covers up its origins as 'rehearsing talk' but is challenged by the ambiguity of all talk as both ampliative and defeasible, able to spread or withdraw, and become modified when challenged. Structures are appealed to as 'rehearsed talk', equivalent to 'precedence' in legal terms (in lay terms, examples of occasions when certain claims were accepted); but the act of appeal is always in the form of 'rehearsing talk', in claims which may not be successful. Thus (as several chapters argue and demonstrate) everyday strivings and the pronouncements of institutions are not related as essentially different levels of discourse, but are different strategies for making claims about relations. A judgement in court may be couched in the language of finality and objectivity, but it remains a claim of social reality that seeks wider support.

To sum up, portraits depict actions on social reality, in which strong actors emerge and become socially visible. In their attempts to place themselves as persons within certain social relations, individuals interpret the actions of others by relating them to their own. They utilize whatever materials are available, redefining them in their actions.

My argument so far has been cast in a synchronic mould, concerned with how beliefs about common practices and customs are constructed by individual strategies in a claim-based elicitative context. It could, with a mere conceptual flick and considerable mutual benefit, be recast as an enquiry into the relationship between historical knowledge and autobiographical knowledge; or, as Francesca Cappelletto (2003: 257) has put it, 'how historical knowledge is generated from individual, factual, autobiographical knowledge'.[10] Since I am concerned with action, a *doing*, the concepts suited to my purpose are those of eliciting and rehearsing talk/action, versus a rehearsed discourse. This pair is connected in being expressed as claims to tradition and proper practice, yet still subject to negotiation. Cappelletto demonstrates the inextricable link between episodic and semantic memory, neither of which can be entirely restricted to its so-called domain of (respectively) factual memory or abstract knowledge of the world, being instead combined in 'emotion as memory' (ibid.: 256). I argue for an analogous relationship between rehearsed and rehearsing talk, which are further correlated with tradition and elicitation respectively, in the same way as episodic memory is correlated with memory proper and semantic memory with tradition. Finally, I follow Cappelletto in treating communicative interaction as a form of intersubjective knowledge rather than a 'unanimous, collective endeavour' (ibid.: 257), but also adapt her insight to my ethnography by adding that the rules of interaction are themselves negotiated knowledge. Kewa people negotiate interpretations of those rules in subtle and nuanced exchanges.

Conclusion

Part II develops aspects of the negotiability of social reality and knowledge through concrete slices of ethnography presented as portraits or minimal narratives, accounts of what people say but combined with their actions and their joint outcome. Though Carrithers provides the crucial features of minimal narratives, I expand their purview to include action, stories, gossip and everyday talk. These are all seen as eliciting strategies which demand recognition and response, sometimes forcefully and aggressively, at other times subtly and insidiously. Eliciting talk is an attempt to make explicit both meaning and intent. Thus when Kewa persons, perceiving the unpredictability of social encounters, say 'we don't know what's in other people's heads', they mean that they must wait for the meaning of their actions to be manifest in their effects on others (Strathern 1988). Action demands to be acknowledged, but the form of its acknowledgment cannot be known in advance. The portraits allow the delineation of a particular theory of action, which emerges from action itself as it is performed or recounted. Throughout this book, but most forcefully in part II, a major motivation for this action emerges as the desire for the acknowledgment of one's social self. When we view the portraits in this light, we see that people did not merely respond to situations; they responded to their implications for the perception of the self (Josephides 1998a: 164). Their actions, then, subvert so many generalizations about social action and cultural institutions.

This short chapter is offered as a theoretical introduction to the two chapters that follow, being in a sense the key to how they should be read. Rather than cover the same ground, chapters 7 and 8 plunge straight into the ethnography.

Notes

1. The mutuality of explicans and explicandum is an insight I gained from my ethnography, before reading Ricoeur on the phenomenological method. In his terse expression, 'All phenomenology is an explication of evidence and an evidence of explication. An evidence which is explicated, an explication which unfolds evidence: such is the phenomenological experience' (Ricoeur 1981: 128). In Josephides (n.d.) I elaborate on the meaning of this mutuality in an explanation that expounds the phenomenological method: 'As a methodology, phenomenology interprets the meaning and develops the implications of the evidence (in this case, ethnographic data or experience), while at the same time that ethnographic datum or experience is the evidence for the interpretation'. Substituting 'explicans' for 'explication' and 'explicandum' for 'evidence', I offer an example of this operation expressed as a deductive argument drawn from a case in chapter 7. Rarapalu left her husband Waliya following a dispute in which she claimed he did not treat her with the respect and consideration befitting marital relations. When she returned to challenge his attempt to take another wife, the arguments offered by both sides in the ensuing court case and magistrates' decision revealed the extent to which the meaning of 'marital duties' are negotiated. Thus Rarapalu's desertion of Waliya and the subsequent court case (explicandum) are evidence for the claim that marital duties must be negotiated (explicans). Conversely, that 'claims about marital duties must be negotiated' is the explication (explicans) of the ethnographic datum (evidence: explicandum) of Rarapalu's desertion of Waliya and subsequent court case.
2. For a discussion of talk in Melanesia from a different perspective, see Brison 1992.
3. Carrithers (n.d.) has now refined his analysis with the introduction of a new term, 'story seed', developed in his work on rhetoric in a new fieldsite in Germany.
4. In her work on witchcraft in the Bocage, Favret-Saada notes that any story told there is either to fascinate or to frighten, thus possessing powers of elicitation. The minimal narratives – though not so called by her – have dangerous implications, being in fact a fight to the death for meaning. Just as with Kewa disputes, nothing is ever settled but everything threatens to flare up again, being ever-present: 'in witchcraft, any episode one mentions necessarily refers to something which happened before, since the spell was always there' (Favret-Saada 1980: 148). See also chapter 2 note 24.
5. There I called them portraits when I was referring to the pictures they presented of Kewa people and their culture (what they communicate), and stories when I was concerned with what went into their making (how they were constructed and

how they communicate) (Josephides 1998a). This distinction is less relevant here. Another possible term, vignette, suggests a static description from the outside of a state of affairs, or pictures used to illustrate a point; but portraits are dynamic, they *are* the point, not illustrations of something else.

6. Far from constituting an over-reliance on words and exact utterance (Wikan 1992: 478), this literal scrupulousness facilitates a more 'pragmatic view of language', a better understanding of how people use talk to construct the self and their social world. It is in this sense that this is a *critical* ethnography (Abu-Lughod 1993: 17). In her article 'Beyond the words: the power of resonance', Unni Wikan argues for a 'pragmatic view of language' that 'leapfrogs' words as ways of producing effects rather than entities conveying intrinsic meaning (to paraphrase Wikan, who is paraphrasing Donald Davidson paraphrasing Richard Rorty). For her, pragmatics and meaning cannot be separated (Wikan 1992: 464), and it is necessary to transcend words in order to attend to the speaker's intention. We should also transcend context, because it is not a given (ibid.: 467). These convictions sometimes push Wikan to pose questions that hover on the brink of unintelligibility: how important is knowing what words 'mean'? (ibid.: 472). May good knowledge of the field language in fact hinder rather than facilitate better understanding? (ibid.: 474). Even taking notes made her uncomfortable, as it violated speakers' intentions by fixing them to the narrow vocabulary meanings of the words they used. As westerners (and anthropologists), Wikan argues, we are in this fix because we cannot admit that no one can think [and understand, presumably] without the heart (ibid.: 463), so we sacrifice 'resonance' with the people (that is, empathetic and compassionate understanding, thinking with the heart) to an all-out effort to 'produce effects on the anthropological community' (ibid.: 473). Wikan's argument is tied to a larger one, to do with 'sameness in the face of diversity' (ibid.: 461). I was drawn to her article to the extent that it expressed the need for anthropologists to shed the relativist view 'that others are essentially different from us, to be understood only by means of their 'culture' (ibid.: 471), that is their culture in all its difference. I agree that we must endeavour to understand beyond words and beneath words and in spite of words – but for all these understandings we do need the words. Words have more than a surface, dictionary meaning in any language or culture, and anthropologists do not as a rule restrict them to such meanings. It is not enough to understand general feelings of empathy; we also have to understand specific intentions. Wikan's Muslim friend's response to the Hindu traditional healer's diagnosis of her sickness reveals the goodwill of both to communicate by opening up their religious beliefs to other idioms and symbols, acknowledging each other's humanity and viable religious and cultural beliefs, but it does not thereby demonstrate more specific understanding or reveal communication at any deeper level.

7. Where I talk of 'eliciting talk and action', Bruner (1986: 13) talks of 'intention and action and the vicissitudes and consequences that mark their course'. These uncertainties lead Carrithers (1992: 91) to conclude that narrative thought is not infallible.

8. As Bloch writes elsewhere, 'Only people have agency and they use whatever tools are available to them to achieve their ends' (Bloch 2003: 101).

9. Mead's definition is similar to mine, minus the pizzazz of dynamic negotiation and plus lashings of reification: 'an institution is, after all, nothing but an

organization of attitudes which we all carry in us, the organized attitudes of the others that control and determine conduct' (Mead 1964: 239).

10. Cappelletto (2003) refers to Bloch (1995) in her discussion of the relationship between autobiographical memory and historical memory, otherwise understood as the move from private representations to public representations. Bloch argues that when someone who, as a witness, has an autobiographical memory of a momentous or traumatic event and subsequently represents that event by recounting it, the listeners in their turn re-represent that event and tell it as if they had experienced it. This is how oral traditions are made. Episodic memory is descriptive of the (facts of the) event that is connected to the self. Semantic (or interpretative) memory is abstract knowledge of the world, a generalized description of what we know of these events. Acquired biographic memory, as in Bloch's description, creates a common historical text – a mnemonic community (Cappelletto 2003: 253). A further distinction is between implicit emotional memory (of feelings rather than words, the emotional significance of the event held in the amygdala) and explicit emotional memory (of conscious intentional recollections of episodes – a simple account of factual details stored in the hippocampus). Since the two types of memory are held in different parts of the brain, it is not necessary to remember an experience in order to feel an emotion associated with it. '"Emotion as memory" means that emotion itself is a form of memory which can be transmitted' (ibid.: 256). Hence episodic memory cannot be equated absolutely with the factual, nor semantic memory with the historical, as both the factual and the interpretative contain historical and autobiographical elements which are inextricably combined (ibid.: 257). For a neuroscientist's account of these questions, see Damasio 1999.

Chapter 7

Love and All That
Negotiating Marriage and Marital Life

The materials that make up this chapter include rehearsed talk, individual persons' accounts of things that happened, and events I observed myself. I switch from one type of source to the other, and from one person's narrative to another's. My informants also switch codes in their narratives, from the collective ideal to the individuating, from apparently descriptive, uncontested rehearsed talk to the domain of fantasy. The section on polygyny and conflict zooms in on actual conflicts as they occur and the responses of those affected by them. In the concluding sections I proceed as in chapter 5, first summing up the accounts in terms of their political and social claims and then examining their deeper levels, where they construct the self and other and reveal the nature of relationships and communication. At this level, the analysis will show how people use 'norms' to position themselves, rather than being constrained by them

Courtship

Descriptions of courtship emerge in many of the autobiographical accounts. Pig kills were prime occasions for courtship, when men dressed in finery of woven tree-bark aprons stained with colourful dyes and idiosyncratic arrangements of plumes on their netted caps, or else headdresses of long cassowary feathers. They stuck bamboo knives or limestone adzes (*are*) in armlets which, like their anklets, were woven out of strips of beaten bamboo, and hung bailer shells round their necks. With painted faces and bodies glistening with tree-oil they danced in line, axe in one hand and maraca in the other, while women, a ceremonial digging stick in one hand, cut in the line of men, and snatching the axe of the man they fancied, danced alongside him. Courting sessions were held in adjoining rooms or in the women's house, where girls arranged themselves in a circle interspersed with older chaperones who made way for the boys to sit next to their chosen partner. A young man would bend his lips to his sweetheart's ear and caress it with courting verses (*rome*) purchased at great cost and certain to 'turn the young woman's liver'. They worked by convincing her of the inevitability of the union between her and the *rome* owner, as the sample below shows.[1]

> I tell this *rome* to you and you listen
> By the fence the sugarcane ripens quickly
> We have ripened like the sugarcane
> What shall we do?
>
> Up there by the bank in the glade
> the river Yaro makes a lapping noise
> your head my head we put together as one
> Now what shall we do?
>
> I tell this *rome* to you and you listen
> Many *wano* trees with teeth like little birds
> are close to the house
> The Kewa child comes close to the house
> Sugarcane and pitpit
> are almost at the house.

Plate 7.1. *Tanim het* courting session. (11 December 1979)

Women's courting songs (*wena yaisia*) were performed by young women in praise of men, who loaded them with gifts in appreciation of their beauty and performance.

> The special cooking leaves are ready
> but where are you?
> Where has my netbag gone?
> You've gone somewhere, they say
> Where have you gone?
>
> In our gardens at Yamu
> Cordyline leaves grew in profusion
> But now they have been replanted
> by the water on the coast.
>
> As among the casuarinas
> so among the many men of Wata
> Their great shadows obscure the place
> Yet Rame still stands out among them
> oil pours down his body.
>
> Where many casuarinas cast shadows
> it becomes dark
> Though you are a man, I cannot call you so
> for at Yamu the areca palms are few
> Answer me!
>
> At Yamu a new banana
> will always replace the one that's plucked
> So just look, and go.
>
> Red sugarcane at Yokere, if I cut you
> it will be with a heavy heart
> So let the wind break you off
> and lay you down before me.

Marriage is achieved through several exchanges (for a full account, see Josephides 1985: 57–61). Prestations from the groom's side to the bride's side are known as *wena nu laapo*, 'woman-netbag-both', netbag being *siapi* for womb or vagina. In his characteristic theatrical manner Mapi enacted the exchanges as he described them, each item handed to the bride who passes on a pearshell to her brother, a pig to her father's brother (*mai*), a sow to her mother, a pig to her father, another pig to her sister. Items left over (such as indigenous salt, pearlshells, piglets, *wabala* tree oil, skirts or skirt fibre, cowry shells) are distributed to remaining kinspeople and to the bride's skirt-maker. The amount of brideprice varies with the number of likely recipients, explained Rimbu, citing the example of the bride's father's sister (*aropa*) who demanded a pig, which the protesting groom had to raise by canvassing kin and partners. The bride's side follows with a return gift (*yagi*) of a sow to start off the couple's herd. The last gift in the cycle is from the groom to the bride's parents and consists of pearshells, cowry shells, *aipa* salt and pigs, and now tinned meat and fish. If the brideprice is accepted, the bride with her mother and sisters stay overnight with the groom's mother while he sleeps in the men's house with his father and brothers. The following morning the groom must go to hunt marsupials and other small game and bring his catch to his affines, together with sugarcane and greens. He may not look at his bride or use her name. After her kinswomen have gone his mother takes her to the gardens and sets a few plots aside for her, then returns to tell her son where she has left her. The son makes up a story for his friends, saying he is going to the forest to hunt, and taking his bow and arrows sets out in that direction, but actually takes a circuitous route to his wife's garden. In the garden the couple consummate their marriage, and at three in the afternoon, Rimbu specified, the man follows the same circuitous route home. He invents a story for his agemates about meeting a man and falling into conversation. But to his father and brothers he tells the truth, and they respond that if she does not run away she is truly his wife.

Until the woman conceives, Rimbu continued, the husband may not stay in the same house as his parents-in-law or even look at them. When they visit he must ensure they are well-fed and housed, then make himself scarce. The reciprocal term for son- or daughter-in-law and mother-in-

Plate 7.2. *Tanim het* courting session with Rimbu in the foreground. (11 December 1979)

law is *aya*, and *kasua* for son- or daughter-in-law and father-in-law. The son-in-law may never use his *aya*'s proper name, and it would be an insult for him to be subjected to hearing it from anybody else's lips. If his wife uses her mother's name in his presence the mother is shamed and must present him with a pig. In the first two or three months of marriage the husband will not accept food from his wife's hands. She will give the food to his mother who will give it to him, enabling him to maintain the pretence that the food was cooked by his mother. After the period of avoidance is over (typically when the woman has given birth to her first child) the husband may use his *kasua*'s proper name and sit and eat with him. But though he and his wife may sleep in the same room as his *aya*, his *kasua* must sleep with his brothers, because *kasua* may not see each other's genitals. Men's traditional dress comprised a bark belt (*aago*) worn at the waist, cordyline leaves (*ramu*) in the back to cover the anus, and a string apron (*konapu*) in the front to hide the genitals. When a man lay down to sleep he took off his *konapu* and removed the cordyline leaves, retaining only the *aago*. Women simply changed skirts, removing their outer grass skirts (*kura*) – normally knee-length but ankle-length during mourning – and donning old sleeping-skirts.

Some of these practices are clearly no longer observed, and dress habits have certainly changed. In Lari's account, her father-in-law did all the cooking in the first three months, and there was no marsupial-hunting. But I was assured that the sleeping rules are still observed.

Plate 7.3. *Tanim het* courting session with Rimbu in the foreground. (11 December 1979)

Problems with Brideprice

Brideprice is central to marriage. In one court case involving non-payment of brideprice, the man was given the option of treating the marriage as fornication and paying compensation, or completing brideprice payments within six months. Six months later the bride's mother and brother brought the errant couple back to court. Magistrate Rusa stated the moral position. It was disgraceful, he said, for a woman to go to a man who can't afford her simply because she likes him, and it was disgraceful for the man to draw the woman to him when he didn't have the brideprice. It's no use blaming each other or claiming to have been seduced; this is 'bullshit'. Both had followed their desires and were equally responsible. Deliberation on the case lasted an hour, during which the brother and mother spoke a lot, the husband a little and the wife not at all. The court ruled that the husband be given a further six months to complete the payment.

Brideprice and its collection are especially problematic when marriage is contracted with people from distant places, not an unusual event these days when young women follow relatives to plantations in the hope of finding husbands there. This was the case with Koai's daughter, who met a man from Kundiawa in the Simbu Province. Koai dictated a letter in answer to this man's brideprice proposals. He rejected the suggestion of 'half pay', which means partial rather than half payment of brideprice, and complained that the advance payment of K100 did not even cover expenses incurred on his journey to Kundiawa. Koai's comment – that he would know if the brideprice was sufficient only after he had made the distributions – underlined the connection between amount of brideprice and obligations to recipients. He finished the letter with a warning: other men had made substantial brideprice offers for his daughter.

The Kundiawa man's reply contained serious breaches of etiquette. He addressed the letter to the girl, whose name he wrote over and over again, omitted mention of brideprice, and repeated requests for the girl to go to him, otherwise he would come for her at Christmas. The response was dictated to me in Tok Pisin.

> Dear Mr J. P.
>
> I have just received your letter, but you did not respond to any of the questions raised in mine. Now I'll explain to you the position of Koai, Lapame's father. At the time of your feast for us in Kundiawa I set the brideprice for this woman at K1,000 in cash and ten pigs. Now you write and just ask about Lapame, how you miss her and how is she. You don't mention brideprice. In our language in Kagua we are ashamed to use our girlfriend's name. Only after brideprice is paid can we use her name. A lot of talk has gone back and forth, now only time for lining up the payment remains. You must send the brideprice, take your wife and go before this year is out. Next year will not do. You are holding back my business, I can't stock my tradestore. This is the end of Koai's talk, you must listen to this man.
>
> Koai.

The marriage did not come off. Four months later Lapame married a local Koiari man, with brideprice of fourteen pigs and many pearlshells.

Rimbu explained discrepancies in the amounts of brideprice in terms of a falling rate of profit, consequent on the first daughter's brideprice being seen as the return for her mother's. Since most of the mother's brideprice is recuperated in the first transaction, daughters get cheaper as they go on. If the rationale for brideprice is that men get back what they have had to pay for their own wives, it would not be justifiable to ask for a high brideprice for all of their women. While it may be true that individual men's strategies are informed by such considerations, in general this is not how things turn out. What Rimbu calls a rule is simply a strategy that must fight it out with other strategies by other actors, all rehearsing their part. Brideprice for a daughter cannot be seen as a return to the husband, because the mis en scène is so different. The wife/mother herself has an interest in her daughter's brideprice, seen from her perspective as repayment for nurturing, as do many other people not involved in the earlier transaction. What seems in practice to determine the size of brideprice is a compromise between the interests that need to be satisfied (the number of persons who have earned the right to receive brideprice) and the amount of wealth the bridegroom is able to raise.

It was seen in previous chapters that women talk of brideprice as an expression of their value, a material indication of men's desire and appreciation for them. Men take a different view. Though they like to emphasize their achievement in raising brideprice, they try to minimize the amount paid, even affecting nonchalance towards the marriage itself. It is a point of prestige to have provided the wealth oneself, and an indication of sexual prowess to draw women with a small amount of brideprice. Yasi, a young man recently returned from plantation labour, carried this nonchalance too far. He talked in slighting tones of his wife Kalinu, claiming he had not wanted her when they met in Mt Hagen but she latched on to him. How could he trust a woman who had had four husbands? It was his brothers who insisted that he give the brideprice of two pigs to her brothers. He would prefer to get rid of her rather than complete the brideprice payment, but she gave him no pretext. He would provoke her, he said, until she showed pig-headedness, then divorce her and take back his pigs.

Yasi was protesting too much. Being painfully aware that Kalinu's past marriages were public knowledge, he preempted criticism by insisting he was bent on catching her out. This studied indifference to one's wife is not uncommon. The truth was that far from being pressed by his brothers, Yasi himself had wanted to give brideprice. When Kalinu's brothers came for the brideprice, Waliya, who had promised Yasi a pig in return for some help he had given him, argued that it belonged to the forthcoming pig kill, but he was eventually prevailed upon to give it up. Yasi added a second pig, together with a promise of more pigs in the future. If the marriage lasts, Yasi will not be talking like this in a few years' time.

The story of Poreale, whose brother Yadi took her away from her husband because he had not received her brideprice himself, demonstrates the importance, for the stability of the marriage, of *who* receives brideprice. Through the male line Poreale was Yadi's father's father's brother's son's son's daughter, therefore his classificatory sister by Kewa reckoning, but he was also related to her through his mother; by this reckoning she was his mother's brother's wife's sister's daughter. Poreale's maternal relations 'pulled' her to them by means of gifts and services and married her to a man in Minj in the Western Highlands. When Yadi discovered that they had 'eaten' the brideprice he went to Minj and fetched Poreale back. The bridegroom's people took him to court over the unreturned brideprice, but Yadi was not liable for this. When I asked Yadi if Poreale had wanted to leave her husband and return home with him, he found the question irrelevant. 'Well, I'm her brother and I received no portion of the brideprice.' Poreale expressed similar sentiments. I explained that I was interested to know her inclination, her own desires in the matter, but she reiterated the order of events: her brother Yadi had come and fetched her away because he hadn't received a share of the brideprice, which the matrikin had 'eaten'.

The girl's wishes in determining a match must not be underestimated, however, and clearly some girls have stronger desires than others. Loma, the daughter of Mayanu and Rama, was the most wayward of brides. She was first betrothed to a local boy but nothing came of it. When her clan sister Kamare married Lari's brother Lenda, Loma married his kinsman, so that she and Kamare would be neighbours. Her paid-up brideprice was K400, seven pigs and two shells. Rama kept K200 and three pigs for himself, his wife Mayanu kept one pig and a pearlshell, and the rest was distributed to clan brothers and father's brothers. The girls returned from their visit to the grooms' home bringing cooked pork, shells and money. Then their kinswomen (Mayanu, Ipa and Demanu) accompanied them back to their husbands' place. They were to sleep there for two nights, but Loma returned home alone the following day. Her mother Mayanu came later in the day, crying, 'U-huuu, u-huuu, Loma's left her husband.' The groom and his relatives followed, and the brideprice was collected and lined up. Then Rimbu spotted Ragunanu, Roga's daughter, standing by the water drum, and whispered in her ear: 'This man is having to take back his brideprice, are you interested in marrying him?' Ragunanu said she didn't mind, if her father agreed. Roga did agree, so Rimbu addressed the groom: 'Cousin (he was of his mother's line), a woman is a woman, will you take a different one?' The groom's brothers welcomed this solution: 'The brideprice is already at your place, it would be hard work to carry it back.' But the groom demurred. 'A woman's a woman, but Loma shamed me when she left. Will your child do the same?' Ragunanu gave assurances, and Roga began his distribution of the brideprice. Rimbu received a pig for his services, and Hapkas and Roga gave one pig each to Ragunanu as a bridal gift.

Ragunanu did not leave her husband the next day or the day after, but the marriage was childless and ended two years later. Biru, her long-suffering suitor who had been giving her people small sums of money towards brideprice, courted Ipanu briefly while Ragunanu was married. When her marriage was dissolved he returned to his first love, and his patience and constancy were finally rewarded.

Some two or three months after the incident at the drum Loma contracted another marriage. Two days after brideprice was accepted and distributed, she returned home. The man's mother came to take back the pigs. Nobody seemed particularly angry with Loma. The two marriages had not been consummated, they said, so her behaviour was not reprehensible. (Loma did eventually marry, and had a child by the time of our 1993 visit.)

Not all desertions were tolerated, however. One man was serving an eight-year sentence for killing his ex-wife and her sister. She had left him for another man in Erave, and when she was visiting her sister in Tiripi he axed them both down as they walked along the road. The women were so pretty, Biru said. 'All the men desired them and he killed them just like that. What a shame!' But other men muttered darkly that women had no business to leave their husbands and expose them to the ignominy of desertion.

Irregular Unions

Some marriage attempts provided amusement for the village. Kaporopali became the object of derision when he tried to marry one young woman after another. He was over sixty years old and already had two wives when he tried to marry Pisa's daughter, Wareame, who was in her twenties and a Catholic. She favoured the match; there was something wrong with her eye, which may have been the reason for her single status. At a public showing Kaporopali lined up ten pitpit sticks, four long ones representing pigs and six short ones standing for shells. But Wareame's mother upbraided her daughter: what was she thinking of, a baptized

Catholic, considering marriage to a man with two wives? Kaporopali tried to save the situation by promising to divorce his other wives, but the match fell through; Wareame was too afraid of the disapproval of her parents and brothers, and the brideprice was deemed insufficient.

A month later Kaporopali came to pay court to Pupula's daughter Kamare, also a Catholic. (This was before her marriage mentioned above.) He repeated his assurances that the second wife would be discarded. The first wife, who had come for the brideprice showing, had for some time been living with her children. I described elsewhere (Josephides 1999) how Pupula shamed Kaporopali, reproaching him with his age and polygamous state, with the words that his son would have been a more suitable match. An old man trying to marry a young girl, Rimbu commented, should foresee the possibility of rejection and never make a public offer without prior consultation. Rimbu tried to argue that Kaporopali needed wives to care for his many gardens, but then gave it up and said that Kaporopali simply wanted a fresh girl in his bed.

Kaporopali was not the only man to be shamed by having his overtures rejected. Wola's attempt to marry Karupiri, his younger brother's (Rake's) widow, was far more reprehensible, beginning with a rape and ending in public disgrace. While Karupiri was still in mourning and alone in the longhouse, Wola came in displaying obvious physical signs of his intentions. She was afraid he might kill her and did not resist, but the following morning she took him to court. The magistrates condemned Wola's behaviour and he became a laughing stock. Though he kept out of sight for several weeks, and had to give Karupiri K40 in compensation, he was still not quite abashed, and a month later he was trying to get her to marry him. He took her to court over her rejection of him, and again he earned derision. The magistrates told him he had gone about it the wrong way and forfeited his chances. If he had looked after her for a year or so, he would have been in a stronger position, as it was not uncommon for a man to marry his brother's widow. Some women added that there were objections to Wola himself: he had neither good sense nor good address, a sad old man who recently took to decorating and trying to pass for a younger one. (Yet at his brother's funeral, as will be seen in chapter 8, Wola is presented as a man of dignity and substance. Thus a man is not totally defined by his behaviour at one juncture of his life.) The magistrates gave Karupiri permission to abandon her widow's weeds (*kura yaai*, a long grass skirt, *mumu*, a voluminous netbag on the head, and *karupiri*, thick strings of Job's tears round the neck); since her husband's brother had not treated her like a widow she did not have to behave or dress like one. On her return home to Aka, Roga gave her K40 to 'straighten' (placate) Wola's line. When Karupiri remarried, I understood what Roga had done: with this money he had bought brideprice rights in her.

Reverse cases, of old women marrying young men, were rare. In 1981 Loketa's elderly mother Waminia became first wife of a young Perepe man. My enquiries elicited responses in terms of the young men's reasons for marrying old to middle-aged women ('they want to eat sweet potatoes'), but no hint as to why middle-aged women should want to marry young men. Women were reluctant to discuss this and seemed unwilling to differentiate this kind of marriage from any other. When I asked Lari if Waminia would have children, which was my coy way of finding out if the couple was likely to have sex, Lari, not taking the hint, responded that Waminia was past childbearing age but might conceive if she used magical preparations. Forced to be blunt, I suggested there would be no sex between them. 'Oh, there'll be sex,' said Lari laconically. 'What the two do is their business.' Though Kaporopali's attempts at marriage were greeted with restrained amusement, there was disinclination for ribald joking in this case. Yone's wife was teased for wanting to sleep with her husband (see chapter 1), but she was a young wife. While old women are mocked in other contexts, as women past childbearing age their sexuality may be too taboo for jokes.

A more irregular marriage was contracted by Kalisi's mother. When her first marriage to Kalu was terminated, she married Likasi, by whom she had Kalisi. When Likasi died she married Kondo, who was Likasi's son by his first wife. Thus she had married her stepson. By then she was too old to have children. The marriage was considered improper and Kondo was too ashamed to show his face in the village. Only after the woman died and he was getting on himself did he return to live here permanently.

Polygyny and Conflict

Women's protests against polygyny abound, and the ensuing events often have devastating repercussions. Lu's sister came to stay with him when her husband Kare took a second wife, but while Kare was away she went to his store and gave the second wife a tongue lashing. When Kare rebuked his estranged wife, she retorted that it was thanks to her he had become a 'company', rich enough to marry another woman. He responded by ramming his boot in her stomach, causing internal bleeding which eventually killed her. (The presence of an enlarged spleen due to untreated malaria was a strong contributory factor.) Her brother Lu collected a large compensation payment following her death.

The main burden of this section is marital conflict, specifically how women in five marriages responded to the threat of polygyny or acted within a polygynous marriage. Ainu's story in particular shows that a woman's interests in her husband's subsequent marriages are socially acknowledged as legitimate, and the woman, especially if she is first wife, has considerable de facto power to veto such marriages.

Ainu and Yako

Ainu and Yako invested some money in Rimbu's store when he first opened it, but soon after Yako asked for it back, to use for brideprice. Ainu pursued him to our settlement, screaming that she wanted her own investment to remain, but Rimbu returned the whole sum to Yako, without interest since it had been taken out too soon. It was almost a year before Yako's marriage plans came anywhere near fruition, when he offered brideprice for a married woman with two children who happened to be visiting Mapi in Aka. Rimbu, feeling sorry for Yako, who lamented his lack of 'replacement' (he and Ainu had a daughter but no son), promised five piglets and three shells. Roga, who was church deacon, warned Lari not to allow her husband to use her own things; as a churchgoer she should not support polygyny, especially when the prospective bride was already married. In the middle of the well-attended marriage negotiations, Ainu appeared and began to attack the lined-up pigs. Her consent had not been sought and she would kill the pigs rather than see them given in brideprice, she screamed. She and Yako grappled together, and the bride-to-be fled, protesting she would not marry a man whose wife did not agree to the match. Then her brothers started shaking hands and moving off, stopping to say to me, with an apologetic air:

> We came to marry our sister, but found that things were not well-done here. The old woman had not consented to the match. If he (Yako) had explained to her that it was only because she had no children, that he wasn't rejecting her so she shouldn't fear for her position, and the old woman agreed, the marriage could have gone ahead. As it is we can't proceed, there would be trouble afterwards. If he straightens things out with the old woman then we can talk.

The brothers made a dignified exit, while Yako and Ainu screamed at each other from opposite ends of the settlement. All bystanders were splitting their sides with laughter. Yako, a very small man, physically the proverbial 'rubbish man', was thought too old to be marrying and this contributed to his lack of success, while Ainu was considered a good worker who did not complain when her husband purloined her money and other goods – except, as we have seen, when he wanted to use them for brideprice.

Giame and Yadi

Giame often fought with her husband Yadi over his alleged infidelities. I always remember how she had laughed at the part in Yakiranu's story (chapter 3) about her husband killing his previous wife because she played around with other men: 'She's just like Yadi, whom I've been beating for the same reason.' The incident below describes one of their more serious fights, at a time when Giame was heavily pregnant.

One night at about eleven o'clock a truck drove into the settlement and parked by the longhouse. After an evening of drinking in Kagua, Yadi was home, bringing the truck owner, Councillor Kengeai, and a carton of beer. Yadi knocked Giame out of bed and asked her to prepare some food for them. Giame retorted that he had just been eating another woman's vagina and she had no intention of cooking for him. 'I haven't been playing around with other women,' returned Yadi, 'I've been working hard driving about and now I want my supper.' Giame attacked first, kicking him on the neck as he sat down, then hitting him on the head with a stick. The truck owner made himself scarce, while Giame and Yadi proceeded to rip each other's clothes to shreds. Rimbu told them they were quits. 'Cut off what belongs to her, give it to her and go.' This insult was a way of getting at both of them, the woman for being interested only in her husband's penis and the man for not being able to control his wife. Yadi (who spoke only Tok Pisin when drunk) told Giame she stank; he didn't want her and would marry the other woman tomorrow. Giame picked up her things and made for Mapi's house, while Yadi picked up *his* things and drove to his girlfriend's place in Waluare. Mapi would not let Giame in, so she came back and sat moaning outside Rimbu's door. Early next morning she followed Yadi to Waluare.

Later in the morning some church-bound women stopped on their way and one of them, Mayanu, harangued the whole settlement for allowing a pregnant woman to be beaten. Giame returned in the afternoon and sat outside the longhouse, surrounded by her children and belongings. She sniffed and looked a little shamefaced, but also defiant. She blew her nose when she saw me, said, 'Nasty cold', and looked away.

The following morning Rama, Yadi, Rimbu, Sipi, Papola, Lari, Kabenu, Rorepame and Kamare were sitting at the building-site of Rimbu's house, discussing Yadi's marriage. As usual, the men sat on the one side and the women on the other. Giame's children were there but not

Giame herself. He would divorce Giame, Yadi said. If another woman wanted to come and live with him, fine, but he would not get married again. Rama blurted out angrily that he didn't like these two women, Giame and Lari. At Thursday's court hearing they would oust Giame, then they should get rid of Lari. These women were jealous and possessive and made their husbands miserable with their suspicions and unfounded accusations. Anyone could see there were no shells or pigs for brideprice in Yadi's and Rimbu's houses, so how did their wives think they would get brides? No one disposes of daughters for nothing. I asked Rama, who was a Catholic, if he knew about the Catholic law on divorce. He didn't champion divorce, he said, it was the women who brought it on themselves with their bad talk. All the men did was flirt. If they really had sexual relations with other women they would be landed with a string of compensation payments. No, they just went to the market and flirted with the young girls. Rimbu summed up the general feeling on behalf of the men. 'Giame should be told to piss off.'

Much of this was rhetoric. Giame and Yadi had three children and nobody believed they would be divorced. Rimbu said that the problem was Giame's rapacious sexual appetite. He himself sleeps apart from Lari because she is breastfeeding, but some people don't observe these rules. His own mother was 'strong', so Wapa sent the two of them away until Rimbu was weaned. If this was Yadi's strategy, said Rimbu, it was a good one.

Lari was upset that I might think she had given 'bad talk', and she was angry with Rama for tarring her with the same brush as Giame. Rimbu also objected. If Yadi was having trouble with his wife, that was his problem, but no one had any business to tell *him* to get rid of his wife. 'If my wife had given me bad talk,' Rimbu told Rama, 'I would take her to court. I don't need anyone to tell me.'

Two days later Giame was at the market, looking downcast. She dismissed the men's claims as so much hogwash, especially as she had heard from Lari that they were organizing a whip-round for brideprice. The money was there, she said; everybody had promised a contribution and as a wage earner Yadi had his own savings. She didn't want a divorce, she was pregnant after all, but she had been evicted and thought the magistrates would be against her. She admitted that she had hit Yadi and made 'bad talk', but that was because of his intention to marry another woman. Tomorrow she would collect the summons from the court. Some women standing around us showed their support by offering to accompany her, but Giame, though despondent, was resolved to go on her own.

When I returned to the village after a few days' absence, Giame was back in the settlement as if nothing had happened. As on a previous occasion, she sheepishly ran the back of her arm across her nose and said, 'Nasty cold!' Rimbu laughed. 'Didn't I tell you she'd be back?' (Well, no.) Lari told me there had been no court case. Instead, Yadi had sent Busi and Pasaroli (two very young men) to fetch her back from her natal village. Giame had repeated to the girlfriend's brother what she had told Yadi to do with his sister at the beginning of the fight, and the court awarded the girlfriend K20 damages. Instead of paying, Giame did debt-labour for a fortnight. Yadi did the debt-labour with her.

Lari and Rimbu

Rimbu had briefly taken a second wife before my fieldwork, but the marriage came to grief (see Rimbu's story in chapter 5). During my fieldwork Lari sometimes had cause for concern. One girl was heard to say she would accept brideprice from him after a courting session. When Lari saw Rimbu go into Yadi's room, she suspected it was an attempt to raise brideprice, so she pulled a picket from my fence and hit him with it. She had dealt three blows when his clan brother Michael stopped her. Rimbu ran off to Mapi and asked him as village magistrate to have Lari sent away for a year, but he refused, as did the village court later. Adding insult to injury, the magistrates remonstrated with Rimbu for his flirting when he was aware of the problems of polygyny. He returned home in high dudgeon, vowing to give brideprice for the other woman right away, though he had no desire for a second marriage and its costly obligations. In a deft move, Lari conciliated him with a gift of K2, which Rimbu passed on to Michael. Though Lari and Rimbu often laughed over Wapa's attempts to procure another wife for Rimbu, Rimbu himself took a second wife much later, when Wapa was dead and I was away from the village. On my return Lari told me how it happened.

From Lari's account: When Marc and I left the village they mourned us for a week, weeping and barely eating, until the other villagers accused them of hiding money and keeping everything we had left for themselves. They would not believe Lari's protestations that we left no money, so they opened up the house and let it be plundered. Lari kept a mattress, some blankets and dishes, and Rimbu took the pressure lamp and the laundry-tub. Giame was one of the grumblers, and she 'greased' Kuri, an Amburupa woman like herself, to make up to Rimbu. This Kuri was a woman who would go with anyone without brideprice, an *ali pake wena* who had several pregnancies but only one surviving son, who lives with her parents.

Soon Rimbu was spending the nights with Kuri. When Lari caught them in Yadi's house 'holding each other tight', she said to Rimbu: 'If I didn't work well or had no children [she was carrying her fifth by this time], then you could marry another woman.' Yet she herself took Kuri's hand and put it in Rimbu's, telling them they could not carry on like adolescents; if they were serious, they should marry. But when Rimbu attempted to collect brideprice she withheld the pigs, drawing angry words from Rimbu: 'All these pigs and gardens and wealth, did you bring them from *your* home? They belong to my land!' She gave way when he wept and threatened in turn. Brideprice comprised one sow, one medium-sized pig and Lari's piglet (which she had tried to hide), four or five pearlshells and K40 in cash. Koipe contributed K10 and one pig. Rimbu handed these items to Kuri, who gave them to her kinspeople.

Lari watched these transactions with dismay. Immediately after, she took her children to the garden and cut down the sugarcane, giving to everyone to eat. Other women in similar circumstances may kill pigs or even pull down houses. For one night they all slept together, but the next day Kuri told Rimbu she didn't like this arrangement, he looked at his first wife too much. So while Lari was in church he divided up all their possessions, taking the best things for himself and his new wife, and partitioned the house. He also divided up the gardens and asked Lari which half she preferred. But Lari would not speak to either of them. Everyone told her that gardens, pigs and shells belong to men, so she should not complain. Rimbu ate only at Kuri's then.

Two months after this marriage Lari gave birth to a boy, Nadawa, and Rimbu proposed a new scheme. They should divide up the children, Lari taking Lisette, Amasi and Nadawa, while he kept Wapanu and Ruma (the older boy and the eldest girl). But the magistrates told him he had no good reason for sending away the mother of so many children. What compensation could he pay her? (The suggestion being that no amount was sufficient. It should be remembered that this is Lari's gloss on what happened, her claim or elicitation.) However, Lari's kin – her mother, sister and brother – insisted that she leave a husband who rejected her. As she began to walk away with them, her Yala affines wept and blamed Rimbu. But in the meantime, Rimbu had taken another route, arriving at Lari's natal village (Yawelea) before her, and then asking her to return home with him. Her people were divided. Those who favoured her return said she could demur if he had taken three weeks or more to come for her, but he had pursued her immediately. One brother gave her a sow, and she came back.

This did not please Kuri, and she and Lari were always arguing. But the marriage was finished when Kuri was caught in adultery with Yasi. Rimbu's skin had changed as a result of eating his wife's food while she was fornicating, and the transgressive lovers had to 'compensate the man's skin' with two pigs (Kuri), K220 and some pearlshells (Yasi).

Rimbu gave K40 to Lari and sent Kuri back home with a blanket, a spade, some dishes and a saucepan. Yasi ran off to Erave. The brideprice was also returned. End of marriage. I asked Lari why she thought Rimbu had wanted to marry again. Her reply was terse: 'It's men's way, to pack off one wife and marry another.'

From Rimbu's account: He had not wanted to be rid of Lari, but she was always cross and refused to give him food, telling him to go to his new wife for his meals. But he was still hungry after eating with Kuri, and wanted Lari's food too. (As the expression 'to cook food for one's husband' refers more broadly to conjugal relations, Rimbu may have been hankering after more than food. Likewise, Lari's admonition to Rimbu could be read as 'Eat where you have sex'.) Then a misunderstanding brought everything to a head. Kuri's mother came to collect some of the outstanding brideprice, and Rimbu gave her K60. As (bad) luck would have it, Lari's mother, her sister and her brother were visiting at the same time and witnessed the transaction. They were affronted that one wife's mother should receive a gift of money while the other merely looked on. No amount of explanation could placate them, though Rimbu repeated over and again that this was Kuri's own money, earned from contract work on the road, which she now provided for her own brideprice. Eventually, tired of the bickering, he told Lari she could go home with her relatives. He thought he would finish with her.

But when he returned home after Lari had gone, he found his barely three-year-old son Ruma quite inconsolable. Neither he nor Kuri could stop his tears. He thought over the situation, and early next morning he lodged a complaint at Kagua police station against his mother- and brother-in-law, for taking a three-day-old infant on a perilously long journey. He was told there were no police officers to spare, so he went after Lari himself. Contrary to Lari's account, he refused the sow her brother had offered because he did not want to create a debt, and they returned home empty-handed. There was no trouble afterwards, but Rimbu was tired of the arguments and left for Mt Hagen, staying four months. In July 1984 Yasi's delict with Kuri was discovered, and in November Rimbu sent her home and recovered the brideprice.

He did not marry this woman just for sex. If he had thought this was her sole interest he would have sent her packing. But she came to his house in an open manner, indicating she was serious. He thought only of her labour, forgetting about the trouble and expense of a second wife. But though she was good with the children, her garden work was poor. She had two thoughts in her head: sex, and eating without having to work.

Liame, Rosa and Kiru

Liame was notoriously irascible; the slightest word could send her into a rage. I have seen her strutting up and down the settlement, waving her bushknife and giving Yago a tongue-lashing, because he had complained about her pig spoiling his garden. At church her voice drowned all others in singing to the Lord. Her husband Kiru, commenting on her defiant full-day hunting trip (see chapter 1), owned she was a very hard woman. He had reason to say so, for in their fights she generally gave as good as she got. When he took her to court for allegedly twice giving him 'bad talk', and she was fined K50, she gave the court the finger: 'Why should I pay you K50? Come and eat my finger.' As a result, she was handcuffed and carted off to prison in Kagua. As Rimbu was telling me this story, Liame walked into the settlement with a hand of bananas on her head. When I asked what had happened, she insisted that her kin had not bailed her out, as Rimbu surmised; she herself decided not to go to prison because she was sorry for her old mother who was sick. She may go to gaol in January; it was up to her to decide when to serve her sentence. In any case, Kiru and his brothers were lying, she had not given bad talk to anyone, but never mind, she would go to gaol, 'no worries'. Later I saw Kiru. 'She's lying, of course,' he said. 'She did say all those bad things and we'll take her to court again.'

One morning Liame appeared with a bruised face and bloody ear. The night before, she and Kiru had returned very hungry from their garden in Pepeawere, and Kiru offered to cook the sweet potatoes if she fetched the greens. But when she got back she found only marita (red pandanus fruit eaten by men) cooking in the saucepan. A farce worthy of the stage ensued. Laime threw out the marita and put in the sweet potatoes. Kiru threw out her sweet potatoes and put in his marita. Liame attacked him with a stick, he grabbed her by the hair and punched her face, then dragged her to a *kot kros* (a village prehearing with a magistrate). Liame, incredibly, declared that Kiru was lying; she had hit him with an axe, not a stick. The magistrate (Mapi) told them they were both well-fleshed and there was no case to answer.

In 1985 Liame was no longer living with Kiru, who had taken another wife (Rosa). She had been gone eight months and Kiru talked about bringing her back, but I left the field before this happened. Many years later, at Payanu's funeral in 1993 (see chapter 8), I observed at close range the actively hostile relations between the two wives. Liame and Rosa began to argue a little before six in the afternoon, after Payanu was buried and the 'mumu' (earth oven) had been opened and the food disposed of. Once again, red pandanus was the trigger. Kiru had asked

Rosa to give the marita to the girlfriend of Nadisua, his son by Liame, but she failed to do so, and Liame was berating her about this and accusing her in addition of eating her (Liame's) share of pork. Rosa retorted: 'I earn my own money, I look after pigs, everything I have is from my own labour and I give it all to Kiru, whereas you give him nothing.' 'What are you on about,' Liame lashed back, 'he sleeps with you, he gives you everything, what do you have to complain about? He is not my husband, he has left me.' Lari whispered to me, 'It's true, he said last night that he had left this woman and doesn't want anything more to do with her; she can keep her gardens and her children and stay on here but he won't share anything with her like a husband, because she is not a good woman, she is always fighting.' I commented that if Kiru returned to live in the settlement the fights would be terrible (since his marriage to Rosa they lived on the mountain.) 'He can't come,' Lari assured me, and Rimbu added that he would banish him from the settlement. Yet I was sure he was included in Rimbu's men's house building and pig-killing plans.

The altercation was around the mumu pit to the left of my house. Kiru had gone to Papola's house and the two of them were squatting outside. As Koke walked past the women on his way out of the settlement, he said, 'Have you women bought this ground that you should fight in it?' Rimbu, sitting on the doorstep of his store, added his bit. The men implied that the ground did not belong to the women and they had no right to fight on it. But the women were not abashed by the remarks, which were oil on their fire. Liame recoiled in mock fear when Kiru began to walk towards the settlement: 'Oooh, he is coming to beat me up now!' But Kiru merely said, in Tok Pisin (the women had been speaking Kewa), 'You two go and sit down somewhere else' ('*Yupela go sindaun long narapela hap*'). Liame spat back in the same language, her words dripping with venom: 'Why should we go and sit down somewhere else?' In the angry Kewa exchange that followed, the Tok Pisin phrase 'sindaun long narapela hap' was repeated in scathing tones by Liame, as if it had been the deadliest and most preposterous of insults. Her final taunt – that she would chop Kiru in half with a bush knife – left him no alternative but to withdraw to the '*haus kuk*' (kitchen), mustering all the bravado he could in his Tok Pisin Parthian shot: 'You two can kill each other, I'll just get another wife.'

The two women did look murderous. Liame's eyes were burning coals, scorching the ground around her; Rosa's like boiled sweets, hard and round, rolling around her face balefully. Each told the other to go away, to go home; they were ferocious and meant business. Rosa was breastfeeding her baby throughout these exchanges, while little Lisette cuddled Rosa's older child. From time to time Kiru and Rimbu shouted from the kitchen, 'All right, that's enough, you are spoiling the ground, go home now', but Liame and Rosa would not call a truce. Liame's youngest son kept setting fire to the brushwood and throwing it in the mumu pit. Finally, Rosa got up and went with her baby into the kitchen while Liame, with a theatrical gesture, took a stick and furiously lashed at the flames her son had kindled, as if she were beating Rosa. Rosa made a brief lunge out again to deliver another insult, but it was over and we all dispersed. (I learned in a letter that Liame died two years later.)

Rarapalu, Karupiri, Foti and Waliya

Throughout this fight, Karupiri, Waliya's wife, flirted outrageously with Rimbu. I described elsewhere the turbulence surrounding her own marriage to Waliya, which his first wife Rarapalu desperately opposed as it entailed a repudiation of herself (Josephides 1998a). Over a long period Rarapalu felt that her husband did not acknowledge her place in his relations and affections. She returned to her natal village in a move which she later described as offering him the opportunity to remedy these deficiencies, through gifts that recalled her home by acknowledging her value as a wife. But instead he sued for divorce and made overtures of marriage to Karupiri (widow of Rake and importuned by his brother Wola). Rarapalu returned post-haste to contest the divorce, arguing that her flight was occasioned by what she perceived as Waliya's breach of proper marital relations. The court took an inflexible view: it was always wrong to leave a husband. Each side gave a different meaning to Rarapalu's actions, revealing a disagreement over what constituted marital duties for each sex. Despite the court's decision Rarapalu stayed on, in a ménage à trois that kept the whole settlement awake with its incessant bickering, violent fights, the clatter of flying kitchen utensils. Any attentions Waliya paid to Karupiri, Rarapalu interpreted as a slight to herself.

Rarapalu's childlessness as a reason for Waliya's desire to remarry was never cited publicly, either by the court or the people. Privately it was said that it must have weighed on Waliya, yet the woman he was proposing to marry was the childless widow of a man whose other wife had borne him children. When Waliya married his third wife, Foti (Rarapalu had left by then), he finally became a father for the first time. Foti, who was Rosa's sister by a different mother, now looked on the fight raging between Rosa and Liame, and assured me that she and Karupiri never fought; only now and then. 'Why should we fight? Karupiri has no children, and we look after my children together.' But I hear sounds of fighting, I ventured. 'Well, just sometimes, like when Karupiri gave bad talk to my daughter

Walame.' There was embarrassment when I pressed her for details. 'She told Walame to eat her mother's thing. We don't say things like that to our children. It was my child, not hers. So I cracked her head open with a stick.' Lari added that the pastor and the 'deacon' (as she now refers to her husband Rimbu) settled the dispute by asking Foti to give Karupiri a pig, or else go to prison. Foti had the last word: 'Waliya's father's brother could not allow a woman with young children to go to prison, so he brought me a pig, valued at K300, to give to Karupiri.'

Another time Foti's pig had spoiled Karupiri's garden, and Foti responded flippantly to Karupiri's protest: 'So what, if the pig is hungry it can plunder your garden after it's eaten everything else.' The two women came to blows and Karupiri cut Foti's head with a bushknife. The case was dismissed by the village court; perhaps it was considered payback for the previous infraction. Though the magistrates said that Karupiri should compensate Foti, no amount was set and Karupiri did not give anything. Foti finished by claiming, once more, that the two of them never fought.

While Liame and Rosa were fighting, a young woman with a swollen eye and cheek and a baby at the breast came up to listen and join in the laughter. Terry (an in-married woman) told me she was Lalo's sister, married to a man from Kalu who regularly beat her. 'It's another man with two wives. This one's his first.'

Negotiating Marriage and Marital Life

The minimal narratives in this chapter have shown how at all levels the marriage process is negotiated, whatever rehearsed talk may be used. The negotiations include the strategies I discuss in chapter 6: elicitation and rehearsing talk through a process of making explicit. The cases of Loma and Ragunanu most clearly exemplify the gaps between ideal accounts and practice. In the case of the murdered ex-wife we see that men are divided in their comments, some seeing divorce initiated by a woman as compromising their manhood and others regretting the wasteful loss of nubile women. Poreale conforms with the 'rules' when she accepts Yadi's interpretation of her brideprice transactions, but she was not committed to the marriage and liked the idea of her 'brother' caring enough to fetch her back. Yasi protests too much in complaining of his wife, preempting criticism and covering his back. The village court magistrates give Wola rehearsed talk, but only because Karupiri had objected to his advances.

The ethnography also showed how brideprice rights can be acquired and negotiated. Brideprice itself is a negotiation; it is not a foregone conclusion, what will be given or received and by whom. Rusa, though a conservative who champions 'rehearsed talk', still recognizes breaches of law (as custom) caused by concupiscence. From an economistic perspective, Rimbu's explanation of brideprice in terms of a falling rate of profit is clearly a pragmatic strategy that must fight it out with other strategies by other actors, all rehearsing their part. Koai's attempt to define marriage exchange with a non-Kewa prospective husband in times of change represents a real struggle for the control of social practice. Notice how he himself begins to use his daughter's name in a letter to the distant suitor, a practice which he condemns in the very same letter. New practices cannot entirely be kept at bay, so best is to try to keep oneself in the frame, to effect/maintain some influence on the main picture. Koai is conceding something here, indicating his willingness to negotiate while laying down the law. He provides an excellent instance of eliciting and rehearsing talk.

Mixed messages surround the practice of polygyny. While it is a sign and symbol of men's prestige, women have widely-acknowledged rights and de facto powers to veto their husbands' remarriages. The term 'rights' in this connection is a problematic one, because it evokes a Western legal term with which it has nothing in common. While the word is my gloss on the actions of women when they contest polygynous marriages, the ethnography also reveals that in practice women have such a veto, and, moreover, that their concerns in exercising it are generally viewed as reasonable. Yet the cases examined here have also shown that women must fight tooth-and-nail for such 'rights'.

The category of 'rights' is thus ambiguous when interests clash. As Terry's comment attests, women believe that wife-beating is more common in polygynous households. But there is no 'rehearsed talk' that accounts for this perceived reality. Unlike other world traditions, Kewa norms do not specify or even suggest conditions that may require the chastisement of women. Specific accounts of women exercising the right of veto suggest that though women accept there may be adequate reasons for husbands to take second wives, these reasons never apply in their own case. In three out of the five cases discussed, the marriages which wives opposed came off, though one of them was short-lived. Women have good reason, then, to consider it a very real possibility that their husbands are negotiating marriages. Thus men's and women's perceptions of men's desire to marry, and their ability to find brideprice, clearly diverge. This is a disagreement about social reality, or else an attempt by men to hoodwink women. In either case it is not a reality which men seek to make explicit. As court cases have shown, magistrates do not necessarily support men in their attempts to divorce their wives and remarry, nor do their decisions express any accepted law. The full account of Rarapalu's story (in Josephides 1998a) shows that the more the village court magistrates tried to fob Rarapalu off with 'new laws', the more their statements sounded like claims trying to establish their social reality.

From the other end of the spectrum, the five cases also illustrated that whatever men's claim about polygyny being an accepted cultural practice ('rehearsed talk'), a right to it is not automatic but must be negotiated with other interests. The example of Liame, unchastened by the village court, vividly brings into relative equilibrium the institutional discourse of the court and her own counterclaims. Rimbu's attempts to send Lari away also show up the court as an institution which is open to rehearsed/rehearsing talk, being used by people as a battleground. What Rimbu really wanted was to force Lari to change her ways and accept his point of view, not have her sent away.

Love and All That

The courting songs provide the best entry into the discussion of the construction of self and other in cross-sex relations.[2] They express, in a formulaic way, what each sex considers marriage to be, and show how each constructs the other as a desirable sexual partner. Both sexes use metaphors of nature, but while men's *rome* verses stress the inevitability of marriage following arousal, women's songs have more social and political content. At the outset, though, both men and women stress that *they were desired*: quite apart from any rules and structures and custom and rehearsed talk, in *their* case their partner desired them personally. This is why Rimbu's ('a woman's a woman') attempts to broker a marriage between Ragunanu and Loma's dumped husband fail and Biru's steadfastness wins – this is love, beyond mere desire or attraction, social or economic ambition. In a similar way as in the courting songs, Lari, in her account of how Rimbu came to marry a second wife, constructs him as a particular kind of man and herself as a serious person and responsible wife. By contextualizing her actions within a state of affairs which showed Rimbu's behaviour as less than exemplary, she saved both their faces: her own, as a good wife who will not allow her husband to make a fool of himself, and Rimbu's, by offering him a way out. Lari's eliciting strategy was complex. By constructing Rimbu as a man worthy of respect, she challenged him to break off the relationship. But by showing him what a responsible man would do in such circumstances, she forced him to behave like one; that is, marry the girl (see Josephides 2001). Lari was eliciting the first response, but there was no 'rehearsed talk' that would have assured either outcome.

Liame's strategies appear to be diametrically opposed to Lari's, though the end-aim is the same. Liame is always locked in power struggles, aggressively determined to prove her worthy personhood. While transcribing the text of the fight over the marita, I added in parenthesis following the word 'marita' that it was a fruit eaten only by men. Suddenly it hit me: marita is the male food par excellence while sweet potato stands for women, especially wives. If I had said that Liame and Kiru each attacked the food that symbolized the gender of the other, how would this illuminate the incident? Kiru was cooking something Liame could not eat, after promising to cook sweet potato; this was sufficient reason to throw out his marita and fly at him. But why did Kiru do it? Although marita is a male food it is not a hunger appeaser, in fact it 'puts your belly on fire' and makes you sweat. Men eating marita look like they are going through a necessary but uncomfortable ritual, or as if they are taking prescribed medication. They force big dollops of it down their throats, often needing to get up, walk around and sweat it out before repeating the ordeal. Sweet potato, on the other hand, is a staple as well as a symbol. If Kiru had not given cooking precedence to the marita over the sweet potato, this may have been taken as a statement about his priorities, even about how he defined his own gender. So perhaps they were consciously fighting with gender symbols. Or maybe they were just being bloody-minded.

Liame's interactions were often agonistic. Several conclusions may be drawn from the fight following which she gave her husband and the court the finger. The most general message is that one true version of events cannot be pursued, because social actors see the meaning of their actions differently, depending on positionality (the extent to which they see themselves as injured and thus responding), intentionality (whether they meant to offend) and outcome. Or it can be inferred that women suffer no false consciousness, in the sense of convincing themselves of the 'truth' of men's constructions of the state of affairs. They stick to their guns, insisting on their own stories and perceptions of events. Or again, it can suggest that the social effectiveness of men's power, as it is made visible through institutions and institutional decisions, may be shown to be a sham. A male court found against Liame, she was fined and upbraided; but she does not pay the fine and remains unchastened and unrepentant. No really powerful sanction has been applied and she continues her life as before. What then is the power of these institutions that anthropologists study so fervently? The court emerges here as an institution people use as a battleground, to further their own claims and desires.

Within polygynous households, conflicts and open fights could usually be seen as struggles for recognition of one's value. All Rarapalu's actions and strategies were pleas to be acknowledged in this way. Though her grievances concerned unfair treatment, it emerged that she viewed as preferential treatment anything that Waliya did for his other wife. Her reactions can thus be read as an objection to polygyny itself. It would not be an exaggeration to argue that a wife always experienced her husband's remarriage as a repudiation of herself. The acid test for this conclusion is found in the reasons women give for polygyny. What these reasons are is not as important as the fact that the speaker never thinks they apply in her own case.

Germane to this point is how women fight for their reputation, always swooping down on words and actions that tarnish it. It impugns women's personhood when men tell them they cannot fight on a certain ground because they do not own it. Women care nothing for ownership in this sense, but they insist they can fight there. On the one hand, they try to score against each other, pitting their worth, value and reputation, and ability to draw support. On the other, there are glimpses of female solidarity or empathy, as in Terry's tone when she tells me about the battered wife in a polygynous marriage: '[Her husband's] another man with two wives. This one's his first.' Terry expects me to understand her emotional meaning, expressed in the sparsest words, a minimal narrative. Nor is the anthropologist immune from an over-sensitive concern with her reputation. Lari's covert criticism, which compromised my own personhood by implicitly questioning my liberality, needed my active collusion: it was my interpretation that sniffed out the slight in Lari's words as a wisp of disappointment at my failure to leave money on my departure.

This chapter has shown portraits that enact the distinction between rehearsed and rehearsing talk, by revealing that the idioms of rehearsed talk (and the rhetoric that informs court judgements), cannot be taken as sufficient descriptions of social reality. By retaining the specificity of individual experiences, actions and responses, I wanted to avoid giving a generalizing picture, showing instead people in their individuality as agents of their actions, undertaken in order to attain certain results. These actions are not necessarily subversive or rebellious; to argue that they are would suggest a prior, accepted cultural practice from which they deviated, while my intention is to allow them to construct cultural practice, as in my perception they did. Nor was the eventual outcome of any event entirely predetermined. While people live their lives as individuals, we write about them as responding to norms (or rebelling against them); but they do not necessarily see their actions as so determined. They use those norms to their advantage, rather than see themselves as imprisoned by them. They always fight for their own definitions of themselves, which place them as moral and social agents at the centre of their universe. In this endeavour they do not need to deny centrality to anyone else; and for this reason specific outcomes may well frustrate individual agents' aims, and look like the products of imprisoning forces. To unpack this (possibly too condensed) sentence: in my own accounts and interpretations I place myself at the centre of the moral universe; but in practice I must negotiate those interpretations with others, whose competing centrality I acknowledge in the act of negotiation. Because the outcome of this negotiation is likely to be different from my original intention, it may look like my ability to act was severely restricted by social or cultural forces ('imprisoning forces'). However, the limitations on the outcome of my actions, and thus my modified strategies, can equally be traced to the countervailing actions of others rather than the presence of restrictive rules. The strategies of elicitation and rehearsing talk mediate such interactions.[3]

Notes

1. All songs are taken from Josephides 1982, where the complete verses can be found with the original Kewa text and line breaks. For fuller discussion of current courting practices see Josephides (1999 and 2005a).
2. See Marilyn Strathern's *The Gender of the Gift* (1988) for a seminal analysis of the construction of other in cross-sex relations.
3. I omit discussion of how minimal narratives organize consciousness and experience, and how they act as forms of communication with moral implications, as previous chapters contained such analyses.

Chapter 8

The Politics of Death

Early on in my fieldwork, when I first witnessed death ceremonies, I noted the tendency for smouldering troubles to be rekindled and become urgent on these occasions. In this chapter I describe events surrounding the deaths of three people: a middle-aged man (Rake) who had been a Councillor and politically influential; an old man (Wapa) who had been a great warrior; and his wife (Payanu), who followed him thirteen years later. The three reports thus span the whole of my fieldwork period, and encapsulate three key questions of crucial interest to the Kewa. Rake's death gave rise to questionings of political organization and power at a time when postcolonial political changes were beginning to have local impact. Wapa's death chronicles reconceptualizations of kinship and social relationships as traditional ideas of rights in persons and duties to clans become challenged, and also shows the workings of a fledgling village court. Finally, at Payanu's death everybody is brought up short, forced to face the end of an old order and the need to position themselves within a new one.

Who's the Big Man of Us All? Rake's Death

On an August night in 1979, a few months after I had started fieldwork, Yadi brought news of Rake's death. He had discharged himself from hospital in Kagua while suffering from dysentery, and gone on a beer binge. Early the following morning many of us from Yakopaita trouped off to Aliwi to mourn the big man (Fig. 2 traces the walk to Aliwi). Rake was completely dead, we were told; only his 'lewa' remained (*pu*, heart, is always translated as Tok Pisin '*lewa*', liver). A woman or a child would have died by now, but a big man's heart is strong and will not leave his body so easily. Rake was still breathing fitfully when we arrived in Aliwi.

He had been laid out in front of the men's house and was surrounded by fifty or so keening women with faces and bodies smeared with white clay, waiving their outstretched arms as they wailed. From time to time a man would get carried away, leap over the women and wail over Rake while bobbing up and down. But mostly the men kept away in the men's house or at some distance from the circle of chief mourners. Suddenly, Warea Rambe of Roga village appeared, took Rake's hand in his and began to talk to him with breathless urgency, sobbing all the while, for a full twenty minutes. His tears, mixed with mucus and clay, ran onto the ailing man's face. Rake seemed to be listening intently, looking up at the mourner with wide-eyed surprise, while a woman constantly wiped his face.

Then a wailing of a different magnitude broke out. Newcomers had arrived from Katiloma, bringing boards for the coffin and lengths of colourful cloth. One of them, in a cowboy hat, tore away and ran up to Rake, screaming *'Na ame! Na ame'* (my brother! my brother!). He continued to wail, bobbing up and down vigorously, until the men standing around Rake started chanting: *'Komada pime! Komada pime!'* ('a man has died and we are having a wake.') All at once the chanting reached a heart-wrenching crescendo, and Waliya whispered, 'That's it now, he is dead.' I rushed up there with the others and saw some men lift Rake into a sitting position. But he was supporting himself on one arm, and when he was laid down again on colourful rags I noticed that he was still breathing. He was carried into the men's house, washed and changed, then brought out again into the *tapada polo* (men's house porch). Men were chief mourners here.

Throughout these proceedings men and women sang their own dirges (*temali*, 'cry-sing') for Rake. In typical fashion, men highlighted his political importance, especially with reference to his land, while women used the idiom of physical attractiveness. I recorded some examples of these *temali*.[1]

Men's *temali*:
Our big man has died but
will he come back again
or is he tricking us.

My brother Rake of Loi [name of his land]
I cannot take his teeth
but why can't I?

Women's *temali*:
Our handsome brother,
his nose sloping elegantly like a bird's hook
Is he sleeping with the spirits
or will he get up again?

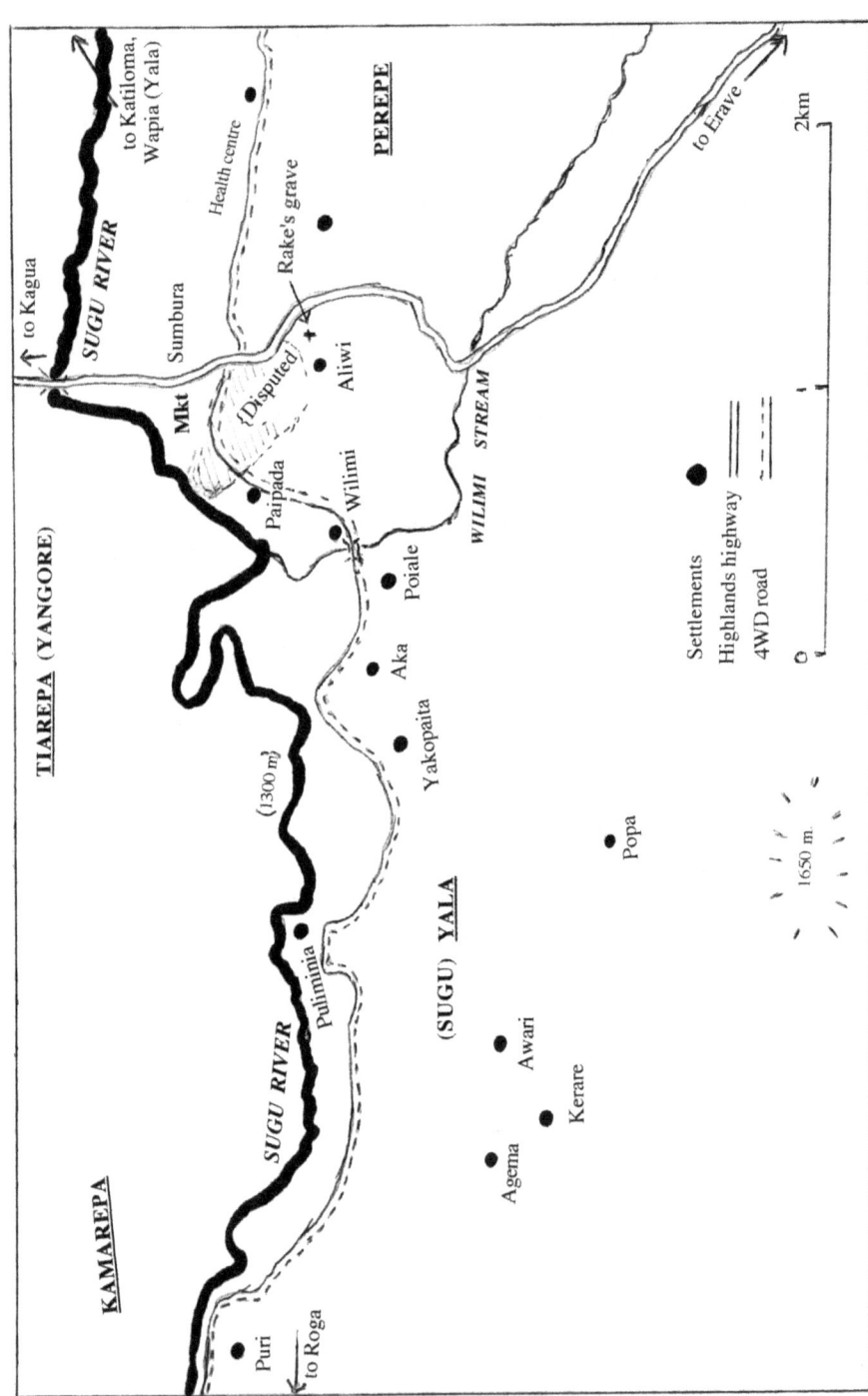

Figure 8.1. Rake's Grave and the Walk to Aliwi

Mourners bearing gifts of food had arrived from Erave, and Yadi the driver was busy ferrying more from Katiloma. He would bring another load from Mt Hagen the following day. Rake's brothers levied a 'tax' of K2 on each mourner, to be used (depending on whom I asked) to settle Rake's debts, or towards the funeral feast.

Next morning the cry went up that Rake had died in the night. When I arrived at Aliwi the atmosphere was tense as several men jumped over the fence by the men's house and ran into the bush. 'There will be trouble,' Lari foresaw; 'They have hidden the body away.' By a tragic coincidence Rake's little son had also died in the night. Then, from the opposite side of the men's house, several men carried the body behind the longhouse and set it down there, guarding it silently and grim-faced. Rimbu kept me in the picture: 'When everybody has come, they'll carry out the test to find out who's responsible for the death, and then there'll be trouble.' The food contributions were now collected, Rake's body was brought from its hiding place and put in the men's house, and Rake's older brother Wola distributed food to all those present (the Tiarepa of Kuare, the Tiarepa of Mamburi, the Koiari, Kamarepa, Erave and Katiloma Perepe, and the Yala). Rake's wife Mulunu was also said to be dying, in a hospital in Kagua, but his other wife Karupiri was by his side.

When we returned to Aliwi at about six in the afternoon, Rake's body had been taken away again. I was led to a little clearing in the bush behind the men's house, where the body was trussed on a tree-trunk like a pig ready for spit-roasting, with each end of the trunk resting on a forked pole planted in the ground. A man from Rake's mother's clan placed the flat end of a spear on Rake's breast, while he whispered the names of various clans. This was the *pulu* test: if blood appeared, the person responsible for the death would be found in the clan whose name was being whispered. No speck of blood appeared, so the body was taken down and returned to the wailing women in the men's house. Rimbu told me that another form of divination would be performed in the night. Rake's body will be carried over all the settlements, and whenever blood appeared on the body, they would know that the owner of the nearest house was the culprit.[2] As on other occasions, I noticed how sheepishly people talk of these customs and beliefs.

The following day we were on our way to Aliwi with our contribution to the funeral feast, when some Yala people from Aka advised us to turn back. The Perepe (Rake's clan) intended to kill us, they said. After some heated discussion we went on, while the Aka residents remained behind. The general feeling was that the dispute was between the Tiarepa Yala and Rake's clan, and did not involve the Umba-Paripa sub-clan from Yakopaita. Our men were carrying firewood and a hand of bananas, and Lari carried the rice and tinned fish. At Sumbura there was more discussion, but we continued on our way. In all our walks to and from Aliwi we were like characters in search of an author or a script. When we came to the Aliwi turn-off we first let another clan through, then our men followed and I led the women in. We put down our offerings outside the men's house. A lean-to on the left was designated ours; the women settled there while Rimbu went to cry over the body, then sat with the Perepe contingent in the centre of the settlement. The body had been hidden again.

At noon a long procession of men came bearing the body, and carried it inside the men's house. Some of the men began to make speeches. Pepena, a Perepe big man from Katiloma, opened the debate with the observation that since Rake had died on this land, the Yala would be prohibited from building on it. Then Rake's older brother Wola spoke. He didn't know, he said, who had told the Yala that harm would come to them in Aliwi. Yesterday they came but today they stayed away. Tomorrow, he said, they would bring the Yala to Aliwi and together they would bury the big man. There was an unspoken consensus on this occasion that the Umba lineage was more Perepe than Yala – Wapa's mother had been a Perepe, and his and Rake's lineages maintained close links. The Tiarepa Yala (Mapi's lineage), on the other hand, shared a name with the Tiarepa clan to the north of Yala territory (see Fig. 2 and Josephides 1985: 19–27 for a fuller discussion of clan genealogies). Clan genealogies, always fragile and full of discontinuities, unravel here: are the Yala, the Tiarepa and the Perepe different clans, and how are the overlaps to be accounted for? Can loyalties be assured?

The Tiarepa Yala responded with this message the following day: 'We saw your axes and your faces; we fear for our skins and stay home. We had a dispute with the dead man. We didn't kill him with sorcery, but there were hard words over land and now we are afraid. If the man died as a result, we will give compensation. Send us word and we shall bring two or three pearlshells to straighten this matter out.' Wola replied: 'I cannot accept your pearlshells as payment for the death of this man, who was the leader of us all. We will bury him without your presence and without compensation.' His rejection of compensation was phrased as a rejection of the reality such a compensation would create – a diminution of Rake's sphere of influence. Wola's tone and words were more moderate than those of other big men and office holders present, and he earned praise for his food distribution.

Three questions were on the agenda the following day: when and where Rake should be buried, and who should replace him as Councillor. Genoka, to the west beyond Aliwi, was picked as a suitable burial-place. It was the site of Pipi, the ancestor-tree of the Yala and Perepe.[3] On the subject of Rake's replacement, the prevailing opinion was that since the Yala, Tiarepa and Kamarepa each had their own magistrate, Rake's magistracy should remain in Rake's lineage.

To Wola's dismay, the Tiarepa Yala, hearing that the Perepe still carried axes, stayed away the following day. The coffin was made, the grave was dug, and Rake's little son was put in first without any fuss. Then Rake was brought and the wailing followed him until the pastor called for silence. He read from a Tok Pisin Bible and then spoke in Kewa. The coffin was lowered into a grave that was barely four-feet deep; kunai grass was followed by strips of foam mattress, tree bark and many planks, before the earth was shovelled in. The grave was decorated with roofing iron and guttering and finished off with a cross bearing the inscription: 'Council Rake. Em indai 10 Ogas 1979.' ('Councillor Rake. He died on 10 August 1979.'). In the old days they would have laid the body on a bed of kunai grass and banana leaves, said Magistrate Malepo, and later retrieved the skull to exhibit in the men's house.

The dispute between the Perepe and the Yala came to a head after Rake's funeral. As Wola put it, 'This dispute started over the land in which you Yala wanted to build. You said to this man, "You die." Five times you said this. I sent word to you to come so that we could bury the man, but you stayed away. For one month we shall sit inside our houses, mourning the death, but in the second month we will go to the village office and hold talks to settle this matter. If the talks do not go well, we shall leave off talking. Only two days you came and sat with us, then you got scared and ran away. Why did you run away? This big man belongs to us all.'

A hearing was held ten days after the funeral. The magistrates asked Mapi why he had not waited for the land dispute to be resolved, as Rake had asked, before building his store behind the cow fence. Mapi laughed and said that a stinking pig had come floating on the Sugu river; he smelled it and was happy. On hearing this, Rake's kinsmen retrieved the weapons they had hidden behind Rake's defunct store and chased Mapi and his kinsmen all the way to Aka. At Paipada they raised their axes as if to hack down the store on the disputed land, but they lowered them again and returned home. This was the signal for the Yala of Aka, Puliminia and Poiale to begin their mobilization. To Mapi's dismay, Rimbu asked the Umba of Yakopaita to stay out of the dispute. Why, he demanded to know as he stormed into Yakopaita, were his brothers not preparing to help when he was under attack? In response, Wapa flew out of his house, brandishing a spear at Mapi, but Rimbu checked him. Furious, Mapi warned Wapa he would take him to court. 'You are a better candidate for prosecution,' Wapa retorted. 'A magistrate who rouses people to battle!' He, Wapa, could fight better than any of them, but times had changed. Mapi, who had never been a warrior, had no business to egg his (Wapa's) children on to fight.

Just before first light the following day, Wapa threw out his voice in a clarion call: 'You Perepe men, where are you when we are being attacked? Where's your protection and assistance?' Within minutes Perepe warriors [Wapa's affines, as mentioned earlier] from the surrounding heights descended on Yakopaita, armed for combat. Alarmed, Rimbu thanked them and asked them to withdraw. Mapi and Ipa later played down the near-fight, complaining instead that Mapi was being blamed for his dream. In this dream Mapi had seen Rake's men's house surrounded by decorated men singing dirges, presaging the death of its owner. Mapi had made matters worse by saying to Rake: 'If this is not your land, you shall die.' While Ipa and Mapi argued that such challenges were common practice in attempts to determine ownership of land, Rake's kinsmen viewed the words as a powerful curse. Mapi, concerned that he would not get an unbiased hearing from the local village magistrates (Rusa of Puri, Malepo of Yago and Kalepea of Katiloma), dictated this letter to me:

> You three village magistrates have summoned Lope Gapea (Mapi's patronym), but he doesn't want to come. He wants the case to be heard by magistrates from Sumi, Kagua, Koali Lombo and Ita, because you Sumbura magistrates stood by while men took up axes and almost killed me and my kinsmen. They damaged our house with the corrugated iron roof, threatened to pull down our other houses and chased after us. We didn't see you stopping their spears. Now I want faraway magistrates to hear our case. Malepo, you must send for all these court chairmen. I will come only if they are sitting, and the police are also present.

Rimbu took his own precautions, dictating a letter to the magistrates clearing him of any complicity in accusations levelled at Mapi. Biru, the agricultural extension officer, gave this account of the court hearing. Wola addressed Mapi: 'We are not saying you gave the man poison, but you marked the day on which he was to die, in two ways. You said in words to him that he would die now, and you saw it in a dream. You dreamt in the night, then came and spoke of this in a public place in the presence of everyone. You may say you are just a dreamer, it is not your responsibility and you did not make it happen.' Mapi, however, wanted the land question settled first. This angered Wola: 'The land is ours, there is nothing to discuss. In days long past your people were chased by the enemy and took refuge with us. We welcomed you and gave you land to garden. Can you deny this?'

The discussion sought to define the main issue of the dispute. Roga was present but silent; Mapi was the only one of his lineage to speak. The distant village magistrates were not presiding as Mapi had requested.

Some time afterwards, the Tiarepa Yala made a compensation payment to the Perepe. Mapi's lineage displayed K214 on ceremonial bamboo poles, first planted outside the Aka longhouse and then taken to the court area, on both occasions accompanied by debates and speeches. By four in the afternoon all talk was exhausted, and the bamboo poles were handed over to Wola under the watchful eye of police officers. Of the Umba lineage, Waliya had contributed K4 and Hapkas K6. Mapi stressed that the payment was to 'straighten the talk', make talking easier, and did not constitute admission of responsibility for Rake's death. However, the land question was settled and Ipa was given permission to go ahead with building his trade store.

Duties to Persons, Rights in Persons: Wapa's Death

In 1980 Wapa had been sick on and off for some time. Various reasons were considered as contributing to his ill-health, primarily disagreements with his daughter-in-law over childcare and frustrated attempts to get a second wife for his son, and resentment that his sons were slow in building him a new house. Once or twice he withdrew to the home of his youth, lofty and stony Agema, but was lured down again by a feast in his honour. In late November he took a turn for the worse. Visitors from neighbouring settlements crowded into our hamlet, all trying their best to elicit from him the cause of his affliction. One suggestion was of *nembu* witchcraft, which causes diarrhoea or dysentery. As a warrior Wapa had killed many men and made several enemies likely to want to poison him (that is, kill him with witchcraft or sorcery). In the past Wapa could take ginger with tree-bark, but this antidote could not be administered since his conversion to Catholicism. If it had been *romo* witchcraft he could have received medical treatment, but against *nembu* nothing could be done.

In early evening, *temali* singing filled the settlement. Liame in particular exerted herself, while Payanu (Wapa's wife) kept up an accompaniment of low cawing. Rika was sent for, a clan brother of Wapa's from Wapia, where Wapa had spent his adolescence. As guardians of his youth, the Wapia Yala had to be propitiated for his illness. Several *kalu sekere*, 'head pearlshells' with names and known histories, were gathered together for Wapa to distribute to Rika and members of his own matrikin (the Perepe clan) who had given him food in the past. Following more *temali* singing, we prepared to drive Wapa to the hospital in Kagua, accompanied by Hapkas and Waliya. In a swift change of mood, the chief mourners moved away and began to joke and laugh. The journey promised to be eventful, as Waliya was notoriously prone to car sickness. The potholes at Wilimi bridge sent us into such a jolt that Wapa started up, calling out for his father: '*Apaya! Apaya!*' We had to stop the car three times for Waliya to be sick on the road, while Wapa stared uncomprehendingly. At the hospital Wapa was put on a drip and Father Apea gave him extreme unction. The orderly diagnosed malaria, pneumonia and dysentery, but assured us he would recover. We returned home, leaving Waliya with Wapa.

In spite of the reassurances, Wapa died in the night. Councillor Kengeai's truck (he had succeeded Rake) brought Wapa's body home the next morning. Before his arrival, mourning noises slowly arose from the village until it vibrated with grief. As the news of the death spread, the whole area came alive with low lamentations. But when the truck bearing the body came in sight the threnodies turned into screeching. Everybody started arriving then: from settlements near and far, from plantations where the truck that brought the body home took the news that filled it up with returning kinspeople. The threnodies continued unbroken throughout the night. I recorded Wata's song:

> I am a daughter of Ragetaperosi
> From foreign parts speaking foreign tongues
> I made my way,
> Like a spider I wove my way
> down Ialibu and came.
> But shame followed me,
> and I went again.
>
> From my father-in-law's place at Yamore
> Where he fed me like a cassowary
> from the breast under his arm
> I followed him and came.

Rimbu was to remember this months later, and pull Wata, his brother Komalo's would-be bride, back into the settlement when, tearfully, she was induced to leave (see chapter 1). But now Rimbu asked me for a Coleman lamp, to light the wake in the longhouse. The others wanted to send to the mission for one, but Rimbu said why do that when the sister here has two?

The coffin was made the following morning, as women continued their wailing in the longhouse and Wapa's body had been removed and hidden. About four hundred people came, bearing gifts of food: sweet potatoes, bananas, taro, yams, sugar cane, corn, pitpit, tinned fish and rice. One man from Kambia proffered a pig, with the words 'I finish your dead' (*kome regato*). The pig was to be killed when the period of mourning (*komada*) was over, and distributed to all those who had contributed food. While Rimbu, Hapkas and others were sorting out the food offerings into piles, Mapi held forth on the causes of Wapa's death.

> We don't know about sorcery here. If we have enemies who kill us, we have no counter-sorcery to avenge ourselves.[4] Gapea, Rombala and Rekari, all these traditional men are dead, and only we are alive, who have no knowledge of these things. But there was an unsolicited sign (*pareo pia*) when a cricket (*maita*) and two kinds of grasshopper (*ayakera* and *wake*) appeared on Wapa's body. This was a clear sign that his mother's lineage (*amara*), the Maita-Perepe, were responsible. But I will not point a finger at you, or take you to court. The man's sons (Rimbu, Komalo and Hapkas) would like to take you to court, but they won't. It's their decision, I can't put pressure on them. I just wanted you to know about it.

Mapi went on to recount an idiosyncratic version of the old testament, starting from the creation and Noah's flood and ending with the ethnographer's arrival (see Josephides 1982: 12–13). He concluded with an extended version of the Lord's prayer, advising individually named clans to settle their differences and come together in God. But his efforts did not avert a fight with wide ramifications. This is how it came about.

While Mapi was talking, food distributions were in progress. Rimbu took a hand of bananas brought by Peawali, Kiru's father-in-law (a Perepe man), and put it on the pile prepared for the Wapia Yala, the companions of Wapa's youth. It will be remembered from the narratives in chapter 3 that when the Yala were chased off their land in the big war, Wapa's lineage fled to Wapia, where they remained for many years. In the rest of this chapter I will use 'Wapia' for the Wapia Yala and 'Agema' for the local Yala. The local lineage divisions are not relevant at this death, as they were at Rake's death and will be again at Payanu's.

Sipi, Agema Pisa's son, sharpened a piece of bamboo and put it on top of the bananas on the Wapia Yala pile. Bamboo knives traditionally carried messages of pig carving, so the Wapia interpreted this gesture as a promise that they would be given Wapa's big boar. Nothing was further from the Agema Yala's intentions. The fight flared up in seconds, gaining momentum when the Wapia seized Wapa's body and vowed to bury him in Wapia. In the ensuing scuffle the Agema Yala recaptured the body, the Wapia demanded some other token as compensation for Wapa's sojourn with them, and the Agema reminded them that Wapa had already given them a head pearlshell just before his death. A kinsman who was Provincial Village Court Officer in Mendi told me off the record that he thought the Wapia had a just claim, but he was careful to leave before fighting broke out.

Within minutes, axes were being brandished and sticks waved about. Some women picked up long pieces of firewood and swished them menacingly. Yasi attempted to keep the peace in the customary way, by stepping between two warring parties and throwing out his arms, but in the process he knocked out Wapia Pusa's teeth. Pusa was then also hit by an axe. Like Yasi, Waliya placed himself between two fighting men, and when they shoved him aside he froze on the spot, adopting the traditional mourning posture of pulling his hair while wailing loudly. Papola's wife Rorepame followed suit, and the fighting abated. Though it started up again at the men's house end, it was a spent force, less a matter of shoving and more of shouting. The pastor saw his chance to start a service.

Eventually the Wapia Yala accepted a head pearlshell as compensation for Pusa's teeth and withdrew, after being promised a share of the pig to be killed. Rimbu had kept a low profile during the fighting. Covered again in mud rather than white clay, he came to assure us that what we had witnessed was not a real fight. There had been no anger or disagreement (*rono*), only sorrow (*yara*). There can be no *rono* among brothers.

Wapa was buried at ten o'clock the following morning. The catechist conducted a ceremony, administered communion and sprinkled holy water, but the burial itself was sparsely attended and not conducted in a particularly sombre manner. People joked and laughed as they dug the grave. Rimbu alone appeared still overcome with grief. He stayed behind in the settlement during the actual interment, as he was to do thirteen years later when his mother was buried.

Then the Wapia returned, besmirched with dirt and loud with threats of court action. Pusa, seemingly happy with his pearlshell the day before, had been worked on by his sons and now demanded his legal rights to compensation, backed by the threat to resort to arms. They brought along their local policeman, a beefy man with handcuffs in his belt and an old-fashioned woman's handbag in his hand. Yesterday's pearlshell was rubbed with mud and scornfully returned. Tempers flared. Michael told the Wapia to scram or prepare to fight, his father Pupula said they should be allowed to stay and mourn, while Pisa, the Agema Yala elder, challenged their claims. 'It wasn't you who invited us back to Agema or helped us build our settlements there; it was the Kamarepa. [This historical event is assigned even more significance at Payanu's funeral, where it becomes the fulcrum of political friction among local Yala clans.] The Wapia appear only when there is something to be gained.' The Wapia retorted that they often came to see Wapa but could never find him: 'In Agema they told us he was in Popa, in Popa they told us he was in Modopu, in Modopu they told us he was in Naguri, in Naguri they told us he was in Papolata. You didn't let the man settle down in one place. He didn't have a good life with you.' The Wapia left in high dudgeon. Only Rika, Wapa's boyhood companion, shook hands, but even he was subdued and visibly disappointed, hurrying off with an angry gesture when they tried to hold him back with cries of 'brother!' Pupula and Lu (the same who had shared Rimbu's adventures in Port Moresby) bemoaned the disunity of the Yala clans, but Pisa was angry at the Wapia for manhandling the body and called for the return of the pearlshell Wapa had given them.

Yodelling was often heard across the settlement during periods of mourning, announcing that smoke was sighted. In the wake of a death, especially of a big man, it was considered an affront to the bereaved to hold feasts or burn grass in preparation for new gardens. Threats of court action were made when enemies openly rejoiced at the death of a big man, and men went about armed in readiness for war.

Nine pigs were killed for Wapa nine days after his death. The catechist and the pastor both counselled rejection of the pig from the Kambia man, as representing a tradition at odds with Christian ethic. The prestation was called *ali abulo*, 'buying man', and called for a return far in excess of the original gift, which the missions considered inappropriate and disruptive to business. To be large enough to honour Wapa's memory, the return would eat into the cash on hand and reduce the number of pigs available to kill for Wapa's memorial feast. People juggle the different ways in which prestige can be gained, and temper their actions with considerations of what is affordable in economic terms. There is no hard and fast rule obliging acceptance of a gift, in whatever form it is made. To sidestep the problem, the gift from the Kambia man was creatively reclassified as *roporopo*, 'immediate exchange': Roga simply 'bought' it with two smaller ones plus K60. (In similar strategies, people find ways to bypass the interdictions of their new religion when receiving brideprice.) Marc and I also killed a pig, purchased expressly for the occasion.

Following the pig kill, Rimbu went up to Popa to light a fire in Wapa's old house. He would now perform this service regularly. Just before he died, Wapa had told him he had hidden ten pearlshells in the bush. But who is to find them, Rimbu lamented. I let my imagination roam over this. What sort of metaphor was Rimbu employing? And had Wapa been referring to pigs, or to what his sons might achieve?

The dispute with the Wapia Yala was heard two months later in the village court presided by five magistrates, two of them from the Perepe clan. Damages of K600 were awarded to the Wapia. Pusa brought a doctor's certificate, which did not mention his teeth but only his shoulder, said to have had 'meat pushed into the bone'. There was little probing into the causes of the fight. The medical certificate provided evidence for the injuries sustained and it was now a question of putting a price on them. Pusa testified that the sharpened bamboo led the Wapia to believe they would receive a pig, and they snatched Wapa's body only because they were disappointed. He accused Wasa of hurting his shoulder and Pima of breaking his teeth. Here is a sample of the hearing:

Pima: 'I didn't break your teeth. If I *had* punched you, your jaw would have been broken, not just your teeth. I wanted to beat you because you cut my forearm with your axe.'

Rusa (chairman of village court): 'That was your own fault. You put your arm in the way of Pusa's axe, then you held Pusa down while some boys beat him. Why did you do this?'

Pima: 'If he had been alive and they came and took him it would have been different. But they were pulling a dead body.'

Wasa: 'I saw Pima's hand and thought Pusa had cut him, so I got my axe and hit Pusa with the back of it.'

Yasi: 'It wasn't Pima who broke Pusa's teeth. The old man was bigmouthing and swinging his axe, so I put my hand over his mouth to stop his talking. But he bit my finger, and I pulled it back sharply. That's how his teeth came loose.'

Rusa looked in his law book and announced that the penalty for breaking teeth was K200 per tooth, but as no teeth were actually broken there was no case to answer on this count. Three village magistrates thought the Agema should pay K1,000 damages. Rusa, as chairman of the court, took into account Pusa's reprehensible behaviour and cut the figure to K600: K400 from Wasa, who had used an axe, and K100 each from Pima and Yasi, who used bare hands.

In private, Rusa explained to me that awarding damages (rather a court fine) meant that a term of imprisonment could not serve in lieu of payment. A defaulter could still be imprisoned, but after serving a term (calculated at the rate of one week per K10 owed), she or he will be let out for one week. If still unable to pay, another term of imprisonment of the same duration will be followed by another week's grace, and so on. Only after six such terms of imprisonment may payment be waived. Rusa always endeavoured to settle disputes before they reached a critical stage. If there had been no settlement in this case, the Wapia would bear a grudge, and whenever Pusa died and of whatever cause, they would hold the Agema responsible and demand compensation for 'the whole man'. The option of taking the case to the district court in Kagua would serve little purpose; in his experience this court reversed village court decisions only in cases when the chairman had not been present when the case was heard, or when new evidence had come to light. In the unlikely event that it did throw the case out or cut the amount of damages, the Wapia would not be satisfied and might pursue compensation in more direct ways, whereas the village court tore up the doctor's letter once restoration was made and that was the end of the matter. If the Agema had not hurt Pusa but instead sued him for mishandling the body and generally causing havoc, damages would have been awarded in their favour. Injuries must always be compensated, whether inflicted deliberately, accidentally, or in self-defence.[5]

Rimbu had his own interpretation of the court proceedings. 'Yasi has drawn blood, so he has a case to answer, but in sentencing him Rusa was pursuing two further objectives. First, by bringing an Umba Yala into the proceedings he is ensuring that the Waluaparepa and Paripa lineages will not feel singled out for blame. Second, he is letting two possible cases for grievance cancel each other out. Yasi's offence of drawing Wapia blood is more than matched by the Wapia's in mishandling the body.' Rimbu further argued that three Aka men – Mapi, Sipi and Yembi – had encouraged the Wapia to press their claims to Wapa's pig. Mapi (I heard this myself) had held forth to the effect that 'we as Christian people should not value traditional things but allow the Wapia to carry off Wapa's pig'. Sipi had placed a sharpened bamboo knife on top of the bananas in full knowledge that his action would be understood as signifying the intention to give a pig.

The judgement was passed on two men, who will go to prison for ten and five months if damages are not paid within four weeks, but it was assumed that the whole community would help raise the payment. Collections started immediately, though the recent pig kill for Wapa plus a low coffee season meant that money was not flush. There was vague talk of taking the case to Kagua if the K600 could not be raised by the following Sunday. Rika (Roga's younger brother and an Agema Yala, not the Wapia companion of Wapa's youth), to whom we had given a lift as far as Mt Hagen, went on to Kudjip to see the doctor who was said to have written the letter about Pusa's injuries. This man denied having written such a letter and wrote three letters to this effect, also agreeing to serve as a witness if someone fetched him (that is, paid his fare and put him up). Armed with these letters, Rika thought that his second brief – to collect contributions from migrant labourers at Kudjip plantations – was now superfluous.

Back home, Rimbu had consulted Komeali, the Yala Provincial Court Officer who had been present at Wapa's funeral. Komeali pointed out that Law Book Three specified that for responsibility to be established the injury must be sustained immediately after the act said to have inflicted it, not a month later. Despite this information, collections were taken in the village until they totalled K512. The conversions into cash equivalents was as arbitrary as ever. Only K139 was in cash, the rest being in shells (valued at K323) and one pig (valued at K50). Though pigs are frequently bought and sold, shells (with the exception of very inferior ones) hardly ever are. If these conversion rates are accepted at face value, the Agema might be seen as offering almost the equivalent of the original amount awarded against them. But their achievement was of a different kind: they had taken control of the event by making it their own prestation. There was a delicate balance in their act. While they wanted to appear generous to Wapa's old associates, in honour of Wapa and to maintain their own reputations, they were also careful not to have their actions construed as admissions of neglect and ultimate responsibility for Wapa's death – especially as Wapa's grievance against his sons was well known.

The payment was handed over at Sumbura market, followed immediately by the Wapia redistribution. The people of Roga, Sumbura and Yago received shells, as did some Agema Yala. Yembi received the little pig, Ana and Mayanu a pearlshell each. The last three had remonstrated with the Agema hotheads, and they were now being acknowledged.

Out with the Old, in with the New: Payanu's Death

Payanu fell sick quite suddenly during our visit to the field in 1993. A bed was made for her in the middle of the settlement, and as she lay there her son Hapkas and her niece Ragunanu (the daughter of Roga, her husband's father's brother's son) washed her with soap, while Wapelenu (Ragunanu's mother and Roga's widow) crooned a *temali* over her. It was Payanu who had brought Wapelenu and Roga together, I was told. Rimbu asked Lari to fetch K10 from the store and give it to the old woman. 'If she dies, you can take it back,' he said. A few days earlier Payanu had complained to Hapkas about her share of his daughter's brideprice. 'I looked after Yamunu when she was young, always giving her food, and now you give me just K4.' 'You should give her K20,' Rimbu told Hapkas, but Hapkas preferred to put his energies into praying over her.

While I sat at Rimbu's new bakery (with an oven constructed from an oil drum) with Tama and two visitors from Erave, Rimbu was making a model of a *rimbu rungi*, a ceremonial pole. 'In the past during pig kills this *limbun* [areca palm] would be decorated with pearlshells and bones of marsupials and be planted in the middle of the open ground. Men would throw valuable things at it, such as pearlshells and little pigs, and everyone would fight over them. It was very competitive, but so senseless, a waste of time and a waste of valuables, just for fun.' Rimbu's deliberate irreverence was signalled by his use of the word *limbun*, stripping the *rungi* of its mystical meaning and reducing it to the tree from which it was made. I also learned for the first time about Rimbu's sister, who as a baby was thrown into a pit when Payanu heard that Wapa was chasing after other women. The child cried for a long time and Wapa heard her on his return. Tama chipped in that his own mother had done the very same thing with two babies. This was a revelation for me: Rimbu had had a sister who died and whose ghost I could be, as was always rumoured in the area.

Payanu's wake (*komada*) was attended by many people from the neighbouring Yala settlements of Pulimina, Aka, Poiale, Paipada and Wilimi Kusu. At eleven the next morning the wailing started in earnest, announcing the death. Ragunanu, Lari, Nali and Wapelenu were chief mourners. They dressed Payanu in a flowery dress (the one in which we had taken her picture a week earlier, all smiles), and Hapkas brought a black cloak. Only women sat around the body and wailed. Now and then a man came up, stood over Payanu and wailed aloud. Kiru, the dead woman's husband's brother's son, did this for almost half an hour, then his son Nadisua ran up and threw himself down, keening over her. Yamola (another grandson) was a little further off, crying with his face covered and each leg alternately rubbing the other. Rimbu was crying inside his trade store. Kiru then planted some shade branches, and Payanu was moved under them. The mourners shook out their hands over her, or tremblingly traced the shape of her body (or so it appeared) in the air just above her. They leaned right over her, their mingled tears and snot falling on her face. Nali had the strongest voice, in spite of interference from the toddler in her arms who grabbed her breasts, kicked her and pulled at her face. Karupiri pulled at the dead woman's hair and actually appeared to be delousing her. Some young women were not wailing; they didn't seem to know how it was done.

Then Kiru began to hold forth: 'All the old people are dying now, and only Pisa is left.' Rimbu, speaking for the first time, took up the topic, while some other men – Nagu, Pasaroli, Kuna – were busy making the coffin with planks that Hapkas had brought. There were no men in the circle of women, and no women at the hamlet end which encompassed Rimbu's bakery and our house. At around three in the afternoon a card-playing group was formed on the grass by the drum oven, including Kiru, Sipi, Kuna and Mandali. Next to them were the smokers; then came the coffin makers. Rimbu stayed aloof, sitting on the doorstep of his store-cum-bakery, with Tama and Hapkas sometimes around him. He beckoned to me. Did I have a blanket to cover our mother? I fetched the unused red one and gave it to the women, who proceeded to wrap Payanu like a mummy, then resumed their wailing. Rimbu said to me, she wasn't ill for a long time, she fell ill only on Friday and now she is dead. 'What kind of illness it is, we don't know.'

At four-thirty the coffin makers were hurried on: '*Eh! Yaai ipula,*' 'it's going to rain.' One end of the blanket was used to line the coffin and

Payanu, quite stiff by now, was fitted into it and covered with the other end. The women were in a frenzy, hardly allowing her to be covered. The men who were not occupied with easing her in or playing cards or chopping wood were sitting with their heads bowed. The women were still wailing at five-thirty, when Rimbu asked me to write a message to be broadcast on the radio for Wapanu, his eldest daughter married in a distant settlement, informing her of her grandmother's death. The coffin was taken into the kitchen, where Marc and I joined the mourners after supper. Prayers were being said now, followed by church singing. Kiru's wife Rosa and other married women had brought sweet potatoes which young girls cooked and now passed round. Greens and other vegetables were cooking in pots on top of the drum which was constantly stoked by little Lisette. Malupa read from a Tok Pisin Bible, translating into Kewa as he went along. Biru said his prayers in loud Tok Pisin for our benefit, especially as Marc was videoing the events. It was cosy in that large room with its drum in the centre, lethargically hot and with cockroaches ambling lazily on the walls. The pressure lamp hung over the coffin, partially lighting up the faces of the wailers. Some caught my eye and smiled. Liame was constantly smiling at me.

When prayers were over, Pastor Ore said we should go home. They would stay up all night talking, praying and singing, as was their custom, but we should not waste our time. He was also worried about rascals. Marc was reminded earlier to go and put the padlock on our door. Throughout the service, Ore opened the door and peeped out. 'We wouldn't want any rascals to come.'[6] Many people followed our lead and also left. At around nine o'clock I heard Kiru holding forth, while women softly sang their *temali*. Throughout the night there was talking mixed with laughter. To my question the next day, Kiru answered that they were discussing the large compensation payment after an accidental shooting. I pressed him about the laughing. 'Oh yes, we also talked about women.' The other men laughed sheepishly as he added, 'About marrying other women.' 'You didn't talk about this with the women present?' I asked. 'Oh no, they would get cross. But it's just talk, just for fun.'

At half past six the *temali* recommenced, continuing without break the whole morning. While the women stayed indoors with the body, the men lounged outside chatting, smoking and eating. Grave-digging started at half past nine, and soon after food prestations began to arrive. The pastor's clan (Kamarepa) came from Puri, bringing sweet potatoes, bananas, sugarcane, rice and tinned fish. Mapi's, Kumi's and Ipa's lineage brought firewood, taro, sugarcane, corn and greens. It was an impressive spectacle to see them winding their way into the settlement. The Yala from Puliminia arrived with whitened faces; Catholics were still allowed the traditional marks of mourning that Evangelical denominations had proscribed. When everyone had settled down Mapi began to speak, holding up a new pamphlet of the Tok Pisin Bible bought in Mt Hagen for K2. He started with a historical account of the Yala's first arrival here, the deeds of their agnatic lineage at the time of the Rimbu Robake spirit houses, their massive pig killing feasts and general achievements at Awari, their enjoyment of fighting and killing and sacking, their expulsion by an alliance of enemy clans, and their victorious return and expulsion of others. But now, Mapi ended dramatically, this 'ancestral' generation, with the sole exception of Pisa, lies dead.

Rimbu suddenly intervened. 'I treated my father well, he never had any grievances, and my mother was living comfortably when she died. In the last three years she didn't have to go to the garden, Lari gave her food. Brothers and sisters, you mustn't think that she died because she was treated badly. Her time had come. We are turning over this page, this generation is finished, only Pisa is left. We'll count the years until he dies. We don't know if we'll see our mother again, if the Bible is telling the truth or lying. If her devil will stink or her God will stink, we don't know [that is, if her spirit will rot like her body; this is an example of the words *remo*, satan and devil being used in more nuanced ways than before].' Rimbu then turned to Mapi: 'Whatever talk you have, you must bring it out into the open. You can leave out the heavy talk, this is a funeral.'

Then Pastor Ore spoke. 'You think that Payanu is dead and finished, but you are wrong. When we plant corn it grows, and so will Payanu. This isn't something I made up, or something my father told me. It's God's teaching, to be found in the Bible. The body will rot in the earth, but the spirit will ascend to heaven.' His assistant, Robert, reinforced this point: 'If Jesus rose from the dead, all the dead can rise up.' Taking the discussion in a different direction, Rimbu mused: 'They say it's Jesus' death that opened the way for everything. If Jesus hadn't died we wouldn't have been exposed to all these things – different colour skins, different kinds of food.' Mapi developed this train of thought further: 'Lisette and Marc are not natives of this place, yet Lisette knows our language. I'm so happy about this that if I had wings I would fly. When she says she is a local person, I feel I am flying, my joy is unbounded. She has a different colour skin but she comes back here time after time. Other places don't have white people. I am really joyful.' This salvo hit its mark, and Warea's face drooped: 'It's true, you really achieved something here. You are truly killing all our thoughts.'

Warea, who was from the Kamarepa clan, meant that his clan could not match the achievements of Mapi's. The exchange is a good example of how, through the use of *siapi* (veiled speech) and eliciting talk, things take off, conversations are redirected and links are made, unintended by the original speakers. Mapi had turned the debate, from a discourse on Christianity and modernity, to a triumphalist proclamation of Yala achievements and an implicit criticism of other clans. But this is subsequently revealed to be part of a longer-term strategy (or perhaps transformed into one) when he mollifies the Kamarepa and uses them as a hammer to strike at other Yala sub-clans.

At the pastor's request, Mapi then led the prayer, with an idiosyncratic opening: 'Marc is not some half-man, Lisette is not a black woman, our achievements have eclipsed yours [to the Kamarepa clan]. These two came back many times, making a bridge with Jesus who died on the cross …'

It was now time for the burial. Apart from the principal female mourners, few people accompanied the coffin. The sons remained in the settlement as the coffin was taken to church for another blessing and then to the burial-ground. At first the coffin would not fit as the pit was not the right shape, but after some tinkering it was lowered with lashings. The old woman's tin plate, her cup and her spoon were put in, as well as a bundle which Amasi described in English as 'dirty old clothes'. When we came back from the cemetery Rimbu was distributing sugarcane. Soon the place was reverberating with the chewing and spitting out of pulp. Only Yala clanspeople were present (aside from Kamarepa members of Pastor Ore's clan). I recorded the post-burial debate, which Mapi began with a potted history of the Yala clan dispersal in the 1930s and subsequent regrouping. This was a defining moment in Yala living history. It began with the *mena lo yada* and *mena yada* ('war over a pig', a series of wars mentioned in chapter 3 and described more fully in Josephides 1985: 32–38).

> It's you Yala who started this war in Agema. You shot Rudu. You conspired to kill Tiarepa Pudu's pig. You killed Maita Koyanu, Maita Yadakubu and Perepe Laisia. [Mapi speaks of the Yala in the second person, though he himself is a Yala.] Then all the clans living around us joined together and chased us out of Agema. Our parents dispersed, some going down the Sugu river and using the *ayia* dialect, others going up to Kagua and using the *alia* dialect, still others going over to Kuare and using the *aipea* dialect. Some even went as far as Erave and spoke Polopapi [a different language altogether]. Only our fathers, Rimbu's and mine, kept the *alea* dialect, our true language [this is blatantly untrue – others also kept the dialect]. Only the Kamarepa took pity on the Yala's laments and escorted them back home to Agema, where they regrouped. The first to return was my father [of Tiarepa clan], the second were the Paripa, the third the Waluaparepa. All of you Yala here [i.e. the Rola and Kaureyala], where have you come from? Did the Kamarepa bring you, or where did you spring from?

A brief account of Yala clan sections involved in this altercation is necessary to understand this exchange. The relevant subclans in the settlements of Yakopaita, Puliminia, Poiale and Aka are the Umba

(Rimbu's subclan), the Paripa (Pisas's and Rama's), the Yarepa (Pupula's and Michael's), the Tiarepa (Mapi's), and the Rola and Kaureyala (Koke's, Yembi's and Kalu's). The latter were coupled together in this debate. The Umba and Paripa were usually presented as having a special relationship, separated as a result of segmentation, but it is more likely that the common origin itself was invented, as genealogical links were not available to account for it.

In his speech, Mapi is insinuating that the Rola and Kaureyala clans are remiss in their duties and in debt to his own clan. More covertly, he is questioning whether they are Yala at all. Providing fuel for him, Pisa recalled some of the prestations following the return to Agema: 'The Paripa gave twelve *mena kiri* [singed pigs normally given to war allies – see Josephides (2005a: 186–87)] compensation pigs to the Tiarepa, the last given to Yone when he held his pig kill. Mapi's lineage gave fourteen pigs to the Kamarepa.' Mapi pounced on this substantiation of his claim that the Tiarepa had compensated the Kamarepa and that the Paripa acknowledged their leadership role in this: 'But what did the Kaureyala or Rola give? Is this your place or ours?' The next speaker, Hapkas, intervened from a different perspective, to pre-empt the accusation most feared by the Umba: 'I grieve for my father's lineage, they were strong, they built homes and spirit houses, they held pig kills. I go up to Agema and Popa and mourn them. But neither my father nor my mother died angry, unhappy or unfulfilled. They will not complain of us. I cleaned up the place there and planted flowers. Now I want to kill pigs in their honour. We must all believe.' While a chorus of older women commended Hapkas's general sentiments ('He is telling the truth, if God's name hadn't come …'), Rimbu turned to Mapi: 'You are not coming out with the real cause, you are cutting the hair on top but the sickness is inside the belly. Why don't you come straight out with your complaint? Bad thoughts can kill a man.'

Pisa, anticipating the course of the debate, cut in: 'The Rola and Kaureyala don't have a good debater (*agele le ali*, 'mouth man'). Who will speak for them?' When Rimbu attempted to do so, Kiru cut him short: 'This is not your lineage, just shut your mouth.' Rorea, a Rola man, angrily rose from among the card-players: 'If I had been there at the time I would have given pigs to the Kamarepa, but I wasn't, so let's drop it.' In one of his deft twists, Mapi's next statement apparently changed the subject: 'All this *komada* business is fine, but rather than have a feast ourselves next time an old person dies, let's all throw some money together now and give it to Pisa, so he can enjoy it before he goes, buy his own coffin and choose the blankets he wants to be buried in. Pisa can hold the plate and we will all make our contributions. He gave compensation to the Kamarepa when they helped the Yala settle back. The clans who didn't contribute then can give K10 or K20 to Pisa now, the rest of us can give K1 or fifty toea. We'll name a day for this prestation. If you two clans don't want to participate, the rest of us will do it anyway.'

But Koke (and other Rola clan members) were not satisfied that the attack on them was over and took up Rimbu's offer of advocacy: 'I am not a mouth man, whatever this man (Rimbu) says we won't go against.' His brother Kuna added his own understanding of what was at issue: 'You are really talking about land here. I keep hearing about this Aliwi land, but I'm not the only one using it.' Almost in unison, Mapi and his brother Kumi shouted at Kuna: 'No, we are not talking about land, we are talking about presents for the old man.' There was laughter at this, and Rimbu admonished Kuna: 'You're not thinking, just shut your mouth. They are beating about the bush, they haven't come out with the real cause of their complaint yet.' Despite ticking Kuna off, Rimbu's intention was to get at Mapi and his brothers. Michael summed up the tenor of this slippery, protean debate: 'All the time you talk, it's just like hitting a box; we don't know what's inside.' Thus the conversation which Mapi first turned to an attack on the Kamarepa as unable to match Yala achievements, then to other Yala sub-clans as deficient in their duties, is redirected again and again, as others try to elicit the 'real talk' that reflects their own interests. But a redirection does not cancel out the previous point, it adds to it, as all the complaints and claims were current. Meaning, duties and social reality were constantly being brought into question.

The suspicion of Mapi is heightened by a dream that Hapkas then recounts, which is interpreted to mean that one day Mapi may kill them, and only then will they know his meaning. Tama, however, continues to ruminate on the old political offices and their passing: 'Pisa was a wealthy big man (*amoali*) in the old days, with many gardens, pigs and wives. Yamola was the 'mouth man'; Rimbu has taken over this function. Wapa was the warrior (*yadamudu ali*). When the government first came they picked some men, gave them black laplaps with a coloured border, made them into village headmen and instructed them to teach others and develop a new law.' Tama is cut short by Pastor Ore, who admonishes the whole gathering for their 'rubbishy talk' which will land them in hell, and not impress Lisette and Marc, who can show them the way to heaven (see Josephides 2001 for an analysis of this speech).

At three-thirty in the afternoon the fire was lit for heating the mumu stones. The day was capricious, alternating hot, overcast, sun and rain, but despite the undercurrents it was enjoyable and festive. Diverging interests became apparent in the attention given to talk about the exploits of the older generation and even the enumeration of old people, dead and living. All the men, young and old, listened, some open-mouthed; older women also listened, some very old ones supplying a name here and there. But the young women were totally uninterested, sitting apart and talking of their own things while they netted their colourful bags (see Josephides 1999).

Directly after the burial, plans were made for Payanu's mortuary feast. Papola, Kiru and Wapelenu planned to kill a small pig each, while Rimbu, Waliya, Hapkas, Kiru and Marc and I contributed money towards the purchase of frozen beef in town. Rimbu's and Kiru's early morning departure to Ialibu for this purpose was marked by a long church service, apparently to bless the journey, but it still rained and all four bags of flour were soaked. It was at this feast that Liame and Rosa fell into the fight described in the previous chapter. Mapi hung around the whole time, while professing indifference to everything happening around him. Yet when Rimbu began to announce the names of food recipients he followed him and repeated everything, as if he had been a loudspeaker. The settlements of Puliminia, Aka, Paipada, Wilimi Kusu, and the Kamarepa clan received food. I was shy about making my own distribution, because I knew I couldn't give to everyone. Rimbu cut the meat for me and called out the names as I whispered them to him. Papola, never one to hold back, addressed me in mock complaint: 'You didn't give me any pork!' I spluttered, flushed with embarrassment, 'But I received pork only from you, I couldn't give you back your own pork!' 'No,' Papola quickly laughed, 'I'm being funny, just joking.' Partly in assuagement, Marc gave Papola's son (and his namesake) the last piece of beef, together with a large sweet potato.

Death and Recurring Conflict: Conclusion

The events recounted in 'minimal narratives' in this chapter have a group orientation, while the stories around marriages in the previous chapter foregrounded individual strategies. They bring about group fights rather than personal ones, describing group negotiations over meaning, duties, and social reality. Despite this slant, the three deaths, taken together, do not give a 'rehearsed' account, a general picture of how Kewa view death, nor how they mark the deaths of different categories of persons. What they do show is that the ritualization of death is not separated in time and space, or even conceptually, from the rest of social life (cf Seremetakis 1991: 47). The activities I describe are not contained by those deaths but go beyond them. While their initial concern is the 'good death', a variety of other issues become attached to the events. In the nature of this ethnography, I do not stress the arcane aspects that make up a Kewa belief system or cosmology, but instead describe events I see unfolding.[7]

It becomes clear, in this approach, that each death must be contextualized individually. While the social standing and kinship relations of the deceased are relevant factors, the context of prevailing interests and problems in the village at the time are even more important. A key question that emerges in comparing the three events is the extent of the concern with responsibility for the death. In Rake's case tests were carried out to determine responsibility, because the possibility of sorcery in the death of a mature big man is a first consideration. Wapa had been a warrior responsible for many deaths, but he and Payanu were old, almost ancestors, so in their case the most serious accusations had to do with neglect. The passage of time is another relevant factor. When Payanu died thirteen years had elapsed since the previous death recorded here. People's interests, their agendas and the realities of village life had changed drastically in the interim. I had been absent from the field for some seven years, and different aspects of village life tended to catch my attention. The duel between the two orders, and especially the obsession with Christianity and theological dogma, could not be ignored. This was men's rather than women's obsession; Christianity for men was more of a politically significant arena of contest than for women, who took to it as a life-changing experience. Pastors were moving centre-stage and leading more than just prayers, on occasion causing acrimony. The anthropologists were more strongly cast as intermediaries between the old and the new, the returned kinspeople who inhabited two worlds. Knowledge about that other world was growing, and people of all ages posed searching and informed questions about it. Turning the tables on us, they made us their informants. During the decade leading to the millennium, Papua New Guineans in general were infected with the frenzy surrounding speculations about final judgement and the second coming, made more pressing in a context of disillusionment with the political situation in the country.

But back in 1979, speculation around Rake's death was of two kinds: who had caused his death, and what his death may cause. Through various levels of eliciting talk, two interconnected activities become visible here: political struggles over land and influence, and attempts to define social reality. The first speculation, over who had caused Rake's death, is seen in his brother Wola's repeated attempts to elicit Tiarepa motives for some of their actions (such as not attending the mortuary feast and offering to pay compensation). Are they making explicit their responsibility for Rake's death? In turn, Tiarepa constantly elicit Perepe moods, by asking such questions as whether they are still going about armed. Wola's initial refusal to accept compensation from the Tiarepa is an aggressive elicitation of Tiarepa stance vis-à-vis Rake's status as a big man, an attempt to force them to agree that he was the leader of them all. Wola makes his meaning explicit by claiming this public space for his clan.

The other form of elicitation attempted to negotiate, or gain acceptance for, certain entailments of Rake's death. How had it changed the playing field? More fundamentally, it led to questions of not only who might replace Rake in prominence, but also how social order itself might change. While one person may keep conflict at bay, the removal of that person also presents opportunities for reorganizing relations. The uncertainty over divinations hints at the liminality of the times, when such rituals have not quite been given up but nor are they practised with conviction. They were carried out gingerly and somewhat mechanically, as if nobody expected to learn much from them. In the account of the enactment of divination in Mapi's story (chapter 4), I noted awkwardness and embarrassment in relation to these practices. What were people searching for? What did they elicit? Was it signs of how to reconstruct the community? I tried to show how from a personal perspective these signs were manipulated, negotiated, interpreted and elicited. How can events such as divinations create/produce *explicit* knowledge?

In the end it was the eliciting talk of the dispute that really carried events. Divinations elicit some answers, but they serve primarily as attempts to find *where* meaning should be sought. Divination, of course, is action, and threatening action at that. But no meaning is made explicit through divination. Wola tries to make explicit what the issue is here, by his constant challenging of Mapi's lineage over their absence from the wake: is the issue that Yala presence would acknowledge Rake as the big man for the area? While the Tiarepa Yala are not ready to concede this, nor do they want the Perepe to divine their real intentions. Mapi's interpretation of his own dream is double-layered: as a reflexive metanarrative reading, it points to Kewa cultural conventions, but as an eliciting strategy it exposes those conventions as open to manipulation. Being uncertain of the success of his actions, he makes a tactical withdrawal.

As in chapter 7, we see people fighting over different readings of social reality. Wapa's 'clarion call' to the Perepe, following Rake's death, to protect his settlement from Mapi's lineage, was an attempt to make a particular reading explicit by putting it in public space; Rimbu's demobilization of those same champions countered that reading with another, repudiating that reality. Talk and action combine in attempts to make knowledge explicit, thereby creating that reality. The mode of communication here is agonistic interaction. Minimal narratives thus combine attempts at paradigmatic, rehearsed talk (explicit inference), and shared knowledge of events. But at the same time, I argue, they are *claims* that events are like this, that these are social facts, that this is how society works.

At Wapa's death as at Payanu's, attempts to elicit the causes of the illness span a range of concerns. Mapi's exoneration ('we don't practise sorcery here') is also a warning to the suspects and a challenge to the sons of the victim. The conflict over rights and duties is expressed as a difference of opinion and perception by different people, sometimes even those from the same clan; Pupula, for instance, immediately acknowledges the Wapia claim, in opposition to his clansmen. In the outbreak of the fight, symbols are read differently, but Sipi, responsible for the bamboo knife incident, is generally cast as agent provocateur, a trickster. In order to maintain a kinship fiction that 'brothers don't fight' Rimbu refines a distinction between 'anger' and 'sorrow'. While the issue of group unity is at the fore during the fight with the Wapia Yala, there are also earnest attempts to establish what was done in the past. Such explicit knowledge is sought through interaction, in order to discover the proper thing to do, on which they could agree. People negotiate different ways in which prestige can be gained, balancing the economics of accepting a gift against other prestige-bearing practices.

Here, as in previous chapters, illustrations are found of the court being used in political ways. Even though the Agema Yala made a payment to the Wapia Yala that was almost equivalent to the original amount awarded against them following the fight at Wapa's funeral, something crucial had nevertheless been gained: by their further actions they had transformed a court fine into a prestation that augmented their own prestige, thus succeeding in presenting reality in a particular way. This exposed Rusa's explanation of court fines and their rationale as largely his own interpretation, in the form of 'rehearsed talk' that couldn't pass muster. Though the fundamental principle that 'all injuries must be compensated' is non-controversial, Rimbu's attempt to second-guess the intention behind Rusa's explanation complicated events still further, by offering an interpretation of an interpretation.

At Payanu's death the playing out of a duel between old and new was established right away. Her death had attracted large crowds, but not as diverse as those at the deaths of the two men. The constant refrain was that *all the old people were dying off.* Two months previously a very old man had died (Pupula), followed seven weeks later by his wife (Ragunanu) – both of them storytellers in chapter 3. Now only one man of their generation (Pisa) remained in the village, and his illness during the last funeral heightened apprehension. Thus Payanu's funeral was the occasion for strong expressions of the perception that an old order was dying out.

The idiom in these debates was religious as well as cultural: Christianity versus old customs. An ambivalent relationship to the old order was exhibited in the debates. While its passing was viewed as a loss, arousing a strong feeling that old people should be treated well since behaviour towards them had to be judged in terms of the norms and customs of that old order, the fear that they may die unfulfilled and with a grudge also affected social and political positions which are relevant today in a Christianized community. Men of all ages and older women exhibited to some degree this ambivalent relationship to the old order, though younger women appeared unconcerned about this aspect of the death.

On his mother's death as on his father's, Rimbu received Mapi's eliciting talk as a challenge, a criticism of parent-neglect intended to cast aspersions on his status as a big man. Mapi spoke through several veils of meaning, but Rimbu himself managed a dig at Mapi and his brother Kumi while appearing to be correcting Kuna. (Mapi and Kumi of Tiarepa Yala are disputing with Koke and Rorea of Rola Yala over land; they argue that since their clan compensated the Kamarepa for helping the Yala return to their land, they have a rightful claim to the land; the Rola did not contribute to the compensation payment and therefore their claim is weaker.) The dialogue reproduced earlier is replete with elicitations. Rimbu complains that Mapi is not open in his disputes, always hedging round and using 'veiled speech'. Mapi's strategy as a 'loudspeaker' at these deaths is precisely to make meanings explicit, by putting them in a public space as statements of incontrovertible fact.

In sum, events around deaths bring about group fights and restatements of group affiliations, specifically through negotiations over meaning, duty and social reality. Rake's death created a general climate of fear as the political and the mystical blended together, and men went about armed. Events at Wapa's funeral appear to centre on claims to rights in persons, but could also be seen as understandings of history and political claims for the future. Payanu's funeral gave rise to feelings of profound regret and loss. Pisa now offered the very last chance for placating the ancestors, who would depart this world forever as Papua New Guinea joined the rest of the world.

I have moulded the accounts in this chapter almost unconsciously as theatrical scripts, complete with mise en scène, cues, *sotte voce* comments and episodes of dramatic irony. The idiom of theatre (rather than just repetitive ritual performance) also invokes the idea of a denouement, a movement and a change of conditions. The three deaths, seen consecutively, repeat this theme of denouement. The third death places us in a theatre in which sets and characters are dramatically changed. This is the aspect from which the accounts of these deaths interest me: not as events exemplifying cosmological beliefs that are immutable and taken together reveal to us a coherent Kewa culture, but as social displays of people's current directions and concerns, of how their lives are lived. Starting with a death, the accounts fan out in many directions, as people go about eliciting their understandings of their social world.

Notes

1. In his seminal work on the expressive modalities of Kaluli weeping, poetics and song, Steven Feld writes that 'it is spurious to analyse the content or principles of any aesthetic system without considering the degree of aesthetic intent in the analytic posture', that is, 'how ideas generate actions and how those actions are purposive, expressive forms that constitute an ideology of emotion' (Feld 1990: 217). In the Kewa case as with the Kaluli, '[w]hen textual, musical, and performative features properly coalesce, someone will be moved to tears' (ibid.: 216). To paraphrase Feld's apt characterization, this coded sentiment references both the lived world and abstract qualities and values, allowing people to have a simultaneous sense of things that are, can and should be, and those that are not, cannot be and should not be (Feld 1990: 222). Feld also comments on the difference between men's and women's singing: 'Men's crying ... is less controlled, momentary, hysterical, and often accompanied by physical trembling and angry gestures. Women's crying ... is more melodic, texted, controlled, reflective, and sustained. These qualities parallel general emotional display patterns: Kaluli women typically act more steady, reliable and even-tempered in everyday matters ... Kaluli men on the other hand are given to marked sudden affect changes, moody grimaces and gestures, aggressive or withdrawn posturing, and bursts from sulkiness to exuberance' (1990: 262). But he adds that men regard women's crying as 'a more spontaneous, natural expression' (ibid.). All this is also true of the Kewa (see Josephides 2005a).
2. This is a variation on the *repena lu* bamboo method, in which the jaw-bone of the dead man is tied to a bamboo pole and is carried by two men, each holding on to one end of the pole. As the bamboo begins to 'pull', the two men follow. The jaw-bone will break and disintegrate in front of the guilty party. The taro divination method, *go yawa*, was not mentioned on this occasion. I learned about it on our visit to Kerari, where I saw an open space encircling a tall oak and was told that big men used to meet and talk there, cooking their food by heating stones in the hollow of the oak. When a big man died they would perform the *go yawa* divination. Using a small pitpit cane or a blade of kunai grass they would mark each taro with a design that represented the clan suspected of the killing, then lay all the taros in the mumu pit over the layers of banana leaves covering the hot stones. In four hours the taros would be taken out, and if a taro was found to be burnt on one side and raw on the other, the clan it represented was deemed the guilty party.
3. See Josephides (1985: 19). From this example we can see how, depending on the circumstances, people manipulate stories of origin, stressing some connections and downplaying others. See also Josephides (2005a).

4. He used the word *nusiali*, a form of sorcery said to come from Erave in the south, in which a spirit stone is pointed at the victim from a place of concealment.
5. From my observation and reading I know that traditionally this compensation leans to equalization, so that no side feels that its injuries were ignored. While the village court may not have the power to award the high damages awarded in this case, litigants accept its judgement of what will keep the injured party happy and discourage direct action. My fieldwork revealed another factor: that donors derived prestige from high compensation payments.
6. On rascals, see Josephides (1994).
7. There is a danger in this strategy, recognized by Seremetakis (1991; see also Weiner 1976), who saw that the implications of the tendency to foreground the 'real', empirical, political aspects of such events were detrimental to the cosmological constructions of women. But although Kewa women, as Maniat women, keen over the body while men are the main actors in the spin-offs around the death, I never had reason to believe that women perceived the significance of their laments as creating powerful cultural meaning, as Seremetakis argues for Maniat women.

Chapter 9

Mimesis, Ethnography and Knowledge

In an earlier ethnography (Josephides 1985) I traced a Kewa 'master narrative' as it attempted to account for the production of inequalities in so-called egalitarian societies. It presented a generalized picture of culture and dealt with the problems of a complex social reality by means of a theoretical stratagem that posited a contradiction between ideology and practice.[1] The present work complements that ethnography with a picture of everyday social interactions, including many-layered accounts, whose effect is to break up any putative master narrative about 'Kewa culture'. People's constant endeavours to shape their lives in complex negotiations within specific situations, drawing on the past to create new futures, become visible here as a contest between 'rehearsed and rehearsing' talk and action. The outcome establishes, even if only for a time, a particular understanding of social reality, what I call 'social knowledge'. By focusing on particular actors in specific situations and contextualizing events in terms of motivations, this approach offers a glimpse of a theory of action based on action itself, not deduced from structures. As part of this possible theory of action, people's strategies revealed that a major motivator of action was to force an acknowledgment of one's self.

Stories, Ethnography, Theory

The perception of local knowledge outlined in this book – as constantly negotiated and made explicit through a series of implicit claims – makes it not unlike academic reasoning or polemic. Writing about his fieldwork at a cattle market in south-west France, Jenkins (1994: 442) observes (referring to Bloch 1991) that social life and social knowledge there are 'characterized by a series of apprenticeships', improvised and without explicit principles. This way of talking about the lack of homogeneous insider's knowledge puts anthropologist and insider on a par, reducing the insider's advantage in regard to that knowledge to mere experience and strategizing, and leading Jenkins to conclude that there is no such thing as objective, uninvolved knowledge.

The Kewa stories in this book are part of the mapping of these apprenticeships. This way of putting it enables a clarification of the methodological link between my accounts and two key orientations in my analysis. The first orientation is of knowledge as gained through self-objectification (by means of elicitation); the second is my use of 'odysseys' to refer to the personal investment in the stories as a construction of the self and one's world. These two orientations are represented by the two levels of analysis at the end of each ethnographic chapter. As already mentioned, in each of these chapters I do two things: tell a story (an ethnography) and make theoretical points about the narratives and actions through which the story is told. The stories are people's odysseys (what Rapport 2003 might call life-projects), their active attempts to get hold of and direct their lives and persons. As they force me to follow their formative peregrinations all over the cultural landscape, I realize that their concerns are not alien to me. Beyond the Kewa context, as an observer I recognize the interplay between personal strategies and social meanings, the intertwining of social and psychological needs, the personal dangers of commitment, the suspicions that individual actors are unfair, and the necessity to retain a vigilant watch over my own self-presentation and treatment by others. But personal odysseys also have effects that enable levels of understanding beyond personal strategies, to what their 'doing' does further, or demonstrates. This second level of analysis (or first orientation) explored knowledge as self-objectification, constantly putting oneself out there on the firing line, but somehow escaping without self-alienation (or rather by redefining 'alienation') and emerging as a moral person. By morality I do not mean conscious concerns with duties or the moral 'ought', but acting with the awareness that actions impinge on others, in a world in which oneself is placed, thus making 'care' and responsibility a natural part of life.

It is clear that the stories in this book are not folk models as opposed to analysts' models, the sort of metanarratives that anthropologists collect to give insightful glimpses into people's own understandings of their culture (LeRoy 1985, Narayan 1989, Young 1983). Rather, they take wing in the midst of everyday social life, in people's narrations and enactments, and this practical grounding and relevance distinguishes them from concise theories whose value resides in their explanatory power. My argument builds up through the integrity and cumulativeness of the ethnography, whose excessiveness (that is, exceeding the requirements of the theoretical argument) I needed to develop the argument in the first place. If I gave only as much ethnography as justified my interpretation, my interpretation would act as a coercive force.

But a distinction must be made between excessiveness and cumulativeness. It is misleading to set up ethnography as being cumulative, in the sense that a new insight into local life must be wrung out of every ethnographic observation. I realize something at a certain stage by dint of accumulation of events; a shape, a pattern. Some *events* may be cumulative, building up a narrative, as when a series of eliciting interventions culminate in an event which retrospectively explains them as elicitations with a particular outcome in mind (as when in chapter 8 Mapi asks a string of apparently unrelated questions and makes various suggestions with the sole intention of showing up the ineptitude of another clan lineage). But though events show the denouement of particular situations, and the extent to which their resolution clarifies social practice and its relation to beliefs, rules and norms, I do not understand *more* about the social practices of elicitation and interaction by heaping example upon example. Elicitation as a particular type of interaction is not changed or built upon by the cumulative nature of the events it elicits, except in so far as it shows that the strategy is used over and over again in a cumulative way (Sahlins [1974: 73] makes a similar point about the "endless multiplication of examples").

By way of summing up the arguments in this book, this final chapter sets itself the following tasks: to consider the anthropological project as Aristotelian mimesis, and ethnography itself in three guises: as delimiting and portraying difference, as being regionally circumscribed, and as cultural history.

Mimesis as a Way of Knowing

In *The Prose of the World* Merleau-Ponty writes: 'Myself and the other are like two nearly concentric circles which can be distinguished only by a slight and mysterious slippage ... Nevertheless the other is not I and on that account differences must arise' (1973: 134). This slippage, as well as the idea of superimposition, are important for Taussig's (1993) discussion of mimesis.[2] For my purposes, what is crucial is the relationship between the copy and the original: the copy – in this case the ethnography – acquiring the properties of what it represents.[3]

For Aristotle mimesis was a disclosure of the world that was nobler and truer than reality; for Ricoeur, it was 'a future horizon of undecided possibilities' (1981: 187), whose disclosure of the world was a projection without alienation, only a finding. Applying Ricoeur's perspective, I see the potentialities of ethnography as projection of the world, not an alienation.[4] Turning back to Aristotle, the 'nobility' is in the transformation of the encounter, the ability to overcome the unexamined conventions of one's own background. In this way ethnographies can be seen as the anthropologists' sympathetic magic. Taussig gives to sympathetic magic the name of mimesis, 'the nature that culture uses to create second nature, the faculty to copy, imitate, make models, explore difference, yield into and become Other' (1993: xiii). The mimetic faculty, he believes, is necessary to the very process of knowing, whose two-way street he explores; an itinerary which I mimic in my discussion of the ways in which 'they' also make models of 'us'. But Taussig's most original contribution to the understanding of the encounter is his stress on imperilment. He writes that 'something crucial about what made oneself was implicated and imperilled in the object of study, in its power to change reality, no less' (1993: 253). At the sensuous moment of knowing (Taussig is citing Adorno), a 'yielding and mirroring of the knower in the unknown, of thought in its object' (Taussig 1993: 45), opens up the self to the peril of infinity, or nothingness (the last clause is mine). That moment is a gamble, yet almost unwilled. This unwillingness speaks to the 'authenticity' of the ethnography, or the 'truth' of the copy.[5]

To apply these insights to my ethnographic fieldwork, I return, from a slightly different perspective, to a point raised in chapter 2. By making a copy of me as his sister, Rimbu has 'normalized' my presence within a classificatory kinship structure. But this act of classification also enables him to control me. People in neighbouring villages envy him; they all want to make me their sister so they can protect themselves from me and gain control over what I represent or embody. The ethnography allows for the elaboration of two aspects of copy-making, an extensive and an intensive one. In the first case, making copies is part of a strategy of self- and world-creation. People do it all the time. But the copies are not replications of what went before or what exists outside. They are claims about social reality, described in this book as rehearsed and rehearsing talk. Just as Rimbu made a copy of me as his sister (catching and fixing me in a [not unproblematic] relationship to himself), so Mapi wants to make a copy of Jesus, to fix his own picture of him. But he must have something 'genuine' to take his copy from – that is why he needs legitimation from an 'original' that exists in Europe. It you want to make others into a copy of yourself, that is imperialism, but if you want to make of yourself a copy of others, that is an imperilling of the self.[6] Though with much to gain, Mapi was imperilling himself, just as Rimbu was every day in his relationship with me. This self-imperilment, much beyond the examples just given, is each Kewa person's odyssey, as described in the stories making up this book.

The second case concerns the opportunities for action afforded by one person's copy-making to the one being copied. Simultaneously as this copy of 'sister' is invested with the power of the visiting ethnographer, the visiting ethnographer acquires a presence and reality through that representation. The representation that objectifies me into a sign-object has added a dimension to my identity, and uncovered new types of consciousness that reveal me as a being beyond myself. The fact that Rimbu has made a copy of me (a sister) enables me to make a copy of him (not only a brother, but an ethnography). My enablement is not a passive permission, a toleration to stay in the village and observe while participating. It is an active creation of a situated social self that determines the manner of my observation and participation, both as a result of politico-social positioning (kinship links) and moral fashioning. They define the position from which I am to 'invent' them.

Taussig writes that an ethnographer must possess two qualities (one being a passion): the ability to mime well, and the urge 'to get hold of something by means of its likeness' (1993: 21). Another requirement, arising from my work, is the facility to add on roles and predicates without becoming lost in them or losing previous ones. In magical practice the copy acquires the properties of the original by means of the double action of imitation and contact (otherwise known as sympathy and contagion, or similarity and contiguity, or even metaphor and metonym); in the production of ethnography, imitation and contact likewise work together to impart power and authenticity.[7] The magic is not only in having been there, but in allowing oneself to be caught.[8]

In reflecting on what makes a true copy or an ethnography 'real', I consider a three way relationship: between the original (the people), the copy (the ethnography), and the copier (the ethnographer). Though I use an active noun to refer to the ethnographer, I keep in mind the process of her own invention. The middle chapters of this book give fragmented glimpses of the relationships and transformations in the field. While the people's daily strategies of constructing themselves and their social conditions evince a conventional routine, they also reach out into the unknown; as Mead might say, they exercise the novelty of the 'I'. My presence provided an exciting 'unknown' for novelty to realize itself in. It also provided an excuse for action and a pretext for withdrawal, when action was unsuccessful in eliciting the desired response. Thus it provided new structures for people to actualize their identities.

Ethnography as Difference, Locality and Chronicle

Ethnography as a Portrayal of Difference

A key feature of my approach is its resistance of tacit assumptions of a fundamental grounding in difference. Crapanzano, reflecting on the self-account at the centre of his experiment in interpretive ethnography, takes a different view:

> The subject of Tuhami's tale is ontologically different from the subject of those tales with which we in the West are familiar. Generic differences ... are cultural constructs and reflect those most fundamental assumptions about the nature of reality, including the nature of the person and the nature of language, that are considered ... self-evident by members of any particular tradition ... Wittingly or unwittingly, however, the anthropologist or his reader often causes the differences to disappear in the act of translation. (1980: 7–8)

Crapanzano urges us to acknowledge a different reality, but it is not clear precisely what he is urging. If it is to accept Tuhami as a representative of some sort of difference, despite being so vividly represented as an individual, it is to see him as a *symbol* of something rather than as himself, symbolizing 'difference' rather than being different.[9] Crapanzano clearly intends to capture complexities, and Tuhami's narrative does so, but his call for the acknowledgement of difference threatens to make Tuhami into a representative of that difference – as 'we in the West' become representatives of 'the West', and flattened as persons in the expression. I wrote of my own fieldwork that I was not struck by difference when I first landed at the airport in Mt Hagen. Far from being overwhelmed by exoticism, I felt quite at home. Much later, my examination of the nature of the person and self-construction, and my analysis of people's strategies in story-telling and their deeper meanings, failed to uncover an ontological difference. As discussed in the section on 'Stories, Ethnography, Theory', the relevance of Kewa stories and experiences can be seen to extend beyond the Kewa context.

Cultural Region and the Tyranny of Theoretical Regionalism

No one can deny the dialectical relationship between the findings of fieldwork and the theoretical perspectives used in their analysis. But this book distances itself from a Melanesian ethnographic position in two ways. First, it provides an implicit critique of the approach that sees Melanesia as an ethnographic region that is home to a particular worldview, a particular kind of sociality and a particular kind of difference, one that expresses itself through distinctive rituals of symbolic reproduction.[10] Second, it positions itself differently from my own earlier ethnography, foregrounding what is made explicit in people's interactions rather than what is hidden by social structures. The discussion on the self sets the scene for an ethnographic understanding and inquiry that goes beyond the local and reflects more explicitly on universal practice or capacity. I argue that the self is always a matter of externalization rather than introspection, and cultural traits are overlays. When I write that Kewa narratives are used to 'exchange experiences of practical wisdom, to make claims and to seek feedback' (chapter 5), this statement does not simply arise from Kewa ethnography as a locally specific observation. It is a general statement that reflects an expanded insight into the ethnography, through the application of philosophical insights

Ethnography as Chronicle of Cultural History/History of Consciousness

The accounts in this book delineate a history of consciousness and cultural change. They trace the transition to modernity from the traditional stories of the older generation, describing their movement through the normal stages of life, to the stories of the younger generation on the model of the modern novel, 'that bespeaks [though this is to fast-forward to a future in the making] the fragmented and alienated nature of its hero or anti-hero' (Crapanzano 1980: 11). The landscape is written over in several ways, as each set of stories chronicles the changes (physical, architectural, social, political, and so on) as experienced by the narrators, leading to a transformation of consciousness. This transformation is in response to the larger changes in their world, of which I as ethnographer was but a tiny part, perhaps a symbolic representative. Their stories show how people nowadays think of themselves differently in relation to their culture; no longer taking for granted a representative moral personhood, they do not give their own lives as a cultural gloss for how the Kewa in general live. To return to the palimpsest analogy developed in chapter 5, what is at issue is not erasure of the past but a condensation and an embedding, as each story 'paints over' other claims. Both readers and protagonists find themselves somewhere else by the end of the book, as each chapter builds up understandings and works towards conclusions that are grounded in the people's own narratives. These are their odysseys, and I could not have understood the ethnography without them.

Ethnography itself, as the sum total of life stories, is always a process of objectification, being an object and a text that is already finished when we begin to read it (Ochs and Capps [1990: 4] on written narratives, citing

Lawrence Langer). But it is a living narrative, because its claim (that people through their eliciting strategies create what others call a culture) is itself an eliciting strategy. In this sense, the production of ethnography is the objectification of the production of culture, as suggested in Wagner's comment (chapter 2 note 20) about intentionality taking the picture. All this may sound like so much sophistry in Michael's metaphor of hitting a box (chapter 8): 'All the time you talk, it's just like hitting a box; we don't know what's inside.' The real meaning, locked inside the box, needs to be interpreted, and this interpretation leads to a new level and shows the broader relevance of local interactions. People's desire – or urge – to generalize beyond the obvious, the prosaic and the local, both as cause and effect, and arrive at an insight seen as more broadly applicable (even universal), was amply demonstrated in the narratives.

Notes

1. The 'master narrative' was both theirs and mine; theirs, because of a 'rehearsed talk' salient in social practice, and mine, because I took up the cudgels with a grand theory that squeezed out the personal motivations of particular actors.
2. Jackson believes that one enters the world of the other through analogy, not mimetically (1998: 97), but his understanding of 'mimesis' is different from the one expounded here.
3. In Josephides (2003b) I explored the transformative moment of contact which creates the ethnographer. Going beyond the ethnography as a copy which acquires the properties of what it represents, I considered how the representer herself acquired those properties. Josephides (1997) also addresses these issues.
4. 'Ethnography as alienation' refers to perspectives that see ethnography as a text written by the ethnographer in conditions of a double alienation: the self-alienation of fieldwork, where the fieldworker must renounce or 'bracket' her or his cultural background yet retain an objective distance ('participant observation'), and the 'othering' alienation of the subjects of study from the ethnography, which is presented as the anthropologist's achievement. Postmodernist critiques of ethnography have questioned whether the other can be known at all, and concluded that ethnographies are ethnographers' representations rather than descriptions of other cultures. This is a view I implicitly take issue with by adopting 'ethnography as a projection of the world', which stresses a personal openness to the cultural milieu and in relations with those in the field, acknowledging the involvement of the ethnographer's own subjectivity. Thus our understanding of that culture is through our relationship with its participants, whom we may know as we know others in our own culture. The basis for this argument has been laid in chapter 2, where I discuss the formation of the self through externalization rather than introspection. Throughout the book I show how these concepts, drawn from Ricoeur but modified and extended, map onto the ethnography.
5. Having accepted the stultifying premise of postmodernism that 'everything is constructed', Taussig then asks how we can account for the perception 'that we

live facts, not fictions'; how can our inventions seem so real and culture appear so natural? (Taussig 1993: xv). I do not use the word 'fiction' to describe social realities in my work. It is a treacherous and seductive word, too redolent of the irresistible, labyrinthine narratives of Borges (1998), who tempts and astonishes us with fantastic (but not necessarily untrue) accounts of the world, of knowledge, of time and of the self. My own terms – elicitation, negotiation, making explicit, rehearsed and rehearsing talk – are better suited to the task of showing how the world I describe is put together.

6. I am grateful to Marc Schiltz for this formulation.
7. In her discussion of the place of Diderot as a precursor to Freud, Julia Kristeva (1991, 1993), like Taussig, sees the darker side of mimesis as the repression which becomes Freud's death instinct. She examines the character of 'Rameau's Nephew', an outrageous trickster whose antics in Diderot's work reveal his 'torn consciousness', his awareness that he is 'at least double', exhibiting 'the uncanny strangeness of our unconscious' which is the other within us (Kristeva 1993: 29). Foreignness or otherness is sometimes dissolved as that stranger, sometimes reified as the foreign other who needs a separate existence. We do not see that the 'fascination and horror' the other produces in us is an extension of 'our own psychic dramas of psychosexual individuation' (ibid.: 30), by means of which the child differentiates itself from the mother. Kristeva bids us endeavour, as Rameau's Nephew did, 'to recognize ourselves as strange in order better to appreciate the foreigners outside us instead of striving to bend them to the norms of our own repression' (ibid.: 29). This is what the ethnographer must be adept in.
8. Favret-Saada, in her study of witchcraft in the Bocage (1980), also describes how informants 'invented' the ethnographer, with dangerous implications. She begins with her own elucidation of the task of the ethnographer: 'To be an ethnographer is first to record the utterances of appropriately chosen native informants' (ibid.: 9). But since 'nobody ever talks about witchcraft to gain knowledge, but to gain power', fieldwork on witchcraft cannot be a standard situation 'in which information is exchanged and where the ethnographer may hope to have neutral knowledge about … beliefs and practices' (ibid.: 11). Stories are told 'either to fascinate or to frighten', and whoever succeeds in acquiring such knowledge gains power and must accept its effects (ibid.). In these circumstances the speech and actions of the ethnographer, just as of any other interlocutor, are scrutinised for signs of this power. Favret-Saadat's detailed questions about the 'magic copula' which her closest informants believed to contain their bewitchment, and her actions in unwrapping and examining this object, convinced them that she was an 'unwitcher' (ibid.: 168), someone who takes on herself the dangerous words spoken by the witch in a spell on the victim and turns them back on the sender (ibid.: 9). Favret-Saadat did not immediately realize her informants had invented her as an unwitcher, until their expectations of her became pressing. Then in a dangerous yet effortless move, she slipped into the role. But for any of this to be possible, Favret-Saada had to 'be caught' herself; and some events supported the perception that she had indeed been a witch's victim (or 'client').The relevance of Favret-Saada's formulations to my work is easily seen. Her realization (from observation) that only the 'bewitched' could become 'unwitcher' (ibid.: 175) inspired the snappy aphorism that we must 'be caught' if we are to 'catch' (ibid.: 14). To extrapolate: as ethnographers, we must believe ('be caught', bewitched) if we are to understand or participate ('catch'). Moreover, the more we talk, the more likely we will be caught (ibid.: 64). Engagement is dangerous, and to be 'caught'

in Favret-Saadat's case was not experienced as a positive event, but it was a necessary one, the only way to understand witchcraft. It is a short step to the link with mimesis.

9. Or is Tuhami to be imagined as Borges' Droctulft, '*sub specie aeternitatis* – not the individual Droctulft, who was undoubtedly unique and fathomless (as all individuals are), but the generic "type" that tradition (the work of memory and forgetting) has made of him and many others like him' (Borges 1998: 208)? The problem arises when Tuhami is presented as an individual self, and, simultaneously, the self is proclaimed to have 'essentially metaphorical' boundaries (Crapanzano 1980: 22). Here we are not only in a different realm of reality; we are also faced with the vexing question of the relationship between metaphor and reality, or whatever Crapanzano may consider to be the difference between metaphor and non-metaphor. Is everything in Tuhami's story to be thought of as a metaphor? Do Tuhami and other Moroccans use metaphor in conscious contrast to non-metaphor, or is the distinction Crapanzano's? In either case, how is metaphorical ontology to be imagined (as in Crapanzano's claim above that '[T]he subject of Tuhami's tale is ontologically different')? And when a little further down Crapanzano laments the loss of the ethnographic encounter 'in timeless description', what would be a description 'in time' in a worldview where time may be metaphorical?

10. As I wrote in an earlier review of an approach I dubbed 'cultural-functionalism' (Josephides 1991: 159), 'the New Melanesian Ethnography' shows how an 'already completed' culture 'works in smooth reproduction, recreating the values that structure it'. The task of the analysis then becomes to clear the ground and uncover what was already there, or, as Weiner put it, to demonstrate the primordial existence of the world by '[specifying] the conditions under which [it] is perceived to be relationally based (by ourselves as well as our hosts) prior to our analysis of it' (Weiner 2001: 71). But this labour also disposes of all the ambiguities deposited in social life by the acts of individuals, or recalcitrant actions that cannot be used as a torch to illuminate the core metaphor of sociality in its reproduction through symbolic meanings. Melanesian persons themselves (as 'agents' for their culture) are seen, as part of their everyday lives, to enact rituals whose dual purpose is, simultaneously, to cover up (and thus offer to disclosive analysis) and reproduce the core relations that make sociality possible. (On trends in Melanesian ethnography, see Foster 1995.)

References

Abu-Lughod, L. 1993. *Writing Women's Worlds: Bedouin Stories*. Berkeley: University of California Press.
Austin, J.L. 1962. *How to Do Things with Words*. Oxford: Oxford University Press.
Behar, R. 1994. *Translated Woman: Crossing the Border with Esperanza's Story*. Boston, MA: Beacon Press.
Benjamin, W. 1968. 'The Storyteller', in W. Benjamin, *Illuminations*. Ed. H. Arendt. New York: Harcourt, Brace and World, pp. 83–107.
Bloch, M. 1989. 'Symbols, Song, Dance and Features of Articulation: Is Religion an Extreme Form of Traditional Authority?', in M. Bloch, *Ritual, History and Power*. London: Athlone Press, pp. 19–45.
——. 1991. 'Language, Anthropology and Cognitive Science', *Man* 26(2): 183–98.
——. 1995. 'Mémoire Autobiographique et Mémoire Historique du Passé Eloignée', *Enquete* 2: 59–76.
——. 1998. *How We Think They Think: Anthropological Approaches to Cognition, Memory, and Literacy*. Boulder, Oxford: Westview Press.
——. 2003. 'Literacy: A Reply to John Postil', *Social Anthropology* 11(1): 101.
Borges, J.L. 1998. *Collected Fictions*. Trans. Andrew Hurley. London: Allen Lane, Penguin Press.
Bourdieu, P. 1977. *Outline of a Theory of Practice*. Cambridge: Cambridge University Press.
Brenneis, D. and F.R. Myers (eds). 1984. *Dangerous Words: Language and Politics in the Pacific*. Prospect Heights, IL: Waveland Press.
Brison, K.J. 1992. *Just Talk: Gossip, Meetings, and Power in a Papua New Guinean Village*. Berkeley: University of California Press.
Brown, P. and S.C. Levinson. 1987. *Politeness: Some Universals in Language Use*. Cambridge: Cambridge University Press.
Bruner, J. 1986. *Actual Minds, Possible Worlds*. Cambridge, MA: Harvard University Press.
Calvino, I. 1977[1959]. *The Nonexistent Knight* and *The Cloven Viscount*. San Diego, CA, and New York, NY: Harcourt Brace.
Cappelletto, F. 2003. 'Long-term Memory of Extreme Events: From Autobiography to History', *Journal of the Royal Anthropological Institute* 9(2): 241–60.
Carrithers, M. 1985. 'An Alternative History of the Self', in M. Carrithers, S. Collins and S. Lukes (eds), *The Category of the Person*. Cambridge: Cambridge University Press, pp. 234–56.
——. 1992. *Why Humans Have Cultures: Explaining Anthropology and Social Diversity*. Oxford: Oxford University Press.

_____. 1995. 'Stories in the Social and Mental Life of People', in E.E. Goody (ed.), *Social Intelligence and Interaction: Expressions and Implications of the Social Bias in Human Intelligence*. Cambridge: Cambridge University Press, pp. 261–76.
_____. n.d. 'Story Seeds and the Inchoate'.
Chomsky, N. 1965. *Aspects of the Theory of Syntax*. Cambridge, MA: MIT Press.
Cohen, A.P. 1994. *Self Consciousness: An Alternative Anthropology of Identity*. London: Routledge.
Cohen, A.P. and N. Rapport. 1995. 'Introduction: Consciousness in Anthropology', in A.P. Cohen and N. Rapport (eds), *Questions of Consciousness*. ASA Monograph 33. London: Routledge, pp. 1–18.
Cooley, C.H. 1902. *Human Nature and the Social Order*. New York: Scribners.
Crapanzano, V. 1980. *Tuhami: Portrait of a Moroccan*. Chicago: Chicago University Press.
Cruikshank, J. 1990. *Life Lived Like a Story*. Vancouver: University of Columbia Press.
Damasio, A. 1999. *The Feeling of What Happens: Body and Emotion in the Making of Consciousness*. London: William Heinemann.
Dreyfus, H.L. and Rabinow, P. 1982. *Michel Foucault: Beyond Structuralism and Hermeneutics*. Chicago: Chicago University Press.
Duranti, A. 2003. 'Language as Culture in U.S. Anthropology: Three Paradigms', *Current Anthropology* 44(3): 323–47.
Edelman, G. 1992. *Bright Air, Brilliant Fire*. Harmondsworth: Penguin.
Evans-Pritchard, E.E. 1962. '*Sanza*, a Characteristic Feature of Zande Language and Thought', in E.E. Evans-Pritchard, *Essays in Social Anthropology*. London: Faber, pp. 204–28.
Favret-Saada, J. 1980. *Deadly Words: Witchcraft in the Bocage*. Cambridge and Paris: Cambridge University Press and Editions de la Maison des Sciences de l'Homme.
Feld, S. 1990[1982]. *Sound and Sentiment*, 2nd ed. University of Pennsylvania Press.
Foster, R. 1995. *Social Reproduction and History in Melanesia*. Cambridge: Cambridge University Press.
Gilsenan, M. 1996. *Lords of the Lebanese Marches: Violence and Narrative in an Arab Society*. Berkeley: University of California Press.
Goody, E. 1995. 'Introduction: some implications of a social origin of intelligence', in E. Goody (ed.), *Social Intelligence and Interaction: Expressions and Implications of the Social Bias in Human Intelligence*. Cambridge: Cambridge University Press, pp. 1-33.
Grene, D. and R. Lattimore (eds). 1991. *Greek Tragedies. Volume 1* (Sophocles: Antigone), 2nd ed. Chicago: University of Chicago Press.
Heidegger, M. 1988[1975]. *The Basic Problems of Phenomenology*. Bloomington and Indianapolis: Indiana University Press.
Hewitt, J.P. 1991. *Self and Society: A Symbolic Interactionist Social Psychology*. Boston: Allyn and Bacon.
Ingold, T. 1988. 'The Animal in the Study of Humanity', in T. Ingold (ed.), *What Is an Animal?* London: Unwin Hyman.
_____. 1990. 'An Anthropologist Looks at Biology', *Man* 25(2): 208–29.
_____. 2000. 'The Poverty of Selectionism', *Anthropology Today* 16(3): 1–2.
Jackson, M. (ed.) 1996. *Things As They Are: New Directions in Phenomenological Anthropology*. Bloomington and Indianapolis: Indiana University Press.
_____. 1998. *Minima Ethnographica*. Chicago: Chicago University Press.
Jebens, H. 1995. *Wege zum Himmel. Katholiken, Siebenten-Tags-Adventisten und der Einflusß der Traditionellen Religion in Pairudu, Southern Highlands Province, Papua New Guinea*. Vol. 86. Bonn: Holos.

Jenkins, T. 1994. 'Fieldwork and the Perception of Everyday Life', *Man* 29(2): 433–55.
Josephides, L. 1982. *Kewa Stories and Songs. Oral History* 10(2).
―――. 1985. *The Production of Inequality: Gender and Exchange among the Kewa.* London: Tavistock.
―――. 1991. 'Metaphors, Metathemes and the Construction of Sociality: A Critique of the New Melanesian Ethnography', *Man* 26(1): 145–61.
―――. 1994. 'Gendered Violence in a Changing Society', *Journal de la Société des Océanistes* 99(2): 187–96.
―――. 1995. 'Replacing Cultural Markers', in D. de Coppet and A. Iteanu (eds), *Cosmos and Society in Oceania*. Oxford: Berg Publishers, pp. 189–211.
―――. 1997. 'Representing the Anthropologist's Predicament', in A. James, J. Hockey, and A. Dawson (eds), *After Writing Culture*. London: Routledge, pp. 16–33.
―――. 1998a. 'Biographies of Social Action: Excessive Portraits', in V. Keck (ed.), *Common Worlds and Single Lives: Constituting Knowledge in Pacific Societies.* Oxford: Berg, pp. 137–67.
―――. 1998b. 'Myths of Containment, Myths of Extension: Creating Relations across Boundaries', in L.R. Goldman and C. Ballard (eds), *Fluid Ontologies: Myth, Ritual and Philosophy in the Highlands of Papua New Guinea*. Westport, Connecticut: Bergin and Garvey, pp. 125–41.
―――. 1999. 'Disengagement and Desire: The Tactics of Everyday Life', *American Ethnologist* 26(1): 139–59.
―――. 2001. 'Straight Talk, Hidden Talk, and Modernity: Shifts in Discourse Strategies in Highland New Guinea', in Joy Hendry and C.W. Watson (eds), *The Anthropology of Indirect Communication*. London: Routledge, pp. 218–31.
―――. 2003a. 'The Rights of Being Human', in R.A. Wilson and J. Mitchell (eds), *Human Rights in Global Perspective: Anthropological Studies of Rights, Claims and Entitlements*. London: Routledge, pp. 229–50.
―――. 2003b. 'Being There: The Magic of Presence or the Metaphysics of Morality', in P. Caplan (ed.), *The Ethics of Anthropology: Debates and Dilemmas*. London: Routledge, pp. 55–76.
―――. 2005a. 'The Aesthetics of Politics: Transforming Genres and Meanings in Melanesia.' In P.J. Stewart and A. Strathern (eds), *Expressive Genres and Historical Change*. Aldershot and Burlington: Ashgate Press, pp. 173–200.
―――. 2005b. 'Moral and Practical Frameworks for the Self', in J. Robbins and H. Wardlow (eds), *Humiliation and Transformation: The Making of Global and Local Modernities in Melanesia*. Aldershot and Burlington: Ashgate Press, pp. 115–24.
―――. n.d. 'Speaking-with and Feeling-with: The Phenomenology of Knowing the Other', in A.S. Gronseth and D.L. Davis (eds), *Making Sense: Between Alterity and Identity in Ethnographic Encounters.*
Josephides, L. and M. Schiltz. 1991. 'Through Kewa Country' (chapter 6) and 'Kewa Aftermath' (part of chapter 11), in E.L. Schieffelin and R. Crittenden (eds), *Like People You See in a Dream: First Contact in Six Papuan Societies*. Stanford, California: Stanford University Press, pp. 198–224, 278–81.
Kavouras, P. 1994. 'Where the Community Reveals Itself: Reflexivity and Moral Judgment in Karpathos, Greece', in K. Hastrup and P. Hervik (eds), *Social Experience and Anthropological Knowledge*. London: Routledge, pp. 139–65.
Keesing, R. 1985. 'Kwaio Women Speak: The Micropolitics of Autobiography in a Solomon Island Society', *American Anthropologist* 87: 27–39.
Kiki, A.M. 1968. *One Thousand Years in a Lifetime: A New Guinea Autobiography.* Melbourne: F.W. Cheshire Publishing. (Recorded by Ulli Beier.)

Kondo, D. 1990. 'Orientalism, Gender, and a Critique of Essentialist Identity', *Cultural Critique* (Fall 1990): 5–29.
Kristeva, J. 1991. *Strangers to Ourselves*. New York: Columbia University Press.
———. 1993. *Nations without Nationalism*. New York: Columbia University Press.
Laidlaw, J. 2002. 'For an Anthropology of Ethics and Freedom', *JRAI* 8(2): 311–32.
LeRoy, J. 1985. *Fabricated World: An Interpretation of Kewa Tales*. Vancouver: University of British Columbia Press.
Levinson, S.C. 1995. 'Interactional Biases in Human Thinking', in E. Goody (ed.), *Social Intelligence and Interaction: Expressions and Implications of the Social Bias in Human Intelligence*. Cambridge: Cambridge: University Press, pp. 221–60.
Lévi-Strauss, C. 1963. 'The Structural Study of Myth', in C. Lévi-Strauss, *Structural Anthropology*. New York: Basic Books.
———. 1966. *The Savage Mind*. London: Weidenfeld and Nicolson.
———. 1977. *Structural Anthropology Volume II*. London: Allen Lane.
Linde, C. 1993. *Life Stories: The Creation of Coherence*. Oxford: Oxford University Press.
MacIntyre, A. 1984[1981]. *After Virtue*. 2nd ed. Notre Dame, Indiana: University of Notre Dame Press.
Mauss, M. 1985. 'A Category of the Human Mind: The Notion of Person; the Notion of Self', in M. Carrithers, S. Collins and S. Lukes (eds), *The Category of the Person*. Cambridge: Cambridge University Press, pp. 1–25.
Mead, G.H. 1934. *Mind, Self, and Society: From the Standpoint of a Social Behaviourist*. Chicago: Chicago University Press.
———. 1964. *On Social Psychology: Selected Papers*. Ed. A. Strauss. Chicago and London: Phoenix Books, Chicago University Press.
Merleau-Ponty, M. 1973. *The Prose of the World*. Bloomington: Indiana University Press.
———. 1974. *Phenomenology, Language and Sociology: Selected Writings*. Ed. J. O'Neill. London: Heinemann.
Milton, K. 2002. *Loving Nature: Towards an Ecology of Emotion*. London: Routledge.
Mudimbe, V.Y. 1991. *Parables and Fables: Exegesis, Textuality, and Politics in Central Africa*. Madison: University of Wisconsin Press.
Myerhoff, B.G. 1978. *Number our Days*. New York: Simon and Schuster.
Narayan, K. 1989. *Storytellers, Saints and Scoundrels: Folk Narrative in Hindu Religious Teaching*. Philadelphia: University of Pennsylvania Press.
Ochs, E. and L. Capps. 2001. *Living Narratives: Creating Lives in Everyday Storytelling*. Cambridge, MA: Harvard University Press.
Personal Narratives Group. 1989. *Interpreting Women's Lives*. Bloomington: Indiana University Press.
Polier, N. 1998. 'Recolonizing the Subject: Colonialism, Sexual Violence, and Capitalist Culture in the Life Narrative of a Papua New Guinea Migrant Woman', *Feminist Studies* 24(3): 511–34.
Rapport, N.J. 1993. *Diverse Worldviews in an English Village*. Edinburgh: Edinburgh University Press.
———. 2003. *I am Dynamite: An Alternative Anthropology of Power*. London: Routledge.
Read, A. 2003. *Papua New Guinea's Last Place*. Oxford: Berghahn Books.
Ricoeur, P. 1970[1965]. *Freud and Philosophy: An Essay on Interpretation*. Trans. Denis Savage. New Haven: Yale University Press.
———. 1981. *Hermeneutics and the Human Sciences*. Ed. and trans. John B. Thompson. London and Paris: Cambridge University Press and Editions de la Maison des Sciences de l'Homme.

———. 1984. *Time and Narrative* (Vol. 1). Chicago: Chicago University Press.
———. 1992. *Oneself as Another.* Chicago: Chicago University Press.
Robbins, J. 2004. *Becoming Sinners: Christianity and Moral Torment in a Papua New Guinea Society.* Berkeley and Los Angeles: University of California Press.
———. 2005. 'The Humiliations of Sin: Christianity and the Modernization of the Subject among the Urapmin', in J. Robbins and H. Wardlow (eds), *The Making of Global and Local Modernities in Melaniesia.* Burlington, VT: Ashgate Press, pp. 3–21.
Rorty, A.O. 1976. 'A Literary Postscript: Characters, Persons, Selves, Individuals', in A.O. Rorty (ed.), *The Identities of Persons.* Berkeley and Los Angeles: California University Press.
Rosaldo, M. 1984. 'Toward an Anthropology of Self and Feeling', in R. Schroeder and R. Le Vine (eds) *Culture Theory: Essays on Mind, Self, and Emotion.* Cambridge: Cambridge University Press, pp. 137–57.
Sahlins, M. 1974. *Stone Age Economics.* London: Tavistock.
Sartre, J-P. 1973. *L'Etre et le Néant* [Being and Nothingness]. Poitiers: Editions Gallimand.
Schieffelin, E. 1976. *The Sorrow of the Lonely and the Burning of the Dancers.* New York: St Martin's Press.
Searle, J. 1969. *Speech Acts: An Essay in the Philosophy of Language.* Cambridge: Cambridge University Press.
Seremetakis, N.C. 1991. *The Last Word.* Chicago: Chicago University Press.
Shostak, M. 1981. *Nisa: The Life and Worlds of a !Kung Woman.* Cambridge, MA: Harvard University Press.
Smith, M. 1954. *Baba of Karo, a Woman of the Muslim Hausa.* New Haven: Yale University Press.
Strathern, A. 1979. *Ongka: A Self-account by a New Guinea Big-man.* London: Duckworth.
Strathern, M. 1988. *The Gender of the Gift.* Berkeley and Los Angeles: California University Press.
———. 1992. *After Nature: English Kinship in the Later Twentieth Century.* Cambridge: Cambridge University Press.
Strawson, P.F. 1965[1959]. *Individuals: An Essay in Descriptive Metaphysics.* London: Methuen.
Strecker, I. 1988. *The Social Practice of Symbolization: An Anthropological Analysis.* LSE Monographs 60. London: Athlone Press.
Taussig, M. 1993. *Mimesis and Alterity: A Particular History of the Senses.* London: Routledge.
Taylor, C. 1985. 'The Person', in M. Carrithers, S. Collins and S. Lukes (eds), *The Category of the Person.* Cambridge: Cambridge University Press, pp. 257–81.
———. 1989. *Sources of the Self.* Cambridge, MA: Harvard University Press.
Todorov, T. 1977. *The Poetics of Prose.* Ithaca: Cornell University Press.
Wagner, R. 1975. *The Invention of Culture.* Englewood Cliffs, New Jersey: Prentice-Hall.
———. 1986. *Asiwinarong: Ethos, Image and Social Power among the Usen Barok of New Ireland.* Princeton, New Jersey: Princeton University Press.
———. 1995. 'Hazarding Intent: Why Sogo Left Hweabi', in L. Rosen (ed.), *Other Intentions: Cultural Contexts and the Attribution of Inner States.* Santa Fe, NM: School of American Research Press, pp. 163–75.
Wardlow, H. 2002. 'Headless Ghosts and Roving Women: Spectres of Modernity in Papua New Guinea', *American Ethnologist* 29(1): 5–32.
Watson, L.C. and M. Watson-Franke. 1985. *Interpreting Life Histories.* New Brunswick: Rutgers University Press.

Weiner, A. 1976. *Women of Value, Men of Renown*. Austin: University of Texas Press.
Weiner, J. 2001. *Tree Leaf Talk: A Heideggerian Anthropology*. Oxford: Berg.
Wikan, U. 1992. 'Beyond the Words: The Power of Resonance', *American Ethnologist* 19: 460–82.
Young, M. 1983. *Magicians of Manumanua: Living Myth in Kalauna*. Berkeley: University of California Press.
Ziman, J. 1978. *Reliable Knowledge: An Exploration of the Grounds for Belief in Science*. Cambridge: Cambridge University Press.

Index

Abu-Lughod, L. 160n6
action
　analysis of 44–5
　motivation for 158–9
　Ricoeur's theory of 37–8, 57–8, 144
　see also talk and action
Adalu Rimbu (spirit cult) 73, 74
Adorno, Theodor 219
aesthetic intent 214n1
Agema 68, 73, 74, 87, 89, 93, 127, 195, 197–8, 200–202, 206–207, 212
　Catholic mission in 77, 99
Ainu 65, 147–8n2
　Yako and 173–4
Aka 10
alienation, ethnography as 223n4
Alirapu 82, 83, 84, 105–106, 108, 109, 141
　narrative of 90–92
Aliwi 77, 188, 190, 191, 192, 208
Amasi 10, 84, 177, 206
Amburupa people 75, 176
Ana 87, 202
anthropology
　anthropological abstraction 78–9
　authentication in 43–4
Antigone, Lari as 139
Areali 68, 70, 73
Aristotle 58, 110, 139, 148n7, 219
ascription, self-ascription and 25–30
Asiwinarong (Wagner, R.) 21
Austin, J.L. 156
authority 139
　ancestral authority 41, 49
　challenges to 42
　of God 103
　and intent 41
　patriarchal authority 147
autobiographical knowledge 157–8, 161n10
Awari 67, 70, 74, 76, 77, 87–9, 121, 205

Baba of Karo (Smith, M.) 80n1
Bala people 76, 89
bantering, bickering and 4–8
Bateson, Gregory 21
Behar, R. 80n1, 147n1
Benjamin, Walter 56, 58, 146, 154–5
Biru 133, 170, 184, 194, 204
Bloch, M. 41, 156, 160n8, 161n10, 217
Boas, Franz 111n6
Borges, J.L. 223–4n5, 225n9
boundaries of recognition 19
Bourdieu, Pierre 46n7, 46n9, 53, 156
Brenneis, D. and Myers, F.R. 47n18
brideprice 78, 79, 85, 199, 202
　Ainu, Yako and 173–4
　Alirapu's story 90
　bickering over 4, 8, 13, 14
　courtship, marriage and 68–9
　Giame, Yadi and 175
　Hapkas' story 119
　irregular unions and 171, 172
　Lari, Rimbu and 176–8
　Lari's story 129, 130, 131
　marriage and marital life, negotiation of 182–3
　Papola's story 122, 123
　problems with 13–14, 167–70
　Rimbu's story 123, 125

Rumbame's story 87–8, 89, 105
   variations in, number of recipients and 164–5
   Wapa's story 63, 64, 65, 71
   women, value and 138
   young men and provision of 137
Briggs, Jean 46n5
Brison, K.J. 159n2
Brown, P. and Levinson, S.C. 35, 36, 39–40, 47n18, 49n23
Bruner, Jerome 54, 55–6, 58, 160n7

Calvino, Italo 47–8n20
Cappelletto, Francesca 157–8, 161n10
Carrithers, Michael 31, 47n16, 54, 56–7, 58, 78–80, 143, 146, 153–4, 157, 158, 159n3, 160n7
Catholicism 10, 65, 84, 101, 170, 171, 175, 195, 204
childbirth, pregnancy and 91–2
Chomsky, Noam 156
Christianity 85, 98, 102, 107, 110–12, 138, 146, 206, 210, 213
   Christian missions 19, 77, 99, 128
   facing change and 106–107
clothing 90, 92
   dress habits 166
cohabitation, tensions of 15
   see also polygyny
Cohen, A.P. 23, 32, 45n3, 46n5
Cohen, A.P. and Rapport, N. 142
coherence
   construction of coherent selves 81, 102, 103–105, 109
   narrative unity and 67
communication
   as capability 34–6
   communicative practices of Kewa people 38–9, 44
   communicative strategies, openness in 44
   language and 33–4
   narratives as 146–7
compensation payments, prestige and 215n5
concealment, explicitness and 42

conception, domicile and 165–6
conceptual categories 44
conceptual vocabulary 21
connectedness 109–10
consciousness
   communication and 135
   ethnography as history of 222–3
   experience and 142–4
   organization of experience and narrative as form of 141
   states of 25–6
Cooley, C.H. 46n6
courtship
   courting practices 187n1
   courting songs 164, 184 *see also* rome; wena yaisia
   marriage and 68–71, 87, 90
   portraits of 162–6
   rejection in courting 171–2
Crapanzano, Vincent 80n1, 221, 222, 225n9
Crites, Stephen 142
critical metanarratives, construction of 81, 102, 105–106
Cruickshank, J. 80n1
'cultural-functionalism' 225n10
cultural history, ethnography as chronicle of 222–3
cultural interplay, semiotic 42–3
cumulativeness, excessiveness and 218

daily life of Kewa people 10–15
Damasio, A. 161n10
Dangerous Words: Language and Politics in the Pacific (Brenneis, D. and Myers, F.R., Eds.) 47n18
Davidson, Donald 160n6
death
   divination in *(pulu)* 94–5, 214n2
   duties to persons and rights in persons 197, 206–7, 208–9
   of Payanu 202–9
   politics of 188–214
   of Rake 188–95
   and recurring conflict 209–14
   ritual of 94–5

of Wapa 6, 14, 41, 195–202
Derrida, Jacques 47–8n20
descriptions of events *see* portraits
Diderot, Denis 224n7
difference
    differentiation of self 34–5
    ethnography as portrayal of 221
discordance 110
discourse strategy 38–9, 152–3
Dreyfus, H.L. and Rabinow, P. 33
Duranti, A. 156
duties to persons 195–202

Edelman, G. 142
elicitation
    analysis of action 44–5
    concealment, explicitness and 42
    conceptual categories and 44
    discourse strategy 38–9, 152–3
    and 'eliciting talk' 17–19, 39–40
    explicitness in 38–43, 44, 155–6
    impoverishing effect of explicitness in 42
    meanings and intentions, contestability of 107–8
    moral self-construction and 108–9
    permanence in time, establishment of 109
    schimogenesis and 21
    strategies of Kewa people 22, 30
    use in ethnography of 21–2
    see also negotiation, rehearsed and rehearsing talk and action
emotions
    as cultural givens 46
    distinguishing between logical and emotional explanations 140
    'emotion as memory' 158, 161n10
    emotional associations 29
    emotional connection 66–7
    emotional meaning 186
    emotional responses 14
    expenditure of 136
    as facilitating fieldwork 4
    ideology of 214n1
    marriage arrangements and 139–40
    mastery over 46n5
    weeping and emotional display 214n1
ends and means, link between 48n21
Erave 76, 85, 92, 93, 118, 119, 123, 126–8, 170, 178, 191, 202, 206, 215
ethics and self in paradigmatic accounts 57–8
ethnography
    as alienation or projection of the world 219, 223n4
    as chronicle of cultural history 222–3
    conceptual vocabulary, development of 21
    elicitation, schimogenesis and 21
    elicitation, use of 21–2
    ethnographer, task of 224–5n8
    ethnographic representation 223n3
    as history of consciousness 222–3
    locality and chronicle 221
    Melanesia as ethnographic region 221
    mimesis as way of knowing 218–20
    as portrayal of difference 221
    postmodernist critiques of 223n4
    'reality' in 220
    self and ethnographical understanding 222
    sociality and difference 221–2
    stories, theory and 151–2, 216–18
    Taussig's ethnographer's qualities 220
    theoretical regionalism 221–2
Evans-Pritchard, E.E. 45n1
existentialist distinction, in-itself and for-itself 28–9
explicitness
    against impoverishing effects of 42
    and concealment 42, 152
    in elicitation 38–43, 44, 155–6
    as a locus of disclosure 37
    as placing in public space 42
externalization *see* narrative; self-externalization; self-introspection; social exernalization

'face' 49n22
Favret-Saada, J. 37–8, 47n14, 49n24, 49n26, 159n4, 224–5n8
Feld, S. 214n1
fieldwork
  bantering, bickering and 4–8
  boundaries of recognition 19
  communicative strategies, openness in 44
  daily life 10–15
  elicitation and 'eliciting talk' 17–19, 39–40
  gossip and talk 3–4
  grudges, festering of 6
  'hiding talk' and anger 5–6
  housebuilding 16–17
  ill-feeling 6–7
  indirect argumentation 7
  landscape 9
  meanings, negotiation of 4
  moods, mercurial nature of 6
  movement, often incessant nature of 9
  onomatopoeic talk 3–4
  payment of informants 96
  place, importance of 8–10
  pre-contact practices 67
  rainfall and mud 8–9
  relativization of statements and 'bad talk' 17
  residential mobility 8–10
  scrambling into the field 15–19
  sexual banter 7
  squabbling 4–8
  style of life 3–4
  tensions and violence 6–7, 179–81, 181–2, 185–6
  tone of life 3–4
  whines 4
food prestations 12, 18, 164, 199, 202, 204, 207, 208, 212
Foster, R. 225n10
Foti, Waliya, Rarapalu, Karupiri and 181–2
Foucault, Michel 79
Freud, Sigmund 224n7

Gapea 63, 64, 76, 77, 87, 89, 93, 194, 197
gardens
  magic and 71–3
  planting gardens 71–3

Geertz, Clifford 21
Gellner, Ernest 79
Gender of the Gift (Strathern, M.) 46n9, 152–3, 187n2
gender relations 92–3, 185–6
Giame 66, 70, 84, 85, 124–5, 147–8n2
  Yadi and 174–6
Gilsenan, M. 80n1, 148n3
Goody, Esther 35, 47n19
gossip and talk 3–4
Grene, D. and Lattimore, R. 139
Grice, Paul 35, 40, 44, 49n23
growing up 67–8
grudges, festering of 6

Hapkas (Nasupeli) 10, 70, 77, 94–7, 101, 106–107, 113–14, 116, 125–6, 132
  brideprice problems 119, 170
  and death of Payanu 202–203, 207–209
  and death of Wapa 195, 197
  marriage of 123
  narrative of 118–21, 140, 142–3, 146
  as visionary 137
Heidegger, Martin 49n25
Hewitt, J.P. 46n6
historical knowledge 158, 161n10
historical perspective on concept of self 24–5
housebuilding 16–17
hunting 12, 166, 179

Ili 128, 129, 130, 131
ill-feeling 6–7
illocutionary intent 40
indirect argumentation 7
individual, self and 22–4
Ingold, Tim 45n2, 47n15

intention-attribution 36, 40, 42–3
intention-concealment 39
intentionality 45n2, 146, 185
   aesthetic intent 214n1
   authority and intent 41
   exchange of 35
   'hazarding intent' 22, 47–8n20
   illocutionary intent 40
   meaning and intent 42–3, 158
   perlocutionary intent 64
interactivity
   practices among Kewa people 37–8
   self and 35–6
interest clashes, rights and 183–4
interlocution and denial 30–33, 35, 37
intertextuality 154
Ipa 6, 82, 87, 117, 126
   brideprice problems 169, 170
   and death of Rake 194–5
   and Mapi 96, 97, 98, 99
Ipanu 70, 170
irregular unions 170–72
   brideprice and 171, 172
Isunga, Sepik policemen 76

Jackson, Michael 46n12, 111n3, 154, 223n2
James, Wendy 45n3
James, William 46n8
Jebens, H. 111n7
Jenkins, T. 216–17
Josephides, L. and Schiltz, M. 76, 136
Josephides, Lisette 17, 20, 36, 37, 38, 39–40, 41, 42, 44, 47n19, 54, 75, 76, 101, 106, 107, 140, 146, 148n7, 153, 154, 155, 156, 159, 160, 164, 184, 187n1, 197, 206, 207, 208, 209, 214n1, 214n3, 215n5, 215n6, 216, 223n1, 223n3, 225n10

Kagua 9, 15, 93, 118, 120, 123, 126, 128, 134, 167, 174, 178–9, 188, 191, 194–5, 200, 201, 206

Kalinu 168
Kalu 76, 87, 123, 172, 182, 207
Kaluali *see* Kopayo Kaluali war
Kaluli people 79, 214n1
Kamare 15, 70, 169, 171, 174
Kamarepa people 68, 73, 93, 118, 191, 193, 198, 204–209, 213
Kambenu 118, 119, 121, 122, 123, 147–8n2
Kambia people 75
Kanada 76
Kant, Immanuel 58
Kaporopali 170, 171, 172
Karupiri 171, 191, 203
   Foti, Waliya and Rarapalu 181–2
Kavournas, P. 80n2
Keesing, R. 58
Kengeai 90, 174, 196
Kewa people
   bickering and bantering among 4–8
   brideprice problems 13–14
   childbirth, pregnancy and 91–2
   clothing 90, 92
   cohabitation, tensions of 15
   communicative practices 38–9, 44
   communicative strategies, openness of 44
   conception, domicile and 165–6
   courting songs 164, 184
   courtship and marriage 68–71, 87, 90
   cultural development of 23–4
   daily life of 10–15
   death ritual 94–5
   divination in death *(pulu)* 94–5
   dress habits 166
   elicitation strategies of 22, 30
   gender relations 92–3, 185–6
   gossip and talk among 3–4
   growing up 67–8
   grudges, festering of 6
   'hiding talk' and anger among 5–6
   housebuilding with 16–17
   hunting 12
   ill-feeling among 6–7
   interactive practices among 37–8

interest clashes, rights and 183–4
journeys 'unfulfilled' 9–10
life, non-uniform nature of 12
magic and gardens 71–3
marital relations 98
marriage 13–14
marriage exchanges 164–6
moods, mercurial of 6
movement, often incessant, of 9
multiple marriages 70–71
pig-growing magic 72
pig-killing 6, 12–13, 17–19, 39,
 65–7, 70, 74–9, 85, 87–8, 89,
 91, 94, 97–9, 105, 122, 125,
 129–30, 134–5, 138, 147, 153,
 155, 162, 169, 180, 199, 201,
 202, 205, 207
pig theft 75
place, importance for 8–10
planting gardens 71–3
polygyny in 89, 100, 170–72,
 176–8, 183, 185–6
pre-contact practices 67
pregnancy 68–9, 91–2
rejection in courting 171–2
relativization of statements and
 'bad talk' among 17
residential mobility of 8–10
selves, construction of 30
semiotic cultural interplay 42–3
sexual bantering among 7
sickness 88–9, 100–101
social interactionist practices
 34–5, 216
social knowledge, construction of
 23–4
spirit houses 73–4
squabbling among 4–8
style of life 3–4
tensions and violence among 6–7,
 179–81, 181–2, 185–6
tone of life 3–4
traditional practices, attitudes to
 92–3, 94
veiled speech of 17
warfare and pacification 75–7,
 90–91, 93–4

whines amongst 4
women's reputations 186
women's work 91–2
see also Ainu; Alirapu; brideprice;
 Giame; Foti; Hapkas; Karupiri;
 Kiru; Lari; Liame; Mapi;
 Mayanu; narratives of self;
 Papola; Payanu; portraits;
 Pupula; Ragunanu; Rake;
 Rarapalu; Rimbu; Rosa;
 Rumbame; Waliya; Wapa; Yadi;
 Yakiranu; Yako
Kiki, A.M. 81
Kiru 6, 10, 12, 96, 119, 120,
 147–8n2, 197
 and death of Payanu 203–4, 207,
 209
 Lari and 128, 132, 134
 Rimbu and 125, 126
 Rosa, Liame and 179–81, 185
Koai 16, 17, 89, 131, 134, 167, 183
Koe Rimbu ('bad Rimbu') spirit cult
 73
Kogalepa 73, 74, 133
Koiari people 68, 75, 93, 118, 147,
 168, 191
Koipame 70
Koke 10, 123, 125, 126, 131, 180,
 207, 208, 213
Komalo 13, 14, 69, 120, 130–31,
 196, 197
Kondo, D. 23, 45–6n4
Kopayo Kaluali war 76
Kristeva, Julia 224n7
Kuare 70
Kumi 8, 12, 85, 92, 204, 208, 213
 Mapi and 95, 96, 99, 100

Laidlaw, J. 79
landscape 9
 transformation of 112–13
Langer, Lawrence 223
language
 action and use of 156
 critical ethnography and 160n6
 pragmatic view of 160n6
 talk and action 156

Tok Pisin 5, 15–17, 65–6, 82, 84, 89, 96, 99, 101, 114, 116–17, 123, 128, 135, 152, 167, 174, 180, 188, 193, 204–5
  word choice, relevance of 65–6n4
Lapame 167, 168
Laperepa people 77
Lari 47n17, 62–3, 65, 84, 92, 113, 116, 117–18, 119, 174–5, 180, 182
  as Antigone 139
  brideprice problems 129, 130, 131, 169
  courtship 69, 166
  daily life 10, 13, 14, 15, 147–8n2
  and death of Payanu 202, 203, 205
  and death of Rake 191
  experience and consciousness 142–3
  irregular unions 172
  love and personhood 184–5, 186
  morality 144, 145
  narrative of 128–35, 138–9, 140–41
  narratives as communication 147
  polygyny 173
  Rimbu and 124, 125, 126, 127, 176–8, 184
  talk and action 40, 41
LeRoy, J. 154, 217
Lévi-Strauss, Claude 24, 110, 111n6, 154
Levinas, Emmanuel 145
Levinson, S.C. 33, 35, 36, 39, 40, 47n19
Liame 7, 12, 92, 96, 147–8n2, 181–2, 184, 195, 204, 209
  love and personhood 185
  Rosa, Kiru and 179–81
Linde, C. 81, 103, 104–105
Lisette (anthropologist) 116, 121, 124
  and death of Payanu 205, 206, 208
Lisette (little) 10, 63, 132, 134, 148, 177, 180, 204
locality and chronicle 221
Loma 85, 128, 169, 170, 182, 184
Lords of the Lebanese Marches (Gilsenan, M.) 148n3

love and personhood 184–6
Loving Nature (Milton, K.) 47n15
Lu 127, 172, 198–9

MacIntyre, A. 103, 139, 143, 144–5
magic and gardens 71–3
Malinowski, Bronislaw 79
Mapi (Lopa) 13, 85
  dramatic flair 95
  land expansion tactics 97
  narrative of 93–8
  theatrical mobility of 85
  visionary and dreamer 98–101
marriage
  irregular unions and 170–72
  Kewa people 13–14
  and marital life, negotiation of 182–4
  marital relations of Kewa people 98
  marriage exchanges 164–6
  multiple marriages 70–71
  negotiating marriage 183–5
  see also polygyny; portraits
Marx, Karl 28
Mauss, Marcel 23, 45–6n4
maximal narratives 53–4
  see also narration of self
Mayanu 10, 82, 84–5, 90, 105, 141, 169, 174, 202
  narrative of 92–3
Mead, George Herbert 22, 24–5, 29, 30, 33, 34, 45–6n4, 46n6, 160–61n9, 220
meaning
  contestability of intentions and 107–8
  and intent 42–3, 158
  negotiation of 4
means and ends, link between 48n21
Melanesia as ethnographic region 221
memory
  autobiographical and historical 161n10
  episodic 161n10
men's narratives 135–8

240 Index

Merleau-Ponty, Maurice 46n9, 46n12, 218
metonymy
  metonymic pragmatics 41, 44, 64, 95
  rhetorical use of 41
Michael (Agema) 15, 18, 65–6, 70, 74, 122, 176, 198, 207, 208, 223
Milton, Kay 47n15
mimesis
  as ethnographic project xv, xxi
  and Jackson 223n2
  and Kristeva 224n7
  as way of knowing 216–20
  and witchcraft 225n8
minimal narratives 53–4
  see also portraits
misrecognition 32
modernity
  dealing in changing world with 81, 102, 106–7, 109–10
  modern perspective on self 30–33
moods, mercurial nature of 6
morality
  judgement and narrative 109–10
  moral constructions of self as paradigmatic accounts 77–80
  moral personhood, construction of 57–8, 77–80, 81, 102–3, 108–9
  narration of self 58
  self-construction and elicitation 108–9
  and self in paradigmatic accounts 57–8
motivation for action 158–9
Mt Hagen 9, 13, 14, 88, 119, 122, 123, 126–8, 146, 168, 178, 191, 201, 205, 221
Mudimbe, V.Y. 29
Myerhoff, B.G. 46n5

Nadawa 177
Nadisua 96, 180, 203
Naguri 70, 73, 198
Narayan, K. 217
narration of self
  changing world, dealing with modernity 81, 102, 106–7, 109–10
  Christianity, facing change and 106–7
  coherence, construction of
  coherent selves 81, 102, 103–5, 109
  coherence and narrative unity 67
  communication, narratives as 146–7
  consciousness, communication and 135
  consciousness, experience and 142–4
  consciousness, organization of experience and narrative as form of 141
  courtship and marriage 68–71
  critical metanarratives, construction of 81, 102, 105–6
  ethics and self in paradigmatic accounts 57–8
  generational divisions within 53–4
  growing up 67–8
  magic and gardens 71–3
  maximal narratives 53–4
  men's narratives 135–8
  minimal narratives 53–4
  moral constructions of self as paradigmatic accounts 77–80
  moral personhood, construction of 57–8, 77–80, 81, 102–3, 108–9
  morality 58, 144–6
  narrative and paradigmatic thought 56–7
  pacification after warfare 75–7
  past, linking with present 81, 102, 109
  pig-killing 65–7, 70, 74–9, 85, 87–8, 89, 91, 94, 97–9, 105, 122, 125, 129–30, 134–5, 138, 147–8n2
  production of 54, 75, 76, 101, 106, 107, 140, 146, 148n7
  projection, ethnography as 223n4
  self and morality in paradigmatic accounts 57–8

spirit houses 73–4
storytellers 59–67, 82–5, 113–18
theories of narrative 55–6
warfare 75–7
women's narratives 138–41
see also Ainu; Alirapu; Giame; Foti; Hapkas; Karupiri; Kiru; Lari; Liame; Mapi; Mayanu; Papola; Payanu; Pupula; Ragunanu; Rake; Rarapalu; Rimbu; Rosa; Rumbame; Waliya; Wapa; Yadi; Yakiranu; Yako
narrative
  autobiographical knowledge, generation of 157–8, 161n10
  connectedness and 109–10
  critical metanarratives, construction of 81, 102, 105–6
  cumulativeness, excessiveness and 218
  discordance in 110
  externalization of memories in 146
  historical knowledge, generation of 158, 161n10
  human interaction and importance of 53
  language, action and use of 156
  lived narratives 155
  'living myth' in 79
  'master narrative' 216, 223n1
  moral judgement and 109–10
  origin, manipulation of stories of 214n3
  and paradigmatic thought 56–7
  power and limitations of paradigmatic thought 80
  reasoning and 154
  representativeness in 79
  subjectivization of reality 55–6
  theories of narrative 55–6
  see also stories
negotiation 20–2, 33–4, 37–44, 78, 157–8
  between old and new 107
  conciliatory xix
  as elicitation 154

in Kewa stories 104–5
of marriage 89, 173, 182–7
Mead and 160n9
over meaning, duties and social realities 209–13
and 'mind-readings' 49n24
and rehearsing talk 58
and social knowledge xix–xx
see also rehearsed and rehearsing talk
Nisa (Shostak, M.) 80n1
Noeme 97, 98, 100

Ochs, E. and Capps, L. 222–3
One Thousand Years in a Lifetime (Kiki, A.M.) 81
oneself and selfhood 27–8
Ongka (Strathern, A.) 80n1
onomatopoeic talk 3–4
otherness and self 25–6, 29–30, 33, 43, 219–20

pacification after warfare 75–7
Paisa people 76
Pamerepa people 68, 77, 89
Papola 95, 96, 113, 114–16, 119, 125, 136–7, 147–8n2, 174, 180
  brideprice problems 122, 123
  death of Payanu 209
  death of Wapa 198
  narrative of 122–3
Papolata 73, 87, 198
paradigmatic thought 56–7
  power and limitations of 80
  rehearsed talk and 157
Paripa lineage, Yala people 18, 19, 84, 85, 97, 191, 201, 206, 207
particularity 27
Pasaroli 176, 203
past, linking with present 81, 102, 109
Pastor Ore 114, 204, 205, 206, 208
Payanu 66–7
  death of 202–9
payment of informants 96
Peirce, C.S. 46n6
Pepeawere people 68, 76, 77, 89, 179

Perepe people 68, 70, 75–6, 93, 96–7, 99, 100–101, 118, 120, 172, 191–5, 197, 199, 206, 210–11
perlocutionary intent 64
person
    duties to and rights in persons 195–202
    rights in persons 195–202
    and self 22–4, 45–6n4
    Strawson's concept of 25–9
    Taylor's concept of modern personhood 31–2
Personal Narratives Group 80n1
pig-growing magic 72
pig-killing 6, 12–13, 17–19, 39
    at Aka 87–8
    Alirapu and 91
    Mapi and 85, 94, 97–8, 99
    men's narratives of 134–5, 138
    narratives of 65–7, 70, 74–9, 105, 122, 125, 129–30
    portraits of 153, 155, 162, 169, 180, 199, 201, 202, 205, 207
    Rumbame and 89
    songs of 147–8n2
pig theft 75
Pima 200
Pisa 10, 18, 125, 170, 212, 213
    death of Payanu 203, 205, 207, 208
    death of Wapa 197, 198, 199
place, importance of 8–10
Poiale 10, 66, 100, 120, 193, 203, 206
Polier, N. 148n5
polygyny 89, 100, 170–72, 176–8, 183, 185–6
    conflict and 172–3
Poreale 82, 169, 182
Port Moresby 15, 122, 127, 136, 199
portraits
    Ainu and Yako 173–4
    brideprice, problems with 167–70
    courtship 162–6
    death and politics 188–214
    death and recurring conflict 209–14
    duties to persons 195–202
    elicitation and explicitness 155–6
    Giame and Yadi 174–6
    irregular unions 170–72
    of Kewa life, production of 153, 154–5, 156, 159
    language, talk and action 156
    Lari and Rimbu 176–8
    Liame, Rosa and Kiru 179–81
    love and personhood 184–6
    marriage and marital life, negotiation of 182–4
    methodological shift towards 152–6
    motivation for action 158–9
    norms and claims 156
    Payanu, death of 202–9
    persons, duties to and rights in 195–202
    pig-killing 153, 155, 162, 169, 180, 199, 201, 202, 205, 207
    polygyny and conflict 172–3
    Rake, death of 188–95
    Rarapalu, Karupiri, Foti and Waliya 181–2
    rights in persons 195–202
    social reality, negotiability of 158–9
    talk and action, rehearsed and rehearsing 157–8
    talk and action, rehearsed and rehearsing, distinction between 186–7
    vignettes and 159–60n5
    Wapa, death of 195–202
postmodernist critiques of ethnography 223n4
pre-contact practices 67
pregnancy
    childbirth and 91–2
    Kewa people 68–9, 91–2
The Prose of the World (Merleau-Ponty, M.) 218
projection, ethnography as 223n4
Puliminia 10, 15
Pupula 15, 59, 61, 65–6, 67, 94, 171, 198, 207, 212
    courtship and marriage 69–70

Mapi and 85
pig-kills 74–5
response to taunts 18–19
warfare and pacification 75–6
Ragunanu (daughter of Roga) 169–70, 182, 184, 202, 203
Ragunanu (wife of Pupula) 5, 10, 13, 15, 59, 62, 65, 138, 147–8n2, 212
courtship and marriage 70, 71–2
growing up 67
magic and gardens 71–3
rainfall and mud 8–9
Rake
death of 188–95
Roga and death of 189, 194
Waliya and death of 189, 195
Wola and death of 191, 192, 193, 194, 195
Yakopaita and death of 188, 191, 193–4
Rama 10, 14, 18, 63, 69, 76, 84, 174–5, 207
Alirapu and 90
brideprice problems 169
Mapi and 95
Mayanu and 92
Rapport, Nigel J. 32, 111n5, 217
Rarapalu 6, 84, 92, 138, 159, 183–4, 185–6
Karupiri, Foti and Waliya 181–2
rascals 215n6
'reality' 219, 220, 225n9
consciousness and depiction of 55
in ethnography 220
nature of 221
ontological reality 46–7n13
perceived reality 183
social reality 42, 80, 105, 155, 157–8, 183, 184, 186, 208–209, 210–11, 213, 216
subjunctivization of 55
transformed reality 112
reasoning 25, 26, 79
abstract reasoning 54, 78
academic reasoning 216–17
interactive reasoning 35
narrative and 154

practical reasoning 35, 38, 48n21
recognition, boundaries of 19
Reed, Adam 148n4
reflexivity 25–6, 28, 34–5
rehearsed and rehearsing talk and action xxii, xxiii, 21–2, 33–4, 38–44, 58, 103, 109–10, 140, 153, 157–8, 168, 182–4, 186–7, 216, 220, 224n5
rehearsing *see* rehearsed and rehearsing
Rero 6–7, 14, 18
residential mobility 8–10
Ricoeur, Paul 22, 23, 25, 27–8, 29, 34–5, 37, 38, 46n11, 54, 57–8, 81, 103, 107, 108–10, 142–3, 144–5, 146–7, 159n1, 219
rights in persons 195–202
Rika (companion of Wapa's youth) 195, 198, 201
Rika (Roga's junior brother) 66, 130
Rimbu 7, 10, 13, 14, 41, 116
brideprice in story of 123, 125
importunity of 18–19
kinship, granting of 29, 219–20
Lari and 176–8
multiple pig-killer 74
narrative of 123–8
Payanu and 66–7
prominence of 16–17
Robbins, J. 82, 102–103, 107
Roga 5, 9, 10, 16, 41, 93, 97, 101, 123, 173
brideprice problems 169–70
death of Rake 189, 194
death of Wapa 199, 201, 202
irregular unions 171–2
Lari and 134
Rimbu and 125, 126
rome courting verses 68, 87, 163, 184
Ronali people 76
Rorea 92, 100, 135, 207, 213
Rorepame 147–8n2, 174, 198
Rorty, Amélie O. 23, 45–6n4
Rorty, Richard 160n6
Rosa 204, 209
Liame, Kiru and 179–81, 182
Rosaldo, Michelle 44

Rousseau, Jean-Jacques 24
Rumbame 82, 83
  brideprice in story of 87–8, 89, 105
  Christianity, conversion to 110
  Lari and 128, 129–30
  narrative of 85–90, 102–106, 108, 109
Rusa, Magistrate 167, 182, 194, 200, 201, 212

Sahlins, M. 107, 218
Samberigi people 75, 123, 127
Sartre, Jean-Paul 22, 28–9, 46–7n13
Schieffelin, E. 154
Schiltz, Marc 15, 47–8n20, 111n6, 224n6
schimogenesis and elicitation 21
Searle, J. 40
self
  action, Ricoeur's theory of 37–8, 57–8, 144
  alienation 217
  ascription, self-ascription and 25–30
  communication and language 33–4
  communication as capability 34–6
  consciousness, states of 25–6
  construction of Kewa people 30
  differentiation 34–5
  elicitation, explicitness in 38–43, 44
  ethics and self in paradigmatic accounts 57–8
  and ethnographic understanding 222
  evaluations, shaping of 31–2
  everyday self 33–4
  existentialist distinction, in-itself and for-itself 28–9
  historical perspective on concept of 24–5
  individual and 22–4
  interactivity and 35–6
  interlocution and denial 30–33, 35, 37
  metonymic pragmatics 41, 44, 64, 95
  misrecognition 32
  modern perspective on 30–33
  oneself and selfhood 27–8
  otherness and 25–6, 29–30, 33, 43, 219–20
  particularity 27
  person, Strawson's concept of 25–9
  person, Taylor's concept of modern personhood 31–2
  person and 22–4, 45–6n4
  reflexivity 25–6, 28, 34–5
  self strategies 36–8, 43–5
  self theory 22–4
  social knowledge, negotiation of 20–21
  speech and 34–6
  talk and action, rehearsed and rehearsing 38–43
  see also narration of self; self-externalization; self-introspection
self-externalization xv, xxi, 25, 34, 44, 107, 222, 223n4
self-introspection xv, xxi, 25, 222, 223n4
semiotic cultural interplay 42–3
Seremetakis, N.C. 209, 215n7
sexual banter 7
Shostak, M. 80n1
siapi (veiled speech) xx, 6, 17–8, 22, 39–40, 205
  and sanza 45n1
sickness 88–9, 100–101
Sipi 63, 69, 118, 174, 197, 201, 203, 212
Smith, M. 80n1
social externalization 141
  see also self-externalization
social interaction 34–5, 216
social knowledge
  construction of 23–4
  negotiation of 20–21
social reality 42, 80, 105, 155, 157–8, 183, 184, 186, 208–209, 210–11, 213, 216

explicans, mutuality of
 explicandum and 159n1
 negotiability of 158–9
 see also 'reality'
sociality and difference 221–2
songs 187n1
 church songs 113
 courting songs *see rome, wena
  yaisia*
 funeral songs *see temali*
 pig-killing songs 147n2
Sophocles 110, 139
Sopo 12–13
sorcery 215n4
Speech Acts (Searle, J.) 40
spirit houses 73–4
squabbling 4–8
stories
 ethnography, theory and 151–2,
  216–18
 of everyday social life 217–18
 information and 154
 life-projects and 217
 mapping apprenticeships 216–17
 of origin, manipulation of stories
  214n3
 theory and 151–2, 216–18
 see also narrative
storytellers 59–67, 82–5, 113–18
Strathern, Andrew 15, 80n1, 158
Strathern, Marilyn 42, 43, 46n9,
 152–3, 187n2
Strawson, P.F. 22, 23, 25–8, 29, 33,
 45n3
Strecker, I. 35, 42–3, 49n22
style of life 3–4
Subulu people 68
Sumbura 9, 65, 76, 87, 94, 120, 121,
 130, 132, 192, 194, 202

talk
 and action, rehearsed and
  rehearsing 38–43, 157–8
 and action, rehearsed and
  rehearsing, distinction between
  186–7
 'hiding talk' and anger 5–6

onomatopoeic talk 3–4
 relativization of statements and
  'bad talk' 17
 speech and self 34–6
 veiled speech of Kewa people 17
Taussig, M. 218, 219, 223–4n5
 ethnographic qualities 220
Taylor, Charles 22, 31–2, 37, 43,
 47n16
temali (threnodies or dirges) 14, 82,
 88, 97, 101, 119–121, 189, 194–5,
 202, 204
tensions and violence 6–7, 179–81,
 181–2, 185–6
Tepenarirepa people 68, 76
theory
 action, Ricoeur's theory of 37–8,
  57–8, 144
 ethnography, stories and 151–2,
  216–18
 theoretical regionalism 221–2
 theories of narrative 55–6
Tiarepa people 68, 69, 74, 75, 77, 85,
 90, 93, 96–7, 100, 101, 118,
 191–3, 195, 206–7, 210–11, 213
time
 activity and 9–10
 experience, consciousness and
  142–3
 'government time' 105
 permanence in time, establishment
  of 109
 'time travelling' 81–2
Todorov, T. 56
tone of life 3–4
traditional practices, attitudes to
 92–3, 94
Turili 77

Umba lineage, Yala people 18, 85,
 94, 96–7, 108, 191–3, 195, 201,
 206–207

violence
 tensions and 6–7, 179–81, 181–2,
  185–6
Von Wright, G.H. 38

wena yaisia (women's courting songs) 87, 164
Wabea 76–7
Wagner, R. 21–2, 47–8n20, 223
Waliya 114, 116, 119, 120, 122, 123–4, 126, 134, 136, 147–8n2, 159n1
  brideprice problems 168
  death of Payanu 209
  death of Rake 189, 195
  death of Wapa 195–6, 198
  love and personhood 186
  Mapi and 95, 96, 97
  Rarapalu, Karupiri and Foti 181–2
Waluaparepa people 69, 76–7, 174, 201, 206
Wamili 130, 131
Wapa 59–65, 67
  brideprice in story of 63, 64, 65, 71
  death of 6, 14, 41
  pregnancy, belief concerning 69
  warfare and pacification 76–7
Wapa, death of
  portraits 195–202
Wapanu 10, 60, 126, 127, 132, 134, 177, 204
Wapia 68, 74–7, 93, 114, 195, 197–202, 212
Wardlow, H. 78, 148n5
Wareame 92, 114, 115, 170, 171
warfare and pacification 75–7, 90–91, 93–4
Wata 13, 14, 76, 164, 196
Watson, L.C. and Watson-Franke, M. 80n1
Weiner, A. 215n7
Weiner, J. 225n10
Wikan, Unni 160n6

witchcraft, bewitchment and 224–5n8
Wola 18, 171, 181, 182, 210–11
  death of Rake 191, 192, 193, 194, 195
women
  narratives of 138–41
  reputations of 186
  value, brideprice and 138
  work of 91–2

Yadi 6, 7, 10, 18
  Giame and 174–6
Yagore 69
Yakiranu 59, 62, 66, 67, 70, 72, 138, 174
Yako 8
  Ainu and 173–4
Yakopaita 63, 65, 85, 91, 96–7, 119, 132–3, 206
  church in 135
  daily life 10, 13–15
  death of Rake 188, 191, 193–4
  fieldwork in 16–18
Yala people 8, 10, 11, 18, 59, 70, 72–6, 82, 85, 88, 90–91, 93, 95, 97, 99, 101, 113, 115, 118, 124, 126, 191–3, 195, 197–202, 203–208, 211–13
Yalanu 69, 77, 130–31
Yamola 68, 70, 73, 119, 147–8n2, 203, 208
Yarepa people 18, 207
Yasi (Etali) 7–8, 66, 69, 82, 168–9, 177–8, 182, 197–8, 200–201
Yembi 10, 83, 90, 91, 201, 202, 207
Young, Michael W. 79, 217

Ziman, John 54

www.ingramcontent.com/pod-product-compliance
Lightning Source LLC
Chambersburg PA
CBHW071226080526
44587CB00013BA/1512